D1621315

658.012.5

...on service

16

59479

Secrets of the Wild Goose

Secrets
of the
Wild
Goose

The Self-Management Way to Increase Your Personal Power and Inspire Productive Teamwork

Donald H. Weiss, Ph.D.

American Management Association

New York • Atlanta • Boston • Chicago • Kansas City • San Francisco • Washington, D.C.
Brussels • Mexico City • Tokyo • Toronto

This book is available at a special
discount when ordered in bulk quantities.
For information, contact Special Sales Department,
AMACOM, a division of American Management Association,
1601 Broadway, New York, NY 10019.

This publication is designed to provide accurate and authoritative information in regard to the subject matter covered. It is sold with the understanding that the publisher is not engaged in rendering legal, accounting, or other professional service. If legal advice or other expert assistance is required, the services of a competent professional person should be sought.

Library of Congress Cataloging-in-Publication Data

Weiss, Donald H.
    Secrets of the wild goose: the self-management way to increase your personal power and inspire productive teamwork / Donald H. Weiss.
        p.   cm.
    Includes index.
    ISBN 0-8144-0431-6
    1. Leadership.   2. Teams in the workplace.   I. Title
HD57.7.W4534   1998
658.4'092—dc21   98–4967
                                                              CIP

© 1998 Donald H. Weiss.
All rights reserved.
Printed in the United States of America.

This publication may not be reproduced,
stored in a retrieval system,
or transmitted in whole or in part,
in any form or by any means, electronic,
mechanical, photocopying, recording, or otherwise,
without the prior written permission of AMACOM,
a division of American Management Association,
1601 Broadway, New York, NY 10019.

Printing number

10   9   8   7   6   5   4   3   2   1

Contents

Preface and Acknowledgments

How I Learned the Secrets
of the Wild Goose

The comic strip "*B.C.*," drawn and written by Johnny Hart, often features a guru sitting atop a mountain dispensing wisdom. I've never met such a man, or anyone anywhere near the likes of him. Unfortunately, no one person (including me) has all the answers to anything.

Instead, I've made a more than thirty-year professional journey in the company of thousands of people in an uncountable number of different personal and business situations. I draw some of the quotes in the book and some of the anecdotes or illustrations from that experience, and in most of these cases I have protected the identities of people or companies because of my pledge of confidentiality to them.

As a business manager and executive, I've *practiced* what I teach (at one time or another). As a social work administrator and family crisis counselor, I've helped individuals, families, and whole communities get more control over their lives. As a business consultant and trainer, I've taught countless managers the skills I teach here and I've tested the tools that help them get more control over their agencies or businesses. And I read a lot, as you'll confirm from the large number of notes in a few of the chapters.

Those notes are not intended to "prove" my case, although some of them refer to research results that help support what I'm saying. They serve mainly to direct you to additional sources on the subject I'm discussing, some of whom disagree with me. On the whole, the notes themselves model a point I make in the book: Increasing your personal power requires that you study and learn.

Finally, I want to stress that the wild goose is a metaphor, one that I stretch once in a while. I think it's a fun image, and although it's also instructive, you shouldn't carry the analogy too far. *Goose,* as we all know, isn't a synonym for *bright.*

Acknowledgments

I owe most of what I know and say to those thousands of people in a myriad of personal and business situations. Their contribution of knowledge, skill, or experiences influences my thoughts, feelings, and life. My personal power owes its strength to the individuals, families, business managers, and communities who have allowed me to enter their lives and share their burdens and their successes. I can only hope that my presence has been of some help to them. They and the way they've borne their struggles have taught me more than books or research could, but the many authors and researchers whose works I've read have helped me fine-tune the lessons I've learned from living. In short, I owe much of my personal power to the flapping wings of other people.

Sara, my wife, stands highest on the list of people to whom I owe debts of gratitude. She has not only been my most important critic and proofreader but has been there through the best and the worst of recent times. She has stronger wings than she realizes.

Adrienne Hickey, my editor at AMACOM, deserves my thanks for believing in my ability to write messages that make sense to other people and that can help them live more satisfying personal and work lives. I couldn't get more encouragement from any member of the flock than I got from Adrienne when she said, "It's a Weiss book. What more need I say?"

To the editors, to the readers, and to the critics with whom I shared my ideas as I developed them, I say thank you for making this book easy to read as well as on target.

Introduction

Sharing in the Secrets
of the Wild Goose

I must go where the wild goose goes,
'Cause my heart knows what the wild goose knows.
                    —"The Cry of the Wild Goose"[1]

An eagle soaring. That's the image you may want for your company—a fierce predator with finely honed, competitive skills to wield power over all others.

But the eagle's a loner, a complete hunting machine that relies on no one else for its survival. The eagle image may *inspire* you to greatness, but greatness doesn't come to people perched in an aerie high above the world they seek to conquer. People and their organizations aspiring to conquest pool their talents, skills, and resources: They're more akin to a gaggle of wild geese than to a solitary eagle.

You've probably seen the United Way campaign poster by Barbara Stirling Willson, now used as a motivational poster in many organizations, showing a gaggle of Canadian wild geese flying in formation. That formation contains the secret of their ability to fly hundreds of miles from their summer home to their winter home (and back again).

The flapping wings of each bird provide a stream of support air (uplift) for the bird immediately behind it. The V formation permits the whole flock to add a lot more flying range than if each bird flew on its own.[2]

When a goose drops out to fly solo, it immediately feels drag and

1

resistance and quickly rejoins the formation to take advantage of the flock's lifting power. When the lead bird—which has no birds in front of it to provide lift—tires, it slips back into a wing of the formation and another bird pulls forward into the lead slot. That way the flock never loses the power it needs for speeding to its goal. And geese don't honk just to hear themselves honking. It's cheerleading. The honking from the rear encourages the birds up front to go for it.

Yes, the wild goose knows what many of us have yet to learn. As author Tom Kayser says, if you think building collaboration into your organization is too difficult, "all you and your people need is as much sense as a gaggle of geese!"[3]

As an executive, a manager, an aspiring manager, or a nonmanagement employee, you need to learn the Secrets of the Wild Goose for three reasons:

1. To bring more structure into and get more control over your own life and work
2. To contribute to the success of your organization
3. To facilitate your work with other people in the organization

---

The Power of Self-Management for Individuals and Groups

Technological, organizational, and social changes in the world of work are accelerating too rapidly for you to ignore the two sets of demands that form the theme of this book: (1) increasing your personal power through self-management and (2) using self-management to increase the power of the groups to which you belong. You increase your personal power (i.e., gain more control over your life and your work) by becoming self-managed, and the organization or group increases its power (i.e., gains more control over its effectiveness or competitiveness) by encouraging and coordinating the efforts of self-managed people.

In the new world of work, organizational success depends on the effectiveness of competent, self-managed people, each of whom feels he has a *personal* stake in the group's coordinated effort. Executives, middle managers, supervisors, and nonmanagement employees all have to align their work goals with one another and to take ownership of the organization's vision and mission. Successful executives increase organizational creativity and collaboration by encouraging the individuals around them to think independently but also to come together to work on common goals in a common space, the way Paul H. O'Neill, CEO of ALCOA, does.

At ALCOA's corporate headquarters, few people can close themselves off from everyone else, not even the CEO. To be sure, they have private places in which to think through problems or to concentrate on difficult assignments. But, although no one looks over anyone else's shoulder, by being exposed to all the world, everyone feels compelled to work more productively. They take control over their own work; they become self-managed. The more self-managed they become, the more productive they become; the more productive they become, the greater their individual contribution when they come together as a group. At ALCOA, coming together frequently is the rule, not the exception. O'Neill and his direct reports regularly meet informally in an open space called the corporate "kitchen" rather than hide away in compartmentalized, walled-in spaces.[4] The informal sessions encourage a free exchange of information and opnion, the result of which is peak performance for both individuals and the group.

To be an individual *peak performer*, contribute to the group, and be in control of your own life, you must exercise *self-management*. For an organization today to be a *peak performer*, it must encourage everyone to practice self-management and to take control of their work.

How This Book Will Help You

This book contains very simple prescriptions for increasing personal and group power through self-management.

1. To increase your *personal power*, you need a vision and goals for your life from which you can develop action plans for organizing your life and work. By the time you finish this book, you'll have written or enhanced a vision for your life. You'll have set personal and work goals directed toward becoming successful and for living a

full and harmonized life. You'll also have designed action plans for fulfilling those goals. The outcome will be directions for satisfying the goals of both the organization in which you work and your personal life.

2. To increase *group power,* the organization has to do essentially the same as an individual does: draw on a vision and goals for the organization's life in order to coordinate the efforts of individuals. By the time you finish this book, you will have assessed your organization's readiness to encourage self-management and examined ways to support collaboration and teamwork among self-managed people.

This book is divided into six sections, each one of which focuses on one aspect of how becoming self-managed will contribute to increasing your personal power or the power of the groups to which you belong.

Section 1: Personal Power, Self-Management, and Group Power

Chapter 1 explains that self-management is the ability to control what happens in the mental and physical space you occupy, the ability to control what you do and how you do it, the competence and commitment to manage your own life. Chapter 2 presents the six *learned* competencies of self-management: wholeness, self-confidence, self-awareness, drive, self-respect/self-esteem, and respect for others. Chapter 3 explains why self-management is important to a business organization, how groups outperform individuals working separately, and how to create a vision for your life and work. By completing the related exercises in the appendices, you'll have taken the first steps toward becoming self-managed.

Section 2: Planning, Realistic Visioning, Action Planning, and Dealing With the Unexpected

Chapter 4 shows you how to achieve excellence by setting your sights on *realistic, achievable* goals for increasing the personal strengths on which you want to build. Chapter 5 expands on the themes of Chapter 4 by explaining how to increase your personal power through self-management. You can achieve this by (1) relating your personal vision to the realities of your environment, and (2) managing seven dimensions of your life. Section 2 ends with Chapter 6, which takes one more step toward effective planning by helping you develop a substantial but healthy anxiety about the future (i.e., helping you to expect the unexpected).

Section 3: Group Power and the Core Business, Self-Management as the Force Behind Increasing Group Power

Chapter 7 begins the process of using your individual self-management in the service of increasing group power; it shows you how to focus individuals' attention on specific, measurable or observable goals that satisfy both organizational and individual needs or demands. By doing the exercise suggested by the models in this chapter, you'll be able to identify your organization's core business. Chapter 8 distinguishes levels of commitment, and explains how the care and feeding of self-management produces wholehearted commitment. Chapter 9 explores how developing the competencies appropriate to your role or function in the organization increases group power.

Section 4: Management and Leadership: The Dual Functions of Managers

Chapter 10 puts your dual role as a manager into perspective; the meat and potatoes of management consists of managing process, things, and yourself—not other people; it also distinguishes between management and leadership for the purpose of showing you that the two need not be separate roles. Chapter 11 describes what leadership values and roles you can and should adopt to be a Manager-Leader. Chapter 12 carries the idea of Manager-Leader forward to help you find ways to support the task-oriented activities for which they are responsible at the same time as you find ways of inspiring the group toward excellence, i.e., how leaders manage incentives and rewards ("Managing the WIIFM"). Chapter 13 distinguishes between WIFFM Leadership and Vision Leadership, i.e., the latter being the ability to touch people's lives and move them down paths they would not otherwise have taken had it not been for the inspiration the Vision Leader provides. Exercises in related appendices will give you a chance to look at ways to evaluate other people's motivation and find out if you are already a leader.

Section 5: Collaboration, Teamwork, the Experiences of Groups, and Managing the Storms

Chapter 14 explains that collaboration consists of three basic processes to which the whole group must be committed: contributing, influencing others, and being influenced by others. Chapter 15 shows you what teamwork is, that it's characterized by collaboration and getting the best from other people regardless of how they're organized, and that teamwork is possible even if formal teams aren't needed. Chapter 16 explores six common group experiences: Introducing, Stage Setting, Probing/Testing, Creating, Producing, Maintaining. Chapter 17 helps you deal with conflicts, disagreements, or differences that occur when at least one involved party believes, rightly or wrongly, that his right to satisfy his needs or interests has been denied. The chapter shows you how to prevent storms and how to manage them when they arise.

Section 6: High-Performance Teams, How to Make Teams Work, When Not to Form Teams at All, and Self-Managed Teams

The chapters of this section bring the power of self-management in groups to its logical application: high-performance teams and self-managed teams (SMTs). Chapter 18 explains that, individually, no one person can accomplish as much as the group as a whole and describes the traits and dynamics that separate high-performance teams from also-ran teams. Chapter 19 shows you when to form a team and when not to. Chapter 20 shows you what it takes to make a team as good as a gaggle of geese: the support of the entire organization and the provision by Manager-Leaders of the systems and opportunities that will allow the team to flourish. Chapter 21 then explains what is needed to transform any group of people into a self-managed team.

Notes

1. From "The Cry of the Wild Goose," words and music by Terry Gilkyson. © 1949 (Renewed) Unichappell Music, Inc. (BMI) & Elvis Presley Music, Inc. All rights administered by Unichappell Music, Inc. All rights

reserved. Used by permission. Warner Bros. Publications U.S., Inc., Miami, FL 33014.

2. See Thomas A. Kayser, *Building Team Power* (Irwin Professional Publishing/CRM, 1994), p. 20.

3. Kayser, p. 20.

4. Joan O. C. Hamilton, Stephen Baker, and Bill Vlasic, "The Workplace," *Business Week* (April 29, 1996), pp. 107–117.

Section 1

Personal Power, Self-Management, and Group Power

1

Increasing Your Personal Power by Becoming Self-Managed

Most powerful is he who has himself in his own power.
—Lucius Annaeus Seneca (4 B.C.E.–65 C.E.)

Watch wild geese in flight. Each bird flies alone, in full command of its own wing power. Each bird individually contributes to the flock's progress, while relying on the other geese to do their share. Working together, the birds create synergy, the process in which the whole group produces more than you could predict by a mere inventory or summing of its parts. To do that, however, each bird must be in control of its personal effort—be the center of its own world.

Being at the center of your own world means that you take in the world around you and reach out to it from the mental and physical space you occupy. What you *do* with that space determines if you control what goes on there or if someone or something else does. That's what I mean by "having personal power," and the way to increase your personal power is to become self-managed.

> Self-management—personal power—is the ability to control what happens in the mental and physical space you occupy, the ability to contol what you do and how you do it, and the competence and commitment to manage your own life.

11

Personal Power Through Self-Management

Imagine yourself lying in a hospital bed, propped up on pillows, and facing an open door through which you can watch people walk back and forth. Watching those people is all you can do. You're completely incapable of moving, of feeding yourself, of washing your own face. You're suffering "living death": the incapacitating stroke that leaves your mind intact and your body immobile. That's the height of powerlessness.

Power, by definition, implies the ability to act or to produce an effect; it also implies control. The most fundamental form of power is personal power, the ability to control what you do and how you do it, the competence to manage your own life. That kind of power begins with the simplest sense of the phrase *self-management:* satisfying our basic needs of food, clothing, and shelter.

Most of us would include in our idea of personal power the ability to cut our own meat, climb a flight of stairs, comb our hair—all those little things we take for granted until something catastrophic happens (and we can't do them for ourselves). A common reaction when disaster takes away that control is to feel helpless and out of control, a reaction overcome by people like Christopher Reeves (the actor who broke his neck in a fall from a horse) and Max Starkloff (founder and president of Paraquad, a group set up to speak for and assist people with disabilities). Starkloff describes his life as full of compromises and dependence on others, yet he is still capable of exercising his personal power in ways that make the most of those compromises and dependencies for managing his affairs. "I can't separate my disability from my life. It links me up to what I believe in, my family, friends, people I've met because of my disability. I have *a full and satisfying life."* [1] [Italics mine.] He, and other people with disabilities, must redefine for themselves what "a full and satisfying life" means and find novel ways in which they can exercise their personal power.

Everyone's life is full of compromises and dependence on others, and for that reason personal power also includes the ability to build mutually satisfying relationships with other people, the ability to earn their trust and their loyalty and to be trusting and loyal. As part of the process of becoming self-managed, you recognize your limitations and welcome your need for the knowledge, skills, and opinions of other people to help you succeed.

In short, power is the ability to manipulate (in a benign sense) yourself and the world in which you live to satisfy your wants, needs, and requirements—and to fulfill your loftiest ambitions.

Self-Management

Management of any kind implies more than the exercise of power; it implies *control*. You can control or manage things, processes, and events in your life, even if it appears as if you don't. You choose the processes in which you're engaged, and even when you feel caught up in a tide you can't escape, you have actually chosen not to swim out of it. Choosing to manage what's in your reach to control is the first step toward self-management.

Contrary to what you may have heard, you can't manage time or people, but you can manage what you do, the actions you take. Self-management consists of exercising your personal power over yourself. You, and only you, are responsible for what you do. Personal history and social conditions may influence you, but you make the decisions to do whatever it is you do. Your success or failure lies mainly in your own hands.

And what you do has consequences for everyone associated with you as well. Reciprocity helps Canadian geese fly hundreds of unerring miles. Likewise, what you do affects people you've never seen or heard of, and what they do affects your life as well. One goal of self-management is to make that reciprocity conscious, to knowingly strive for your own personal success and contribute to the success of other people. Managing your activities well (not managing time) and leading other people (not managing them) will propel you and your organization to your destinations.

Self-Management, Not Time Management or People Management

Forget about time management, a meaningless phrase, and don't take literally the notion that we all have the same amount of time. We don't own, use, or operate with time as we would a computer. Coercing time to do our own bidding is impossible. We can't command it to start or stop. We can't keep it for ourselves or give it away. We can't control it. Therefore, we can't manage it. We can only *live it.*

We all live in the conceptual invention we call time, the convenient *fiction* we use for measuring distance in units based on the speed of the earth as it rotates on its axis or revolves around the sun. The units we call seconds, minutes, hours, days, weeks, months, and years correspond to other units of measure we call inches, feet, yards, and miles. "It took me a year to do this," means the same as "The earth traveled 58,404,000,000 miles around the sun from when I started this until I finished it." "A year" is a shorthand method of expressing the number of miles of the earth's orbit. We use time to measure our effectiveness in managing processes or events.

You don't manage time. Rather, you manage what you do with your life (the processes that go into making up your activities) within a measure of time.

You don't manage people, either. You may control things and processes in people's lives, e.g., material resources and their paychecks, but not them. They can always use their own personal power to defy you or reject you and your power. Dictators and tyrants can exercise power over people through force and intimidation but that type of power is limited by the will of those they aim to control: "Go ahead, shoot. I'd rather be dead than do what you demand." Unlike the control you have over things and processes, you possess less power over people in proportion to the degree of power they exercise over themselves.

Managing Things: The Beginnings of Self-Management

Things are resources you shift from one place to another, give away, keep, or use. They consist of energy and have substance, but they have no will that resists what you do to them. If you can't move them by muscle power, you find other means, including mechanical brute force, to bend them to your will. We modern humans may have our evolutionary origins in the ability to stand erect, but we have our psychosocial origins in recognizing our power over nonliving and living things (our "dominion over the earth"). When people exercise that power over other people, we call it "coercion." And coercion is *not* management.

Self-management becomes possible because you decide for yourself to use yourself for a specific purpose; things—even many higher forms of animals—can't make such decisions. Even when you feel you have no control over your life, you are in fact agreeing to let other people or events control or direct you or push you in a specific direction in spite of your conscious wishes: "I'll do this [whatever "this" is], even though I'd rather not."

Managing Processes: The Mechanism That Makes Self-Management Work

Managing processes more than managing things propels your ability to increase personal and group power through self-management. The processes you manage involve the use or flow of resources (including intangibles such as information, memories, and talents) that enable events to take place. Consultants Michael Hammer and James Champy explain that "a business process [is] a collection of activities [tasks] that takes one or more kinds of input and creates an output that is of value to a customer."[2] You can "map" those processes with flowcharts and PERT charts. Managing performance means managing, measuring, or observing the processes by which work gets done, as well as the final product (outcome). The process (how you play the game) is often as important as the results (winning). But, this business definition tells only one small part of this essential but complex, difficult-to-grasp story.

Consider a single moment in your own life: It emerges and unfolds from a collection of processes, a continuous flow of activities, not discrete identifiable or nameable events. Modern management philosophers such as Margaret Wheatley have revived a very old idea—that what we call a discrete or identifiable "current" event consists of processes flowing together to form "actual entities" or "actual occasions."[3] We then assign names to memorable junctures of processes, important moments, e.g., "my wedding," "my bar mitzvah," "my confirmation," like a historian calling certain socio-political-military processes The Battle of Gettysburg.

I live north of St. Louis, where the Mississippi, Missouri, and

Illinois rivers meet, and this geographic fact provides me with an analogy. Just as the three rivers merge to become one river downstream, you at this moment are (your identity is) a confluence of processes, as in the rough depiction in Exhibit 1-1: the sum total of your past and current experiences, and the combination of your own perceptions of yourself and of the perceptions other people have of you. (Many more streams flow through your "present" experience, but these three satisfy the principle of simplicity and stay true to my analogy of the three rivers.)

To talk about the beginning of an actual occasion, in Exhibit 1-1 "You (here/now)," means to trace seemingly independent and disconnected processes to their roots (which most often refer back to still other processes). To grasp that current event (you at the present moment) requires *mentally freezing* the flow of physical, social, emotional, and intellectual processes coming together from the past and organizing them into a perception of what "this moment" is. Drawing on tools and principles of association, selection, and omission, we organize those processes and talk about the present as if it stands still and isolated from everything else. In Wheatley's terms, we "self-organize";[4] we take our perceptions and organize them onto patterns

Exhibit 1-1. Processes that form "the present."

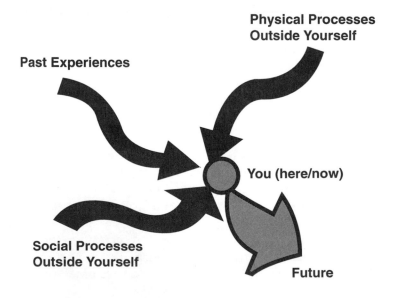

we find useful for defining what we (and our organizations) are and for planning: creating and shaping organizations and directing activities in the future.

"This moment" (the actual occasion) consists of the inputs (mainly the *information*) available to you about your own past experiences and about both the physical and social world outside yourself. How you process and organize the inputs or information about them that you take in defines your unique moment. Sometimes processing and organizing goes on automatically, without your being aware of what's happening; literally physically seeing the world from your perspective (colored with your values, attitudes, past history, etc.) is one such automatic process. Sometimes you consciously process and organize the inputs or information about them, as when you consider why something has happened or why you feel the way you do about it. That processing and organizing determines the next moment and other moments beyond it.

You respond to that organization of information in two ways (outputs): (1) an "inner" response (a thought, a feeling, or an emotion) and (2) an "outer" response (an overt action). Those responses immediately become data for organizing "the next moment." In short, *"this moment" is also a process* through which you convert inputs into outputs of value to yourself or to other people (to confirm Hammer and Champy's definition). The result of this conversion, especially the inner response, can either encourage or block personal or organizational change or growth.

Organic, emotional, and intellectual lives don't start and stop as isolated moments, like still frames in a motion picture or video. They flow like the "same river" of the ancient Greek paradox, which posits that you can't step into the same river twice (or even once, for that matter) because as soon as you lift your foot the water that is the river has changed; it isn't the same anymore. Yet, in another sense, the river and your identity always remain the "same." Wheatley speaks of "self-organizing structures . . . [as mantaining] a coherent identity throughout their history. [Actual entities or actual occasions] are temporary states. What endures is process—dynamic, adaptive, creative."[5]

To talk about the future is to describe possibilities, possible branches into which the river of your life might flow. To get control over yourself (to "self-organize"), you direct the river of your life, but only if you use the information presented to you to plan for the future, and then implement the plan. What happens here and now lapses into the past and merges with the future as it happens. The American philosopher George H. Mead said that the here and now consists of only the coming together of the flow of historical, personal, and social processes into identifiable moments or events we can talk about—that is, the present consists only of certain conscious perception of things in the past.[6] How can you manage people when what you understand of yourself and them are only events *gone by*?

The processes flowing in from outside you and from your own past (forming your present and moving on into your future) create the center of your world. The amount of information you take in from the world around you depends on the extent to which you reach out into that world from the mental and physical space you occupy. The quality of that information depends on how well you examine it, interpret it, and use it. The extent to which you expand and enrich that space, *and use the information you gather,* determines how much and how well you, not someone else, coerces what goes on in your life.

The process of one individual's life and the processes of a business organization are akin to one another. As an actual entity, the organization flows through time, forms, changes, and maintains its identity the same way you do, only in a far more complex way (since so many individuals are involved in forming an organization). And, like the people who make up the organization, it is self-managed to the extent that those people, as a whole, control the organization's destiny.

Managing processes involves managing things, events, activities, or tasks *and determines their value.* The more aware you become of the processes flowing into your present and becoming your future, the more control you can exercise over things and your life—creating actual occasions that are the fulfillment of objectives or goals and renewing yourself by seeking after new goals. The more aware you are of the processes that flow into and through your business organization, the more control you can exercise over its resources and processes—likewise creating actual occasions that are the fulfillment of organizational objectives or goals and renewing your organization by seeking after new organizational goals. The more control over yourself and your organization's processes you have, the more you influence other people.

Influence: An Outcome of Self-Management

Given what I've said so far, it follows that the old-fashioned notion of managing people means making them do what we want, *coercing* them. Yes, we can coerce people to do things. In that sense we can control them, which is the same as managing things or processes.

Put a gun to most people's heads, and they're likely to do as you say (while some would resist). Lock up someone behind barbed wire, and she's likely to submit to your will, but all the while she'll be thinking of ways of doing you in. Coercion passes for management in slave labor camps, old-style military units, and other command-and-control environments. At best, people respond to coercive power or status power with compliance ("OK, I'll do it"); at worst, they react with malicious obedience ("I'll do it, but I'll get you for it later"). An essential goal of exercising self-management is to make coercion unnecessary, replacing it with persuasion and leadership by example. In other words, you influence other people by persuading them to do what needs to be done or by becoming a role model for them to follow.

The traditional and common command-and-control management style (authoritarianism) gets things done in the short run, but the price paid is the loss of creativity, innovation, independent problem solving, and long-term success. Because we now believe that such a price is too high, the workplace is becoming more democratic. Unlike most workers of decades past, a majority of modern employees (nonmanagement as well as management employees) want and expect to participate more in the decisions that affect their lives, and companies that encourage participation get better results than their more rigid counterparts. Moreover, the highly competitive nature of the new global economy demands more from workers, more-creative and -productive minds contributing to the well-being and growth of the organization. But, to get that level of input, companies must encourage democratization, which means developing self-management skills. In a well-run, modern business, effective management of processes and things *and* leadership of people replace coercion.

Few individuals have the kind of power needed for coercing others to do anything. As a manager, you have the status or position power to get people to *comply* with management's wishes; people do what managers require of them out of self-interest (the desire to keep their jobs). On the other hand, in the daily course of your work and personal life, you usually exercise personal power (self-management) to get people to commit to what you want them to do, to influence them, rather than coerce. Influencing includes role modeling (leading by example) as well as persuading because what you do is usually more important than what you say. People see what you do. They see how you manage or control processes, things, and events. Watching you influences the decisions they make about how to live their lives. The more self-management you show to the world, the more power you have for influencing other people.

And, people will watch you; count on it. They follow your lead only if they see that you manage things, processes, and events well—that you have command of the conditions of your own life and work. If, simultaneously, they see that how you manage things, processes, and events benefits them as well as you, what you do has that much more impact on their choices. That's why companies tend to pay higher salaries to managers who share power and decision making with employees. When teamwork is the rule rather than the exception, productivity rises 18 to 25 percent.[7]

Increasing Personal Power

You have to work at developing your personal power; it isn't ever handed to you—it takes self-discipline and a systematic approach for becoming self-managed, for focusing on personal goals and objectives. The personal power you gain through self-management gives you the ability to do what you want to satisfy those goals and objectives. That ability, if exercised, engenders freedom, but self-management implies *responsible* freedom, taking ownership of your life, your work, and the consequences for your actions.

This kind of freedom doesn't come naturally. Responsible freedom is a learned behavior that adults often actively discourage in their children or wards. Until the magical age of eighteen, parents, teachers, athletic coaches, and public officials expect children to respond to and obey rules, to trust and respond to authority. Although grown-ups preach to youngsters about becoming more responsible, for a variety of reasons (including fear), they rarely provide their fledglings with opportunities to practice responsibility.

People in general rarely raise your bar for accepting responsible freedom to the level of self-management, yet—poof!—when you reach age eighteen, they tell you that you too have become an adult and are expected to act like an adult: i.e., to exercise the skills of self-management. Suddenly immersed in an adult world, you find, in most cases, that the demands of family and community to which you responded are now replaced to a great extent by the demands of your bosses.

To take control of your own life and work, you need to exercise personal power. You need a vision for your life. Then, to realize that vision, you need the skills of self-management. As in the case of any other skills, you need to learn and adapt those skills to the life you envision for yourself.

Goal Setting and Increasing Personal Power

Self-management means to use your personal power in the exercise of controlling your own life. You increase personal power to the extent that you improve your ability to act on and to achieve your own goals.

Each person defines for herself what constitutes her basic needs and defines for herself what personal power she must have in order to satisfy them. From those definitions she identifies the goals she has to achieve (and the means for achieving them) in order to live a full and satisfying life.

An old parable tells us that if you give a starving person a fish, you feed him for just one meal, but if you teach him how to fish you feed him for a lifetime. However, another take on the parable says that teaching the person how to fish does not feed him for a lifetime. Instead, it gives him just the opportunity to be so fed. Whether or not the person takes advantage of the chance is a matter of personal choice from among a large variety of possible goals. If the person chooses a goal other than fishing, he will never use the knowledge and the skill (his personal power) he has for fishing.

Begin the program of increasing personal power by turning to the three exercises in Appendix A. The SWOT Analysis will help you identify your strengths, weaknesses, opportunities, and threats. "The Center of Your World, You" will help you identify where you are in relation to others. And, the two parts of the third exercise ("Ben Franklin, John Venn, and You") will help you identify your core strengths and interests. I suggest you do these exercises before reading on.

Notes

1. David Dorr, "No Retreat," *St. Louis Post-Dispatch* (December 13, 1995), p. 5E; Lynn Elber, "Disabled Actors Say They Can't Get Jobs," *St. Louis Post-Dispatch* (August 10, 1996), p. 8E.
2. Michael Hammer and James Champy, *Reengineering the Corporation: A Manifesto for Business Revolution* (New York: HarperBusiness, 1993), p. 35.
3. Alfred North Whitehead, *Process and Reality* (New York: Harper & Row, 1960).
4. Margaret Wheatley, *Leadership and the New Science: Learning About Organizations From an Orderly Universe* (San Francisco: Berrett-Koehler, 1992 and 1994), p. 98.
5. Wheatley, p. 98.
6. See George H. Mead, *Mind, Self, and Society,* ed. Charles W. Morris (Chicago: University of Chicago Press, 1934); Mead, *The Philosophy of the Act* (Chicago: University of Chicago Press, 1938); Mead, *The Philosophy of the Present* (Chicago: Open Court Publishing, 1932).
7. Edward E. Potter, president of the Employment Policy Foundation, quoted in "Work Week" column, *Wall Street Journal* (March 12, 1996), p. A1.

Other Sources

Weiss, Donald H. *Get Organized! How to Control Your Life Through Self-Management* (New York: AMACOM, 1986); *Get Organized! The Personal and Workgroup Performance Manager (for Windows 3.1 and 95),* Version 2.0.

2

Manager, Manage Thyself

Lead your life so you wouldn't be ashamed to sell the family parrot to the town gossip.

—Anonymous

Wild geese in flight work together as a well-trained team, one that depends on each team member to hold up its end of the bargain. And goslings have to learn from their elders the skills and rules that hold the flock together.

The goose metaphor breaks down only when we humans override our innate urges to cooperate and collaborate. Self-managed people, however, make the most of both their ability to control their own destiny (as Jack Welch, CEO of General Electric, exhorts us to do)[1] and their ability to join with others to create that destiny. Self-managed people increase their personal power by making competence, coordination, and commitment their personal and group goals. Six basic competencies of self-management make it possible to reach those goals.

How you think about and act toward yourself and others is determined by the *six learned competencies* of self-management:

1. Wholeness
2. Self-confidence
3. Self-awareness
4. Drive
5. Self-respect/self-esteem
6. Respect for others

The Six Learned Competencies of Self-Managed People

People with personal power usually think and act in ways you admire, but they were born, like everyone else, with only the capacity for becoming self-managed. As I see it, self-managed people exhibit six categories of learned competencies. The first category, *wholeness,* is the ability to see yourself as a whole person. Wholeness supports the other five behavior sets: self-confidence, self-awareness, drive, self-respect/self-esteem, and respect for others.

Wait a minute. Aren't these "learned competencies" traits or characteristics rather than skills? Yes and no. Each of those terms describes the outward signs or outcomes of large sets of skills related to how we take in, organize, and act upon information about ourselves and about the world around us. To be whole, for example, calls for clearly seeing and managing the various processes and connections of our lives. The descriptions we call traits, therefore, are end products of essential abilities to "become something." Contrarily, to "lose confidence" or to "lose self-esteem" means to lose, for some reason, the ability to take in, organize, and act upon information in the way you did previously. So, yes, the words signify traits, but they also signify the processes by which the traits manifest themselves.

Wholeness

The whole person, represented in Exhibit 2-1, provides the background and support for managing yourself—for integrating the experiences, thoughts, feelings, emotions, values, and actions that go into making you who you are. At the same time, the more competent you become at integration, the more secure your wholeness becomes.

The whole person goes to work, and the whole person comes home. You have a work life, with all the intellectual and emotional issues it involves. You have a life outside of work, with all the intellectual and emotional issues it involves. You can't leave one at the doorstep of the other without creating serious crises. Managers who demand their employees bifurcate their lives usually are themselves incapable of doing so all of the time. Indeed, people who think they can live divided lives all of the time are lying to themselves, which creates yet another crisis.

Wholeness also means pulling together two very different ap-

Exhibit 2-1. Portrait of a self-managed person.

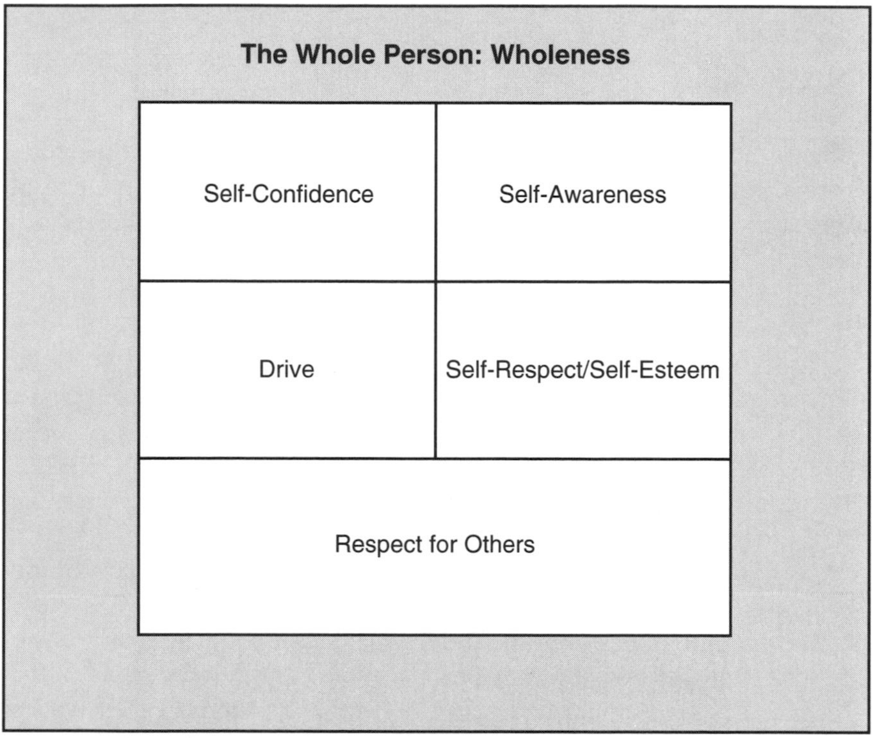

The Whole Person: Wholeness

Self-Confidence	Self-Awareness
Drive	Self-Respect/Self-Esteem
Respect for Others	

proaches to life in general and to problem solving or planning in particular. *Linear* thinking, the step-by-step and analytic methods we use for organizing life and work (what psychologists call "left brain," because that's where analytic thought goes on), takes place only within the bigger context of the vision for your whole life and manages the details within that context. The context of your life's vision is filled with emotional values, creativity, flashes of insight, and subjective decisions (events that psychologists say go on in the "right brain"). Artists look at a canvas and envision a complete scene or pattern, not lines, shadows, and highlights. Still, they then have to execute that scene or pattern with lines, shadows, and highlights. Without the details, the vision will remain forever locked up in their minds. Likewise, well-formulated plans for your life or your business provide the details that make vision come to life. Your objective? *Develop "whole brain" living and managing* in which you integrate both the linear, analytic side of your life and the nonlinear, subjective side.

Self-Confidence

Having a vision for your life, with long-term goals and objectives, brings you a sense of security and self-confidence; it provides you with a recipe for believing in yourself. Self-confidence requires that you:

- ➤ Act on principle. This means establishing a set of values (a moral code) and living in accordance with it. It also means deciding what you want for yourself and determining that it is right and that it gives meaning to your life and adds value to the lives of other people and to the world in which you live.
- ➤ Acquire knowledge and decide that your beliefs are accurate, and that they're useful for yourself and for other people.
- ➤ Develop abilities and translate what you know into what you do, being creative or innovative as well as skilled.
- ➤ Develop strong opinions and feel a passion or intensity about what you believe, want, or need.
- ➤ Accept disagreement and negative feedback without defensiveness or a need to explain yourself; disagree with other people and give them negative feedback; be influenced by other people when you see value in their points of view.
- ➤ Feel and express realistic optimism, having the patience and the insight to follow the lead of other people as well as having patience with events over which you have no control.
- ➤ Take responsibility and be accountable for getting results.

Self-Awareness

Self-awareness comes from ongoing, honest self-assessment and prevents a self-managed person from being smug and self-satisfied. Self-awareness comes from the ability to look into yourself and to become self-critical and thoughtfully introspective. It requires that you:

- ➤ Develop a knowledge of your limitations as well your strengths, and acknowledge those limitations.

➤ Be *un*satisfied with your present situation and its limitations (that is, be willing to move beyond where you are even if you're happy with it), and to see things both as what they *are* and what they *could be.*

➤ Look for new directions in which to learn and to grow, and seek out new and different ways for informing yourself, for expressing yourself, for doing what you do, and for perceiving and relating to the world around you.

➤ Become flexible and adaptable, forming new opinions and ways of doing things when circumstances demand them.

Drive

Drive is the passion to get to where you want to go (not to where life might take you) and to be focused on achieving your goals (to be motivated). Drive means that you:

➤ Develop the energy and stamina (through diet, exercise, and appropriate forms of rest) to do what you need to do, to be self-starting, and to be strong-willed or tenacious about the vision for your life.

➤ Show enthusiasm for your life and what you are doing. (Ralph Waldo Emerson, in his essay "Circles," phrased it this way: "Nothing great was ever achieved without enthusiasm.")

➤ Display vigor of thought as well as deed; develop sticktoitiveness, staying the course when you believe it's right and on target.

➤ Develop the daring to take risks and to make the most of your independence and your need to seek out new opportunities for self-expression, for creative expression, and for innovation in both your work and your nonwork activities.

➤ Take leadership roles when needed, influencing others to follow.

➤ Revitalize yourself regularly throughout each day, renewing your own sources of energy through proper doses of rest, nutrition, exercise, and relaxation.

Self-Respect/Self-Esteem

If you don't care about yourself, who will? Self-respect allows you to care about both aspects of who you are—your mind and body—

provisioning both of them: strengthening rather than depriving, abusing, or diminishing them. It requires that you:

- Recognize you are as valuable as anyone else.
- Find the inner security you must have in order to give yourself permission to need other people to help you fulfill your dreams as much as they need you.

Respect for Others

Respect is the magic bullet that makes cooperation possible. Developing the skills related to respect for others requires that you:

- Recognize the dignity of other people, avoid judging them.
- Care for and about people, accept them as they are.
- Recognize other people's knowledge, skills, creativity; be open to their ideas, thoughts, or feelings, and contributions to your life.
- Recognize others' needs and aspirations.
- Open yourself up to others—listening to them, accepting and acting upon their opinions or suggestions—and learn from and be influenced by them.
- Give people helpful, honest feedback and act as a positive role model for them.
- Cooperate and collaborate with others.
- Be dependable and credible, contributing accurate information to other people.
- Communicate openly and honestly, which requires being available and accessible to others and transferring information to them.
- Seek group consensus when appropriate, supporting the group decisions and acting on them.
- Be *un*satisfied with the status quo for others as well as for yourself, encouraging them to find new and different ways for adding value to their lives and to the world around them.

Notes

1. Noel M. Tichy and Stratford Sherman, *Control Your Destiny or Someone Else Will: Lessons in Mastering Change—The Principles Jack Welch Is*

Using to Revolutionize General Electric (New York: HarperBusiness, 1993).

Other Sources

Graham, Ellen, and Cynthia Crossen. "The Overloaded American: Too Many Things to Do, Too Little Time to Do Them." *Wall Street Journal* (March 8, 1996), pp. R1 and R4.

Greengard, Samuel. "When Successful Execs Fail in Mid-Career." *Wall Street Journal* (July 26, 1992).

Grossman, John. "Working it Out." *US Air Magazine* (July 1996).

Sherman, Stratford. "Leaders Learn to Heed the Voice Within." *Fortune* (August 22, 1994), pp. 92–100.

3

Augmenting Group Power
With Personal Power—
and Vice Versa

The most important single ingredient in the formula of success is knowing how to get along with people.

—Theodore Roosevelt (1858–1919)

Increasing group power through self-management *is* the secret of the wild goose: forming a unified whole out of a group of interacting or interdependent items or parts. No matter how they may squabble on the ground over tidbits of food, once airborne, geese know how to get along with one another and do it well.

It is difficult, if not impossible, to separate personal power from group power because everything we do as individuals takes place in a social, or group, context; every group to which we belong, and many of those to which we don't, influence what we think and do. Before we go on to Section 2 of this book, then, we must consider how as individuals we contribute to increasing group power and how groups help us as individuals to increase personal power.

> Groups outperform individuals working separately when the individuals in the group contribute their personal power to the potential power of the group. In high-performance groups, each person converts his personal power to group power.

Using Personal Power to Increase Group Power

Groups that outperform individuals working separately do so only because the individuals in the group have contributed their personal power to the potential power of the group. In a high-performance group, each person has to convert his personal power to group power. The culture in the United States has raised the idea of the rugged individualist to the level of an icon, which makes the conversion of self-management to group management seem unnatural.

Yet a peak-performing organization happens only when people *capable* of doing so learn and use the skills of self-management. Those skills or best practices help you express your personal power and responsible freedom as positive actions that channel the strengths of self-managed people into a powerful organization. By positively applying your respective personal power, you and your coworkers pull together around a system of common or shared goals and objectives. Freely organizing your lives and work on the basis of a common vision enables you and other self-managed people to align your individual goals and to coordinate your activities into a powerful synergy. Isn't that what we call effective teamwork?

The blending of personal power, responsible freedom, and group power requires that you:

- ☛ Take a long view of your life and work in which you identify their most important aspects or dimensions.
- ☛ Harmonize those most important aspects or dimensions and workable methods for managing things, processes, and activities.
- ☛ Acquire established methods and skills for meeting deadlines, for avoiding scheduling conflicts, and for achieving more-desirable results than you get without them.
- ☛ Pull your organization's operations and its people together around common or shared goals and objectives.
- ☛ Align unshared individual or personal goals and objectives with one another and with the organization's goals and objectives.

Needed: A Systems Approach and Strategic Thinking

Only by taking a systems approach (i.e., seeing both your personal life and business activities as unified wholes) and developing the skills of strategic thinking will you accomplish the pulling together and aligning of goals instinctively generated within a gaggle. To create that unified whole requires that you and everyone else in the organization—regardless of status, age, experience, or professional field—think long-range or strategically and work cooperatively to develop goal-driven action plans. Short-term management thinking, such as downsizing to increase next quarter's profits and shareholder value, produces short-term gains. Effective strategic thinking, on the other hand, can make a success of low-tech (even no-tech) production.[1]

Selecting a Vision for Your Life

Thinking strategically and working cooperatively also promote three essential ingredients of self-management and of successful businesses: competence, coordination, and commitment (the 3 C's).

> *Competence*—the ability to produce desirable outcomes or results
>
> *Coordination*—the connections between different parts of your life or the life of the organization
>
> *Commitment,* the desire and willingness to do what is necessary to succeed

How you apply the 3 C's depends on what you want to achieve—*the vision of your life.* The more confident you are in the rightness of that vision for you, the more personal power you will have and be able to exercise—in short, the more self-managed you will become.

Writing a vision for your life takes considerable thought, and the "Eulogy Exercise" in Appendix B may help you. By completing this exercise, you'll have made some decisions as to what you want the rest of your life to look like. We'll consider other aspects of vision in Chapter 5.

The Need for Clearly Stated Goals

How you apply the 3 C's also depends on setting clearly stated goals (desirable outcomes or results), which is hardly a startling revelation.

No matter how obscure or subtle the goals, human behavior is essentially goal-oriented, often goal-*driven.* The exercise in Appendix C, "What Drives Me?" will help you define for yourself the outcomes you want from what you do, and that list of twenty-five possibilities is probably incomplete. Most people don't know what drives them. Sometimes their goals remain so obscure as to require counseling or even psychotherapy to uncover them, but most times people suffer merely from ill-defined, vague, and ambiguous desires, wishes, and hopes. Since the road to self-management consists of achieving an ongoing series of goals, you should complete the exercise in Appendix C *before* reading the subsequent chapters.

Becoming self-managed overcomes empty dreaming by requiring you to strive for clarity of goals. Expressing goals in well-formulated goal statements helps you identify specific, realistic targets and the conditions you need for hitting them. These goal statements shift your focus away from the clock and away from to-do lists and toward monitoring progress focused on what you truly want to achieve. Your goals give meaning to what you do and to the time it takes you to do it.

Priorities

The best "time managers" prioritize things they have to do during a given period of time, but they don't usually prioritize their goals. What do you want? A happy home life, or a career involving 90 percent travel? A large house decorated with expensive furniture, or money in the bank? How can you decide what's most important or immediate *to do* until you know which of those goals you want to emphasize now?

Prioritizing goals prevents running into goal conflicts that drain your personal power and frustrate you. Sorting through competing goals and setting them in a rank order of importance or immediacy helps you put them into the perspective of your whole life, as it is and as it could be. It helps you *harmonize* competing demands.

Plans

We often have an idea of what drives us, but we don't consciously and deliberately plan for achieving our goals. We take one day at a time and let things happen (sometimes *to* us). We waste personal power on trivial pursuits, and then we wonder why we don't feel in control of our lives.

Systematically managing resources, activities, or processes gives you more control. It requires, however, that you include the ingredients for self-management identified above: a vision for your life and goals. Then you can design action plans to achieve them (i.e., objectives or milestones and activities). Goal-driven strategic thinking keeps you focused on the future and the competencies you need for getting to where you want to go. Goal-driven plans help you coordinate your activities—short-term and long-term. Commitment comes from believing that your goals are good or right and that your plans for achieving them are realistic and practical.

Still, no plan should be written in concrete. What is good or right *now* may not be so later. A *healthy anxiety* about the future and keeping an eye on the demands change makes on you and on other people keeps your plans from growing rusty and grinding to a halt. In the words of John Kotter, writing in *Fortune,* leaders today must "kill complacency . . . before it kills you."[2]

Vision and Mission for Your Organization

Most peak-performing organizations (e.g., Hewlett-Packard, 3M) prize the self-management of their employees. They encourage individuals to develop and increase their personal power by making development resources available to them, by providing training and education, by paying them for learning new skills, and by giving them opportunities to use the new skills they learn. In turn, each person feels in control of her life and work, even when, at times, she feels overworked or underpaid.

Business organizations, no less than individuals, that suffer from vagueness or ambiguity in their stated reasons for existing reach dead ends and burn out. Even many CEOs of Fortune 100 corporations have difficulty expressing their organization's vision or mission in clear, executable terms. One major international company describes its mission as "to increase shareowner value." Its employees find it difficult to translate that statement into action for two reasons:

1. *Shareowner* is too narrow a concept.
2. The mission statement as a whole is too specific and limiting.

To quote one of its managers, "Our mission statement makes it seem our company's good only for making a profit for the investors. We don't feel like it does anything for us or for our customers."

Increasing Personal and Group Power Through Synergy

Organizing your life and work gives you the ability to help your organization design mission statements and goal-driven action plans that identify the competencies the organization needs for accomplishing its goals and objectives. You can help the company prioritize and harmonize its goals to create better coordination, and to help it develop more teamwork, if not teams. Finally, you can also encourage commitment by involving people in the planning process as well as in the execution of the plans. The synergy created as each person contributes his personal power to benefit the group produces greater results than any one person or any group of individuals working separately could produce. In turn, the success of the group contributes to the ability of the individual to increase his personal power.

Notes

1. Mark D. Fefer, "How Layoffs Pay Off," *Fortune* (January 24, 1994), p. 12; Fred Hapgood, "Keeping It Simple" (description of Lantech Inc., a manufacturer of industrial packaging equipment), *Inc. Technology* 1 (1996), pp. 66–72; John A. Byrne, "Strategic Thinking," *Business Week* (August 26, 1996), pp. 46–52.
2. John Kotter, "Kill Complacency . . . ," adapted from *Leading Change* (still-to-be published book by Harvard Business School Press), in *Fortune* (August 3, 1996), pp. 168–170.

Section 2

Planning, Realistic Visioning, Action Planning, and Dealing With the Unexpected

4

Increasing Personal Power Through Planning

Strive for excellence, not perfection.

—Author Unknown

How fortunate for wild geese! They don't have to plan for their migration. The seasons change, and instinct gives them flight. We humans, on the other hand, have suppressed our instinct for simplicity, and, in the absence of that instinct, we must plan. People with self-management skills recognize the importance of planning and strive to become the best they can become and achieve the best of the goals they have set for themselves.

> Perfectionism can drive you and other people insane. Excellence, on the other hand, comes from setting your sights on *realistic, achievable* goals for increasing the personal strengths on which you want to build.

Roadblocks to Effective Planning

The thought processes involved in planning seem too linear and too structured for some people, and the planning model I lay out in this section evokes four distinct types of resisters:

1. People who never plan anything beyond the immediate future
2. People who confuse to-do lists with goals

3. People who set goals without giving thought to how they relate to one another, to their lives as a whole, or with those of the people closest to them
4. People who set ultimate goals and leap into activities without any intermediate goals

Failure to Plan

Some of us just live and take life as it comes. We rationalize, "Well, you can't predict the future so just go with the flow." Floating this way often gives rise to frustration and feeling unrewarded. That frustration and lack of reward then reinforce the aimlessness: "Why bother?" Actually, people who say they make no plans plan more than they think, and their thinking extends beyond day-to-day living.

Like wild geese, we are goal-oriented creatures; we have instinctive goals. Culture and family also fashion goals for children to adopt, and as the children grow up, they don't realize those goals unconsciously compel them to act in specific ways. For example, some might be unconsciously motivated by a desire for security, a life undisturbed by risk or challenge. Even so-called nonplanners actually made unconscious choices at an early age and live accordingly.

Unexamined goals born of nature or of nurture are fuzzy, ill defined, and hard to separate from daily comings and goings, but they exist nonetheless. Getting control over your life doesn't have to involve complex and detailed plans. Rather, it requires (at least) that you recognize the unconscious vision developed early on, and that you become aware of the goals you're attempting to achieve to realize the vision. Doing so will reduce the frustration and help you identify the rewards you are getting relative to the plan you now pursue.

Writing Too Many To-Do Lists

Many people make laundry lists of daily things to do. They usually list the easy-to-do stuff first and save the progressively tougher stuff for later in the day. By the time they get through the mountain of easy stuff, they're too tired to do the tougher stuff. What gets put off until "I'm more up to it" may never get done because the procrastination has ignited a fire (i.e., has created crises) that has consumed the to-do list; the fire now has to be managed. Hear their lament: "No matter how hard I try, my life's just one crisis after another, but I operate better when I'm under pressure."

To-do list writers are just kidding themselves about working better under pressure, and the pressure they put themselves under also adversely affects all the people around them. But, more to the point, to-do list writers often don't know *why* they're doing anything they do and when asked usually reply, "I had to do it." They feel a sense of pride when, at the end of a day, they can put a checkmark in front of every item on the list, but eventually they wind up feeling frustrated and unrewarded. They don't know what *outcomes* they're supposed to produce, and they can't recognize the successful completion of a goal as its own reward.

What you do and when you do it derives importance from *why* you're doing it. Goals and objectives should drive activities, not the other way around. Writing your to-do list as a response to results you want to or have to produce will prevent a lot of the daily fires and make what you do much more rewarding.

Setting Conflicting Goals

Many people don't see how their goals relate to one another, to their lives as a whole, or to other people's lives. Finding it difficult to avoid conflicts, they usually complain, "I can't bring balance or order into my life." They too feel frustrated, although they can claim many rewards for their efforts, but not always the payoffs they would most like to have.

The situation worsens for some people because others make demands on them they seem not able to refuse (for whatever reason). Many "fast track" young and married managers at large corporations find their career goals and family goals constantly pulling them in different directions; their supervisors only exacerbate the problem by making demands on these young people that drag them one way when their families would rather they go another.

It sounded like a dialogue from a movie, but this conversation went on in front of me, beginning when the earnest young woman told her boss, "I'm sorry, sir. I can't go to California next week. It's my anniversary Tuesday."

"So?"

"I do have a life outside of this office, you know," she answered.

"What life?" her boss demanded to know. Without waiting to hear the answer, he said, "Your life's here. Until you're the boss, you don't have any other life." The young woman went to California.

Goals in conflict force people into no-win situations, as in the young woman's case. While she did understand her conflict, she felt compelled by her boss to make her career choice. But some people—without any external pressure from a demanding boss or other person—place the same kind of impossible (contradictory) demands on themselves. Separating their lives into various action arenas (or "dimensions," as I suggest later) and coordinating among their goals and with other people's goals would put an end to many of the stresses they experience.

Diving Into Activities

The same people who write many uncoordinated goals also tend to dive right into things to do without first designing action plans for achieving goals or for monitoring progress. Their desires drive their actions before they've thought about what they have to do to get what they want. They tend to solve problems the same way: See the symptoms of things going wrong and jump on a solution before identifying the real problem or its cause.

Intermediate goals (objectives or milestones) help you keep on track and increase the number of little successes that add up to successfully reaching your ultimate goal. That type of planning identifies the different demands the dimensions of your life make on you, the resources you need, and the barriers you have to overcome. To manage the dimensions of your life successfully takes time, effort, and self-discipline.

Designing Realistic Plans

It's an imperfect world. People make mistakes. They misjudge opportunities and their ability to take advantage of them. They are, in a word, fallible. On the other hand, let's not rationalize away serious errors, misjudgments, or shoddy work. A trainer's game called "When 99.9% Is Not Good Enough" makes clear the dangers of being cavalier about fallibility, but when life and death aren't at stake, cutting yourself and other people a little slack may actually help you and them achieve excellence. Reaching for the one "perfect" goal can, contrarily, diminish everyone's chances.

Consider what happened to the owner of a large Dallas employment agency group in the late 1970s and early 1980s. He would express the group's annual sales income goal as a single target toward which everyone had to work. To determine monthly goals for the whole company, he'd divide the annual goal by twelve. To determine goals of each of the operating groups, he'd divide the organizational goals by the number of operating groups. He'd set individual goals for employees in each group by dividing each group's goal by the number of people in it. And, no matter how unrealistic his numbers were, he wouldn't entertain discussion of historically demonstrated "up" and "down" cycles in the business. When people failed to meet his goals, they felt powerless and humiliated, which contributed to their inability to reach future targets.

When the recession in 1982 hit Dallas, he refused to modify any of his goals. "You set a goal and you never retreat from it," he'd say. He even had people wear lapel buttons that proclaimed, WE WILL NOT JOIN THE RECESSION. A year later he was out of business.

Wanting to reach your highest goals drives your quest for "being all you can be" (as they say in the U.S. Army slogan). Developing your personal power for being the best you can be depends on goals and action plans that take into account (1) a realistic appraisal of your capabilities or competencies, and (2) your willingness (or lack of it) to devote yourself to developing the needed skills.

Take care, however, not to turn commitment into an unrealistic obsession, the way my friend in Dallas did. It can destroy you. Insurmountable barriers can defeat you. Recognizing these realities won't turn you into a loser (as some people say). As Aristotle said, a truly brave person knows when to retreat. Not recognizing when the odds are totally against you and not making the proper adjustments in your life will, indeed, ensure failure. When all your valiant efforts don't lead to one goal, be ready to shift gears for driving toward another—equally great—one. Look for other of your strengths on which you *want* to capitalize and take corrective action before you become too locked into what might be a disastrous effort.

Increasing your personal power takes realistic planning, flexibility, and patience—as well as determination. Realities have a nasty habit of getting in the way of best-laid plans. Hundreds of thousands of people attend touring motivational rallies, yet few achieve the loftiest goals they set for themselves. Not that they don't try, and not that they shouldn't stretch themselves out of their comfort zones. Still, they risk diminishing their personal power rather than increasing it unless they have a more systematic, more realistic method than merely wishing it so.

Prescribing Performance Ranges, Not Perfection

Setting one and only one target for measuring performance overlooks several critical factors: (1) your *readiness* to achieve your goal (your competence), (2) your *willingness* to achieve it (your commitment), and (3) the *internal or external conditions* that might affect goal attainment (coordination within the group and with economic realities). That's why Peter Drucker and George Odiorne,[1] pioneers of "management by objectives," called for *performance ranges.* Rather than set a fixed (usually optimal) target for any of your goals, it makes sense to set a variety of possible levels of attainment.

✦ *Minimally acceptable performance (pessimistic goal).* What you might expect from yourself when you're setting out on a chosen path, with no experience and little training. As a manager, it's what you might expect a trainee to achieve in a given time frame.

✦ *Optimal performance (optimistic goal).* What you might expect from yourself when you feel competent at what you're doing. As a manager, it's the closest to perfection you might expect from the most expert person in a given time frame.

✦ *Realistic performance (realistic goal).* What you might expect from yourself after deciding on your optimistic goal and recognizing the possibility that one obstacle or another may prevent you from reaching it. Only by setting this standard of performance closer to optimal performance can you hope to stretch yourself beyond the minimum. (And, as a manager, this standard is what you might expect the average person, with training, to achieve in a given time frame.)

Just as you approach a physical fitness program in stages, prescribing performance ranges for yourself in all things you do increases your ability to manage your own life. A wise old saying tells us that if you want to reach the moon (realistic goal), shoot for the stars (optimistic goal). Setting your goals high, shooting for the stars, encourages you to strive for optimal results. Should you, for some reason, not reach the stars, you will have at least achieved much of what you do want. By setting the three performance ranges, you avoid the frustration our friend in Dallas produced by having, one, and only one, goal to shoot for.

Yes, like The Little Engine That Could, you should think you can. But, just because you think you can doesn't mean you will. Yet, thinking you can't ensures that you won't.

Planning and the Plan

Designing an action plan for reaching the moon doesn't guarantee you'll achieve your goal, but having no plan at all practically guarantees failure. A strategic plan, either a plan for your personal life or a plan for your business, is a temporary stopping point in the process of planning. Too often a plan grows dust on the shelf—a book that few, if any, people ever read—whereas it should be a launching pad for action. The implementation of the plan also propels planning to another level, another stage, another phase of your life or work—or provides the basis for taking off in a new direction.

Any number of processes beyond your immediate control (including unintended consequences) can force you to rethink where you're going or how you'll get there. Astronaut Jim Lovell tells you how having an unforeseeable problem, the explosion on board his Apollo 13 spacecraft, can abort a well-designed plan.[2] In fact, after you start out on a journey, you may change your mind and decide on a different destination, but that's okay. Regardless of what action you take, your original plan will help you know and understand where your new plan begins.

Pogo, the philosophic comic-strip possum in my generation's funny papers, said, "We have met the enemy and he is us." The lack of a plan is the enemy of action; the lack of action is the enemy of a plan. Lacking a plan is akin to getting in the car and aimlessly "just driving around" at a time when important goals must be reached. If, on the other hand, you start out with at least a destination in mind, you're likely to get there, and if not, you'll have a way to find out the reason why.

"The plan is nothing. The planning *process* is everything," Dwight Eisenhower reportedly said when he was supreme commander of the Allied Forces in Europe during World War II. Actually, the two—the planning process (*strategic thinking*) and the plans that emerge along the way (rather than any one plan)—work together to control your destiny. Thinking on your feet about the future as you execute the plan and overcoming problems with long-range solutions help to prevent obstacles to your goals from subverting everything you do.

Strategic thinking propels you into the dynamic and continuous process of turning possibilities into realities—the process of identifying possible *opportunities* and possible *barriers* to achieving the goals you want for yourself or for your business. It consists of problem solving and decision making, the results of which you might capture on paper (the plan). In a world of continuous flux, looking at your life or your business as a growing, evolving organism helps you stay alert to the demand for taking in a continuous flow of information and remaining flexible and adaptable. *Planning* (thinking ahead, looking for possible snags, dealing in worst-case scenarios) and *the plan* (a list of goals, objectives, and activities) make managing your life and your business effective. One feeds on the other.

Coordination and Planning

Self-management also calls for skills and a willingness to coordinate the goals and activities within your life plans with those of other people. Coordination prevents personal and interpersonal goal conflicts. Consider a graduate student who marries a woman with two children from a previous marriage. It's reasonable to assume, then, that he has two primary goals: to earn the Ph.D., and to be a great husband and father. But the two courses of action that spring from those goals are destined to clash. While he has a deep inner passion for both goals, acquiring the competencies for one diminishes his ability to serve the other. He suffers from goal conflicts that effective self-management can prevent.

Having a plan for your life not only helps you understand what you want, where you're going, and how you're going to get there, but it helps other people as well. Coordinating your life and work with other people helps prevent conflicts that throw barriers into both of your paths. Knowing your plan also allows other people to help get to where you (and they) want to go, or at least to get out of your way if they've nothing to contribute.

Overlooking other people's goals or life plans leads to conflicts with them. You can facilitate coordinating your plans with theirs by sharing common goals or aligning your goals with theirs and vice versa. Planning and sharing your plans with the people around you is a matter of self-discipline, or a high degree of communication skills (skills in self-disclosure, in listening, in giving feedback). Most important, they require a willingness to accommodate your demands to satisfy those of the people you want close to you. Coordination is the first step toward full collaboration and teamwork.

Planning, the Plan, and Action

Even the best plans die aborning when they suffer from a lack of action. Doing what your plan prescribes transfers it from the printed page (or from inside your mind) to reality. Plans are blueprints or road maps that merely sit there and do nothing. Therefore, make *goal-directed action* the purpose of your plans.

If you do nothing to implement your plans, you might as well not do any planning at all. As you implement your plans, simultaneously engage in the planning process, always on the watch for previously unforeseen problems that explode and force you to abort your mission. Fear of unknown barriers and of possible explosions can prevent you from acting on your plans. Indeed, the most common reasons for inaction after drawing up a plan is the inability of the planner to do what is required: the lack of skill or the lack of will.

Commitment and Increasing Power

Overcoming a lack of skill depends on overcoming a lack of will because if you don't have the competencies or skills you need for achieving your own goals, you can acquire them—but without commitment you can't take responsibility for yourself. That's the moral of all those heartwarming, inspiring tales about people overcoming their disabilities to achieve greatness. Taking responsibility for yourself is risky and requires that you have the desire or passion for working plans that make managing your life possible. Passion tempered by reality becomes a powerful force for living.

Notes

1. Peter Drucker, *Management: Tasks, Responsibilities, Practices* (New York: Harper & Row, 1973), in particular, pp. 37–129; George S. Odiorne, *Management by Objectives II* (Belmont, Calif.: David S. Lake, 1979).
2. Jim Lovell and Jeffrey Kluger, *Lost Moon: The Perilous Voyage of Apollo 13* (New York, Boston: Houghton Mifflin, 1994).

Other Sources

Hamel, Gary, and C. K. Prahalad. *Competing for the Future.* Boston: Harvard Business School Press, 1994.

Kallinger, Joseph C., and Karsten G. Hellebust. *Strategic Planning Workbook.* New York: Wiley, 1989 and 1993.

Moore, James. *The Death of Competition: Leadership and Strategy in the Age of Business Ecosystems.* New York: HarperCollins, 1996.

Wheatley, Margaret. *Leadership and the New Science: Learning About Organizations From an Orderly Universe.* San Francisco: Berret-Koehler, 1992 and 1994.

5

Vision and Reality

You must have both vision and a capacity to implement it.
Because if you have a vision without relating it to reality, you
have nothing. You have a fiction, and what we need in politics
is non-fiction.*

—Shimon Peres (quoted in *Newsweek,*
December 4, 1995, p. 53)

The good fortune of wild geese shows itself once again! Their migratory vision is built in. We should only be so lucky. Instead, our culture or family usually charts a course for us. We then have a
responsibility to ourselves to exercise our personal power to bend
that course by relating the vision for our lives and work to the realities
of our world and by managing the dimensions of our lives.

> To increase personal power through self-management, relate the vision
> for your life and work to the realities of your world and manage the
> dimensions of your life.

Vision

A vision is a guiding tool that directs how you set goals for fulfilling
it; the goals then give meaning to the practical actions of your life.
The vision itself, however, consists of a set of broad *first principles*

*I would replace Peres's word *politics* here with the broader but equally valid word
life.

49

from which everything else flows, a picture of possible futures with which you shape your present world. The vision for your life emerges from the answer to, What can be? and, What should "what can be" look like?

Listen in on an imaginary team from the Hilton Hotel chain as they ask themselves, "What can we do with that old L&N railroad station in Pensacola, Florida?" Built in 1912, the depot served the railroad and the town faithfully for many years before the downward spiral of the railroad economy forced L&N to retire the old building. After some debate about the empty and unused depot, a team member says something to the effect, "Why not turn that station into the foyer and function rooms of a fifteen-story hotel?"

The team saw the "what can be" when looking at the "what is" and converted the two-story L&N station into the Grand Hotel. Now the old brick and wood edifice proudly graces the façade of a glass, steel, and concrete tower, and *it gives the new building its unique character.* Seeing what can be is the solid foundation on which all goals and objectives are built.

Seeing the possible expands your vision of what you can be, whereas defining yourself as a specific something limits your vision. Athlete, artist, entrepreneur, those are career goals, not identities. Broadening your vision opens up the possibilities for being a whole person.

Sidney Franklin, the first American bullfighter, told me: "If I had followed my family's wishes, I'd probably be a very unhappy man. Instead, I left home when I was a *pischer* [in his teens] and sought a *life,* not a career."[1] By not defining yourself too specifically or narrowly, you free yourself to express your personal vision as, for example, *To live a satisfying, self-fulfilling, creative life in which I can make contributions to the world and, perhaps, influence it in some way.* Now you can set goals that can fulfill the wholeness of your vision.

Franklin might have given the same advice to a company, and SBC Corporation, Inc. is one company that acts as if he actually had. SBC sees itself as not just a telephone company but as "the friendly neighborhood global communications company," providing cellular phone, cable, and advertising services as well as telephone lines. SBC's vision statement is admittedly broad, and yet it provides clear and unambiguous direction for setting the goals that can fulfill the vision.

On the other hand, to prevent clarity from crystallizing into a rigid obsession, treat a vision as a starting point that guides action for *only as long as it is appropriate to the circumstances.* How do you spell *survival* amid all the rapid changes in our world? A-D-A-P-T-A-B-I-L-I-T-Y.

Who would have dreamed that AT&T would voluntarily break itself up into separate, smaller, more flexible operating units? It's ironic when you consider that previously it took the Justice Department many years to take apart the old company's superstructure and create the Baby Bells. Change or be changed, isn't that a corollary of "control your own destiny or someone else will?"

Often life imposes the demand to change on us. The tragic fall actor Christopher Reeve took has compelled him to create a new vision for his life rather than stay the course or give up.[2] You shouldn't have to fall off a horse and break your neck before preparing yourself to stay in control of life's impositions. That preparation comes from a flexible vision for your life that takes into account many different personally satisfying possibilities of what you can be. In business it also means to see what is possible when you look at what is.

Reality

"Dream the impossible dream" makes for good poetry in musical theater, but impossible dreams are impossible. To succeed, you have to respect the exigencies of reality.

Visioning distinguishes itself from dreaming because it bumps up against reality. Ryder's original dream of being the best and biggest trucking company in the country bumped up against the growth of air and rail freight; Ryder had to change its identity to survive and expand into other forms of transportation. IBM's dream of being the biggest as well the first and foremost in the computer industry bumped up against smaller, more flexible companies; "biggest" had to give way to smaller and more decentralized to realize "first and foremost" (which it still hasn't fulfilled). Reality doesn't care much for dreams.

To make the most of your personal power, think of your life in management terms: areas or spans of control. I've divided those areas of control into seven realities, or dimensions (listed in alphabetical order in Exhibit 5-1) that shape your life and influence the look of

Exhibit 5-1. The seven dimensions of a life.

Career	The work you want to do; it includes the status you want to achieve in your work life (e.g., CEO of your own company)
Community relations	Roles you want to play in society
Family relations	What you want for both your family of origin (parents, etc.) and for your acquired family or families
Finances	Your desired earnings from work and your income from other sources; outlays for tangible and intangible expenditures; luxuries as well as necessities (e.g., food and leisure travel)
Material goods	Things you want to have or own, e.g., house, cars
Personal values	Your goals with regard to moral values, health, and spiritual needs (religious, emotional, or psychological forms of expression)
Social relations	The relationships you want to have with people closest to you other than family (friends) and with acquaintances, neighbors, and colleagues or associates.

your personal vision. Instead of attacking all the realities of your life at the same time or with equal energy, separate them into those that are most important to you *at this time* and over which you need to exercise the most control.

Only you can define which dimension is most important to you, but, when planning, fitting the goals you set for fulfilling your life's vision into at least these seven dimensions would prevent you from overlooking something that matters to you or that has connections with other areas of concern or value to you. When I say "at least" these seven dimensions, I mean you can subdivide your life into smaller units or add more dimensions if you wish.

Separate the seven dimensions from one another only for the purpose of analysis. In the real world, they overlap or otherwise relate to each other in various ways. Take, for example, having things you want (the dimension of material goods); that may depend on conditions of finances, having the financial means (or the credit) to pay the bill; purchasing goods, in its turn, is a financial transaction or outlay. Community relations and social relations may have people in common; the role you play in the community may depend on having acquaintances in high places, or that role could introduce you to them. Your social and community relationships may also depend on your personal values, on your career status, on the work you do, or on the financial standing you have in the community. Sorting out these relationships and setting priorities as well as milestones are necessary for getting from where you are to where you want to go.

Exhibit 5-2 draws the relations between vision, dimensions, goals, objectives, and activities. Here's how to use the model.

Decide first on a vision for your life; the vision as you see it now determines the dimensions that mean the most to you. Choose one or more of the dimensions from among the seven I've listed as a place to start your planning. The dimensions you choose determine the high-priority areas of your life; if you choose them all, you then have to rank them in order of priority. Identify the goal(s) you need to

Exhibit 5-2. From vision to action, personal model.

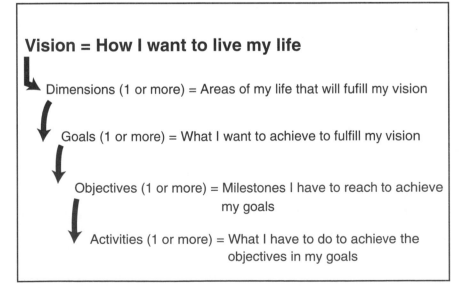

Vision = How I want to live my life

Dimensions (1 or more) = Areas of my life that will fufill my vision

Goals (1 or more) = What I want to achieve to fulfill my vision

Objectives (1 or more) = Milestones I have to reach to achieve my goals

Activities (1 or more) = What I have to do to achieve the objectives in my goals achieve to satisfy each dimension. To achieve each goal, identify the objective(s) or milestone(s) you have to reach; these objectives then define what you have to do (the activities) to reach those objectives. The purpose of this scheme? To replace a thing- or clock-orientation with a goal-orientation. In the model what you do (activities) originates in and serves the plan expressed in the goals and objectives in a specific dimension.

Managing the Dimensions of Your Life

Columnist Susan Shellenbarger raises the Michael Keaton film *Multiplicity* to the level of social commentary when she claims that it pounds this critical nail on its head: "role overload."[3] Today's workers are "driven nearly nuts" by the demands of trying to be good parents, mates to their working spouses, and workers. As the journalist often points out, only a few companies really do anything to help their employees manage these competing demands.[4] Both the movie and Ms. Shellenbarger may exaggerate the solution to the situation most people face, but they both build their premise on the obvious truth that many people are torn in too many directions.

In response to a *Business Week* survey, 42 percent of 8,000 people said that work has a negative impact on their home life, while only 32 percent said it has a positive impact. Sixty percent responded that management didn't give much thought to people's needs when making decisions that affect their lives. Even in family-friendly companies, according to the survey results, employees perceive that the lion's share of the benefits go to white-collar workers, professional staffers, managers, and day-shift workers. Most of the friendliest companies also lead their industries in income (e.g., DuPont, Hewlett-Packard, Motorola), but few companies, according to the answers the surveyors received, operate strategies and programs that satisfy the competing demands of working people.[5]

And, demands do compete—just because different dimensions of your life compete for satisfaction. The competition then gives rise to the lament you read before: "I need to find a balance to my life."

What an image that phrase "balance to my life," conjures up: a scale on which a certain amount of one dimension equals a certain amount of another. But, that image doesn't make much sense because you can't count out wishes, wants, needs, and goals like so many gram weights per dimension. Maybe that's why most people don't get control of the demands on their lives. They're going about it all wrong.

Harmonizing Goals

Rather than try to balance goals against each other, seek ways to harmonize them, ways to make them work together. Sometimes it's necessary to emphasize one dimension instead of another to bring about what the Japanese call *wa* and the Taoists call *T'ai*, or tranquility: feeling satisfied with the relationships among all those things that matter in your life. Stratford Sherman, writing in *Fortune*, and John P. Robinson and Geoffrey Godbey, writing in *American Demographics*, point out that some people are already working toward harmonizing their lives in this sense: deciding first of all what is important to them and willingly subordinating everything else.[6]

The story of the conflicted young woman who went to California instead of celebrating her wedding anniversary isn't a unique one. Although most young career people with families want to be good spouses and good parents (the family dimension):

- Most of them have to earn a living or develop a career (career or finances dimension).
- Most of them want things (material goods dimension).
- Most of them have parents, siblings, and friends with whom they want to spend time (family and social relationships).
- Some of them want to take part in the life of their community, e.g., serve on the school board (community relationships).

Young parents may have to spend less time with friends and their own parents in order to develop careers and spend time with their children. They may have to buy fewer things for themselves and forgo active community relationships until the children are older, but they can still have *some* things and still serve their community in a *less aggressive* way. These are choices with which people are faced all of the time. They're particularly painful for people who want careers and family life while the companies they work for place excessive demands on them. David Whitman in a *U.S. News and World Report* article, "The Myth of AWOL Parents," makes the point that many people do make such choices, decisions that shape who they are and the lives they lead.[7] These are the options with which women have had to grapple for many years, and career tracking systems may not be fair to parent-employees because they tend to penalize people who take time to also be mothers or fathers.

Preventing Goal Conflicts

Creating greater harmony in your life prevents collisions between goals of various dimensions, e.g., climbing a career ladder in a highly competitive environment *and* spending more time with your family. Using strategic thinking to line up various dimensions against each other can reveal the stresses between their goals. A chart like Exhibit 5-3 can help you sort out the possible goal conflicts by identifying where and how goals clash.

In the exhibit you can see that the promotion goal and the goals of the family (the items in italics) compete mercilessly. I could have indicated the objectives and activities for the family and material goods dimensions in greater detail, but you probably can see the conflicts or collisions clearly enough. Something has to give in this scheme of things, and the decisions to make should be yours, based

Exhibit 5-3. Identifying where and how goals clash.

Career	Family	Material Goods
Goal: Earn a promotion to manager in 3 years. *Objective:* Increase influence within 2 years. *Essential Activities:* ➤ Volunteer for committees. ➤ Do extra work, even if that means overtime and working weekends.	*Goal 1:* Spend 2 hours daily with children beginning now. *Goal 2:* Spend 2 hours daily with spouse beginning now. *Goal 3:* Meet children's physical comforts beginning now.	*Goal 1:* Buy entertainment center after first raise. *Goal 2:* Buy sports car after second raise.

on which of the dimensions have the greatest significance for you (and your significant others).

I counseled dysfunctional families in the Fort Worth, Texas, area for four years early in my career life and saw firsthand to what extremes goal collisions can drive a family. As a rule, couples don't sit down with charts like Exhibit 5-3 and ask one another, "Which dimension do you want to emphasize? What goals do you want to achieve first? How can we reconcile the differences? How can working toward one goal help satisfy another?" The failure to work through these issues in this manner frequently leads to spousal abuse, child abuse, or divorce.

Likewise, not many managers sit down with charts like this and ask, "Which of our goals do we have to emphasize now to satisfy our mission? What are our work group's highest priorities?" They rarely look at the priorities in an employee's chart and ask, "Which of these goals should he emphasize? What are his highest priorities?" Failure to work through the issues in this manner frequently leads to missed goals, unhappy managers and employees, and angry customers. On the other hand, many of "tomorrow's CEOs" do make an effort to build relationships with other people in what writer Justin Martin calls "the foundation for progress."[8]

Notes

1. Sidney Franklin's advice to me when I was in my early teens; his family and mine were neighbors in Brooklyn, New York, from 1947 to 1952, and he visited often.
2. Interview with Christopher and Dana Reeve, on *Dateline*, NBC Television Network, December 26, 1995 (and elsewhere).
3. Susan Shellenbarger, "Feel Like You Need to Be Cloned? Even That Wouldn't Work," *Wall Street Journal* (July 10, 1996), p. B1.
4. See, for example, Susan Shellenbarger, "Hewlett Keeps Trying to Reshape Workplace to Help Family Life," *Wall Street Journal* (May 3, 1995), p. B1.
5. Keith H. Hammonds, "Balancing Work and Family: Big Returns for Companies Willing to Give Family Strategies a Chance," *Business Week* (September 16, 1996), pp. 74–80.
6. Stratford Sherman, "Leaders Learn to Heed the Voice Within," *Fortune* (August 22, 1994), pp. 92–100; John P. Robinson and Geoffrey Godbey, "The Great American Slowdown," *American Demographics* (June 1996),

pp. 42–48. See also Diane Crisfall, "How to Manage in a Chaotic Work-place," *American Demographics* (June 1996), pp. 50–52.

7. David Whitman, "The Myth of AWOL Parents," *U.S. News and World Report* (July 1, 1996), pp. 54–56. See also Jerry Adler, "Building a Better Dad," *Newsweek* (June 17, 1996), pp. 58–64.

8. Justin Martin, "Tomorrow's CEOs," *Fortune* (June 24, 1996), pp. 76–90.

6

How to Prevent Personal and Organizational Lockjaw

Even if you're on the right track, you'll get run over, if you
just sit there.

—Will Rogers (1879–1935)

Geese don't have to think about the future. At the right time, when
climatic conditions change, their instincts propel them skyward, to
fly for "home." But that doesn't mean they'll always get there. Something can get in the way: unseasonable weather, disease, hunters.
Geese, too, can suffer from "stochastic shocks": unforeseen, unforeseeable changes or upheavals that undermine your neat and tidy
plans.[1] This is where visioning collides with reality.

Self-management calls for you to look forward as much as possible, but the farther forward you look, the less accurate your predictions will be. Life is essentially a crapshoot that you can't reduce to
sure-bet goals, objectives, and planned activities before sailing forward. You have to act on many vague or ambiguous goals because you
can't always foresee changes over which you have no control. Andy
Grove, CEO of Intel Corporation, put it this way: "You need to plan
the way a fire department plans. It cannot anticipate fires, so it has to
shape a flexible organization that is capable of responding to unpredictable events."[2]

> Self-management requires visioning, which requires a high degree of
> healthy anxiety about the future (i.e., expecting the unexpected).

The future's unpredictability doesn't shield you from the need for planning. Indeed, our justifiable lack of confidence in the future adds to the importance of strategic thinking to undo self-satisfaction. Self-management requires visioning, and visioning requires a high degree of healthy anxiety about the future (which means, simply, to expect the unexpected). Only by planning can you gain control over the directions in which the rivers of your life and organizations flow and create your futures. Strategic thinking that involves communicating with others, collaborating with them, and coordinating your goals creates many cogent ideas for achieving any given set of personal or organizational objectives. That teamwork increases personal power as well as organizational power.

Create the Future

Don't try to *predict* the future. Create it. If you set a goal and work hard to achieve it, you have a better chance of making a future to your liking. Remember why you can't predict the future: It hasn't happened yet. Thus, your future is open for you to help shape it. If you set performance ranges and alternative goals toward which you can direct your energies, you are even more likely to make your future reflect your "predictions."

Expect the Unexpected

By definition, you can't predict what the unexpected will be, but you can expect it to happen. If you drive a car, you know that training and experience have programmed you to expect the unexpected all the time.

Consider this. You can't foresee when a highway crazy will cut you off or otherwise disrupt your drive to work. You don't even consciously think about such potential calamities when they happen. Instead, training and practice cause you to react properly to the situation. On a dry day, you exercise one brake maneuver. On a wet day, a different one. And, most often you avoid the accident. You can be, and should be, that well prepared for business shocks.

Learn Continuously

Watch the world around you, become aware of things happening, not just in your profession or in your industry but also in those events that seem peripheral. They create ripples that can drown you or your organization by the time they reach you.

Have you heard of the so-called butterfly effect? A butterfly flapping its wings on an island in the South Pacific can set off a chain of events that finally drops a foot of snow in Buffalo, New York. In practical terms for a global economy, the butterfly effect means that changes in Toledo, Spain, can and do affect your world in Toledo, Ohio. And yet, sad to say, people in the United States are woefully ignorant of the rest of the world. How much do we in the United States even know about our neighbor Canada?

Communicate With Other People

Especially if you're one of a corporation's insulated leaders, a CEO or CFO, knocking down the walls of the executive suite may not be enough if you're not also talking with people from the front line. Listen to your vendors. Listen to your customers. Read what other people are saying in more than one newspaper or news magazine; *Business Week* and *The Wall Street Journal* rarely ever talk about the same economic news the same way. Make your decisions on the basis of more than one interpretation of the same event. You let events blindside you when you look at them from a biased or otherwise narrow perspective.

Set Flexible Rather Than Rigid Goals and Objectives

Be tenacious about the vision for your life (broad and vague, by definition), but don't be a bulldog about how you get there. After setting goals, identify the milestones you have to reach in order to achieve the goals; then design an action plan for reaching those essential milestones. As you proceed along paths set up by the plan, revise (overhaul) the plan by changing or adding goals, objectives, or activities or by deleting them when they aren't needed or aren't working. Design both best-case scenarios and worst-case scenarios. *What can you do if the world won't live up to your expectations?* Flexibility allows you respond to unintended consequences (what happens as a result of what you do that you neither intended nor expected).

Set Parallel Goals

Follow two or more paths toward two or more goals in the same dimension. Pursuing two careers at the same time—e.g., director of human resources *and* author of self-help books—insulates you from career destruction should you lose your job. Satisfying two family goals at the same time—e.g., strong relations with your spouse and children *and* strong relations with your siblings—prevents unpleasant scenes when competing demands force difficult decisions. Becoming multifaceted not only increases your flexibility; it also makes you a more interesting person.

Shock Your System

Shatter the complacency you feel about the status quo by shocking your system or, as some people would say, by "getting out of your comfort zone." Shocking your system means only to seek out new goals in new directions, to go to "places" you've never been before. In either case, don't confuse this process with "shifting paradigms," which is a very different one.

In business, shocking your system means, instead, to look at what you're doing, to look at what other people are doing (especially at what your competitors are doing), and to make changes that help you leap forward to a different plateau of growth or development. This is what Sony did when its competitors entered the Walkman market. By the time everyone else jumped on Sony's bandwagon, the Walkman's inventors came out with a smaller, more reliable version of their original invention. A few tweaks sometimes can send major ripples through your own world.

Manage Resistance to Change by Teaching

Teaching everyone in his organization the benefits of "open-book management" and *how to read the books* gave Jack Stack the advantage he needed for renewing Springfield Remanufacturing Corporation.[3] To his good fortune, Stack's employees wanted to learn. However, teaching is one thing, ensuring that people learn is another.

When you offer to teach people new ways of doing something, especially if they think that what they are doing is already "good enough," you're likely to meet resistance. People usually resist large, dramatic changes. Unless you are seen as genuinely caring about them, unless they see the benefit to themselves of making the change, they won't dance; you can't make them. The CEO of General Electric, "Neutron Jack" Welch (as his detractors call him), first tried to teach his key executives his new ways of running GE. Their resistance forced him to replace many of them in order to accomplish his vision for GE[4] (whose market value, profits, and assets are now at the top of *Business Week*'s top 1,000 companies).[5] You cannot teach people new ways of doing things if they do not want to learn.

What is the danger inherent in any system? The potential for becoming rigid or, in the case of organizations, rigid and bureaucratic. By practicing self-management, leaders teach by role-modeling the self-management behavior they expect from others, but old, bureaucratic habits are difficult to replace. Jean Batiste Aristide, former president of Haiti, led a peaceful, democratic reformation in his tiny nation only to be ousted by an entrenched military bloc; it took the threat of military intervention by the United States to restore the country's slow crawl into the twentieth century.

Prevent Organizational Lockjaw Through Teamwork

Preventing organizational lockjaw requires the diversity of perspectives, opinions, values, skills, and knowledge of many people. A management system is useless unless it can improve work-group or team performance as well as individual performance.

Expecting the unexpected for an organization and managing it require the same tools self-managed individuals need: creating the future (by initiating change and innovation), continuous learning, communication, flexibility, alternative planning, and teaching people the skills they need for continuous improvement and growth. You treat an organization like a self-managed person when you draw knowledge and information from all sources to fashion a plan for the organization's life (a vision statement) and work (a mission statement with goals and objectives). People can then translate the mission statement into their goals and objectives: what they have to accomplish to enable the organization to fulfill its mission. These goals and objectives can also direct the work group or team's activities.

Team Up to Achieve Organizational Goals

Just as wholeness characterizes a self-managed person, it also characterizes a well-managed business organization.

A business organization consists of people, facilities, capital, equipment, materials or supplies, and a complex of processes by which all that comes together to produce the business's goods or deliver its services. Those processes have goals, namely "process goals," that define how the organization gets its work done, how it uses its capital, facilities, equipment, and materials and supplies; process goals define how the people in the organization relate to one another, how they relate to the organization as a whole, and how the organization relates to them. Seeing the organization as a whole takes into account all the process goals, and the large overview focuses specific individual or group process goals on organizational goals. In short, just as effective self-management consists of a wholistic approach to your life, organizational management consists in taking a wholistic approach to the organization.

By considering the process goals of the work group or team (how it gets its work done and the relationships among the members) as dynamics within the organization's processes, you help the people in the work group or team take a wholistic approach toward their life and work. Learning to take a wholistic approach is sometimes painful, and the painful lessons of others can help you prevent the same pain for yourself.

Consider the lessons learned by McDonnell-Douglas's management when it initially attempted to reorganize how the work on the jumbo military transport, the C-17, was done. Its first efforts almost destroyed the whole organization because it didn't consider the consequences of imposing threatening decisions on the people required to carry them out. You can't expect to manufacture a cost-effective, well-made air machine by sending a top manager to tell 5,000 managers to compete for 1,000 jobs and to threaten union workers with downsizing. Yet, that's what the executives of Mac did at first. After experiencing slowdowns, defects, bad engineering, and a myriad of other problems, especially lost morale, the company sent the right man to do the right job.

Don Kozlowski had managed fighter programs for Mac (its strength). When he took over the C-17 program, he walked the walk down on the line. He listened to the people doing the work, encouraging them to form teams of hands-on experts to find solutions to inefficiencies and mistakes. Although job slots did disappear and people were laid off, he still raised survivor morale by bringing everyone into the process and giving everyone ownership of the product they were producing. The result was a renewal of a company on the brink of disaster.[6]

Large organizations develop flexibility and adaptability not by downsizing but rather by promoting relatively fluid structures (even if they do downsize) that can respond to unexpected events or unintended consequences. What some people call a tiger team (a group pulled together to solve short-term problems) epitomizes what I mean.

Gene Kranz, flight director of the Apollo 13 mission at NASA's Houston Control, dumped standard operating procedures during the emergency and restructured how his flight management teams worked. To satisfy the demands of the emerging situation, he pulled his White Team out of its normal shift rotation and lengthened the duration of the two other teams to cover for the White Team. He then used the personnel of the White Team to create an ad hoc team, the sole function of which was to solve problems as they arose. Guided by the flight's overall mission (which had changed from "land on the moon and return safely" to simply "return safely"), the team shifted its goals with the shifting fortune of the capsule 240,000 miles away.[7]

Some companies have formed skunk works—semipermanent but fluid groups—that, like tiger teams, are uncommon as well as uncommonly effective manifestations of high-performance teams mandated to innovate and invent. Guided by the vision and mission of the organization in whatever they do, they create goals, objectives, and activities to support the larger organization's vision and mission. Rather than react to disasters, they create futures (some of which could produce disasters).

Call on Everyone's Resources

Each and every member of a group plays an essential role in the group's ability "to deliver the goods." If someone is expendable, she shouldn't be there in the first place. You could and should also include in your list of essential resources your vendors and other outside constituents that can affect your organization. Take into account and co-ordinate all constituencies.

To be effective, you and everyone else involved in designing your personal or organizational plans have to examine them for coherence and achievability before you set them in motion. Whether you apply the exercises in Appendix A to your personal life or to your organizational life, they demand that you manage all realities: your strengths, your weaknesses, your opportunities, and your threats. Additionally, as you develop plans for accomplishing your goals, you have to identify the talent or people resources as well as the equipment or facility resources you need for reaching your milestones. The absence of a necessary or essential resource is a barrier. If a milestone calls for completing a computer spreadsheet and you don't have a computer, you're in serious trouble before you start. Design plans to overcome barriers to your success.

Look for and eliminate goal conflicts. Each person or group's process goals, if taken in isolation from organizational goals, could compete with others or contradict the demands for organizational success. By everyone taking a wholistic approach, everyone considers what he is doing in the context of the whole, which prevents the internal struggles that competition and contradiction can produce.

You don't have to do this strategic thinking by yourself, if you're a manager or a business owner. Talents hide within the people around you just waiting to be unlocked. Open the door for employees to contribute to and influence the company's strategies by increasing employee competence, e.g., in problem solving and decision making. Employee involvement increases coordination, productivity, and profitability. Moreover, employee involvement increases commitment.[8] Once people get a taste of taking responsibility for what they do, they don't easily give it up. That's a lesson learned at General Motors' Saturn division. The employees themselves have voted down union efforts to undermine employee/management committees.

Notes

1. Robert H. Waterman, Jr., *The Renewal Factor: How the Best Get and Keep the Competitive Edge* (New York: Bantam Books, 1987), pp. 30–31.
2. Andrew S. Grove, "A High-Tech CEO Updates His Views on Managing and Careers," *Fortune* (September 18, 1995), p. 224.
3. Jack Stack and Bo Burlingham, *The Great Game of Business* (Garden City, N.Y.: Doubleday, 1992).
4. Noel M. Tichy and Stratford Sherman, *Control Your Destiny or Someone Else Will* (New York: HarperBusiness, 1993, 1994).
5. Jennifer Reingold et al., "Business Week 1000," *Business Week* (March 25, 1996), pp. 89ff.
6. Christopher Carey, "After Initial Nose Dive, C-17 Helps Transport McDonnell Douglas To Stratospheric Heights" *St. Louis Post-Dispatch* (December 31, 1995), pp. 1A and 6A–7A.
7. Jim Lovell and Jeffrey Kluger, *Lost Moon: The Perilous Voyage of Apollo 13* (Boston, New York: Houghton Mifflin, 1994), pp. 159ff.
8. Stack and Burlingham.

Other Sources

Albrecht, Karl. *The Northbound Train: Finding the Purpose, Setting the Direction, Shaping the Destiny of Your Organization.* New York: AMACOM, 1994.

Section 3

Self-Management: Increasing Group Power Within the Core Business

7

Increasing Group Power: The Core Business

If we live according to the guidance of reason, we shall desire
for others the good which we seek for ourselves.
—Baruch Spinoza (1632–1677)

A gaggle of wild geese understands its core business: to protect the
flock, to propagate, and to migrate from the cold to the warm and
from the hot to the cool. Simple. Clear. Unambiguous. If only all
businesses would express their core business that well.

For your organization to be as clever as a gaggle of geese, you
must have a core from which you can coordinate your business processes and get commitment from all your stakeholders. You define
your core business by identifying three factors:

1. The core competencies of your people
2. What the market wants you to do
3. What you want the business to do

Group power lies in the core business and in nothing else. Increasing
group power and strengthening your business's competitive edge call
for applying the goal setting inherent in self-management.

> To apply self-management to increasing group power, focus individual
> attention on specific, measurable or observable goals that satisfy both
> the organization and the individual. Otherwise people will fall back into
> "look-good" activity traps.

Self-Management and Management by Objectives

Yes, the proposition in the insert looks a lot like the Management by Objectives (MBO) of old, but just because W. Edwards Deming said some pretty tough things about Management by Objectives[1] doesn't mean that Peter Drucker and George Odiorne, grandfathers of MBO, can't instruct us on the basics of self-management and its application to business.

Applications of MBO in the United States, mainly in command-and-control environments, often encourage people to spend their intellectual capital on ways to beat the system. The idea is to meet the goals, even if you have to cheat. Instead of focusing on the intent of the goals to achieve organizational success, people focus on activities that would make them look personally successful. MBO was designed to prevent getting caught in "activity traps," among other things; therefore, any misapplication of the system that concentrates on activities rather than on goals crumbles in on itself.

At the same time, blaming the theory for human failure makes about as much sense as blaming a quarterback when the tight end drops the ball. Ideally, in MBO properly applied:

➤ Organizational leadership acquires information and feedback from *all* its constituencies (from customers to custodial engineers sweeping the floors) when formulating its vision and mission. That's the image created in Exhibit 7-1.
➤ Everyone associated with the organization indentifies the goals he has to achieve to fulfill the mission.
➤ When strategic thinking involves feedback from all directions, the entire process is collaborative, promoting coordination.

In practice, contrarily, top management usually takes information from only some of its constituencies (usually from within top management itself) and imposes all the goals and objectives from the top.

It seems risky to bank on a management theory that some people believe has failed. Why should an organization's leadership today be more likely to apply the theory any more successfully than they did in the fifties, sixties, seventies, or eighties? Because personal perceptions and management thinking are changing.

Drucker and Odiorne were ahead of their time. Partly due to

Exhibit 7-1. Ideal information flow for formulating an organization's vision and mission.

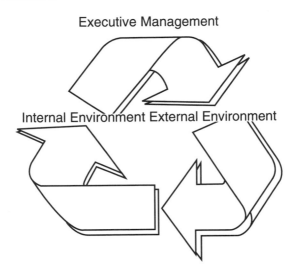

Executive Management

Internal Environment External Environment

Deming's teachings, many in executive management are freeing up their own values and methods and those of their organizations; visioning and strategic thinking are going on at the top. Many managers now "manage the dream" (as Warren Bennis, management teacher and author of *On Becoming a Leader,* says).[2] They then allow (if not encourage) employees to find their own ways to achieve that dream—to become self-managed. In these cases, top-level decisions and performance management processes include a broad feedback loop that takes advantage of the wide diversities in the workplace and that uses information from all sources. Command-and-control still exists, but it's slowly giving way to a more open, more process-oriented workplace.

This slow evolution comes about, in part, because many individuals now think in the language of MBO. They set personal goals for themselves in life plans that harmonize the different demands of their lives. They take in and use more input and feedback from the people close to them (e.g., spouses, children) than they did before. They feel more comfortable collaborating with others than they did. No, we haven't seen a global revolution in human dynamics, but more and more people feel more and more at ease in a participative world.

That comfort with participation spills over into the business environment, as individual managers see the benefit to themselves and to their organization of thinking strategically, of taking and using input and feedback from their constituencies, and of encouraging employees to make and act on their own decisions. Deming has influenced management philosophy, even if he didn't revolutionize it.

One thing Deming did was to replace the word *goals* with *standards,* which are tools organizational managers can use for knowing what they are about and where they are going. The practice of taking a customer focus to ensure meeting the standard of customer satisfaction drives the Deming business philosophy. Still, customer focus and customer satisfaction (when more than slogans) are only goals masquerading as performance standards.

Organizations define *customer focus* and *customer satisfaction* as productivity and quality goals that serve customers best and that help them stay in business. People then find ways of meeting the goals, and here's where self-management meets organizational management: by aligning individual goals and organizational goals in a way that satisfying one also satisfies the other. Self-managed people in a well-managed organization turn *their individual focus toward specific, measurable or observable organizational goals* rather than toward look-good activities. "What can I do to achieve and/or influence the organization's productivity goals? What can I do to achieve and/or influence the organization's quality goals?" The organization's results goals give direction to outcome objectives at operational and individual levels—and vice-versa—which is what Robert Krulwich said happened at a company called Pinnacle Brands.[3]

Vision to Action in Organizational Management

Vision directs goal setting and designing action plans to support its attainment. The flow from vision to action for an organization is identical to the personal flow model in Exhibit 5-2, with appropriate changes, as in Exhibit 7-2.

Vision and Mission

In Exhibit 7-2, the word *vision* refers to how people should see the organization, e.g., as a premier international transportation company.

Exhibit 7-2. From vision to action, organizational model.

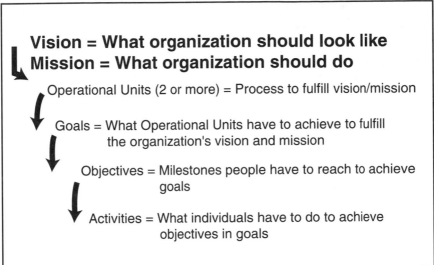

Vision = What organization should look like
Mission = What organization should do

Operational Units (2 or more) = Process to fulfill vision/mission

Goals = What Operational Units have to achieve to fulfill
the organization's vision and mission

Objectives = Milestones people have to reach to achieve
goals

Activities = What individuals have to do to achieve
objectives in goals

Its *mission* encompasses what the organization should be doing, its core business, e.g., "Increase stakeholder value by providing transportation services." While everyone *owns* the vision and mission, managers at the top manage the processes and resources that contribute to achieving the vision and the mission and managers reporting to them manage the processes and resources of operations.

Operational Units

The organizational dimensions through which vision and mission are to be accomplished can be businesses, divisions, departments, work groups, cross-functional teams—any group or processes through which work gets done. At all levels, managers are still needed to manage these processes.

Goals, Objectives, Activities

Every operational unit builds its goals, objectives, and activities with the organization's and unit's vision and mission in mind. The operational unit owns the goals of the unit, and by extention, everyone in the unit owns them as well. The objectives (milestones) necessary for reaching those goals can be divvied up among groups of members and individual members of the unit. Activities designed to reach the milestones can then be assigned to individuals.

The vision and mission are the broad parameters that direct goals and objectives; the operational details are fleshed out by the people who have to fulfill the vision and mission. But, where did those parameters come from? From, as I said before, *all* the constituencies of the organization, *including the people delivering on the vision and mission.*

Delivering on the Vision and Mission

Each and every member of an organization plays an essential role in the organization's ability to deliver the goods. You could and should also include your vendors and other outside constituents that can affect your organization in the list of essential role players. Take into account and coordinate all of your stakeholders.

Stakeholders include anyone and everyone, including society as a whole and its governing bodies, that stand to benefit in some way from the organization's existence and that give input and/or feedback to the organization. These stakeholders are an organization's constituencies:

- Owners (including stockholders and other sources of capital)
- Management employees
- Nonmanagement employees
- Customers (and the market in general)
- The industry as a whole (including competitors)
- Vendors/suppliers
- Society as a whole
- Governing bodies of the society

Ignore any one of those constituencies at your own peril. To maximize their benefit from what you do, they'll do what they can to influence or affect it. You might say they make life and death decisions for your organization through the quantity and quality of their input and their feedback.

To deliver on vision and mission, everyone involved in designing your business plans has to examine them before setting them in motion. Whether you apply the exercises in Appendix A to your personal life or to your organizational life, they demand that you manage all realities: the strengths and weaknesses, opportunities, and threats with regard to all stakeholders. In addition, as you develop plans for accomplishing your goals, you have to identify strengths from people's talents as well as from the equipment or facility resources you need and have or those you still have to get. The absence of a necessary or essential resource is a barrier (a weakness or a threat). If you need to complete a computer spreadsheet and you don't have a computer, you're in serious trouble before you start. Design plans to overcome barriers to your success.

Core Business

Identifying your organization's core business takes the organization's vision to a practical level; here you identify just what it is your organization does that maximizes the core competencies of its people. The turnaround at Sears, Roebuck provides a minicase.

After years of taking a beating from Kmart and Wal-Mart, CEO Arthur Martinez decided that to return to retail industry supremacy Sears, Roebuck and Company had to take some drastic steps: slash jobs, close stores, drop out of the catalog business, and cut loose its securities and insurance businesses. Not at all arbitrary, these turnaround slash-and-burn tactics emerged from a clear-cut redefinition of Sears' core business: retail stores. Now strategic thinking and increasing group power began with Martinez's "five priorities":

1. To focus on the core businesses: apparel, home appliances and furnishings, and automotive
2. To make the stores attractive: "more compelling," "interesting," "fresh, smart and sassy"
3. To focus on local markets
4. To lower costs
5. To instill a new mind-set throughout the company that "today, change is a constant"[4]

Corporations "will be judged," writers C. K. Prahalad and Gary Hamel believe, "on their ability to identify, cultivate, and exploit [their] core competencies [and] rethink the concept of the corporation itself."[5] That rethinking of a core business emerges from the relationships among three basic drivers you can represent in a Venn diagram (Exhibit 7-3). The diagram draws on information provided by people from both inside and outside the organization and follows from these three steps:

1. Identify what your organization does best or better than the competition (core competencies).
2. Find out what your organization's buying public wants you to do.
3. Decide on what you want the organization to do.

Match what the organization wants to do with what it can do best and with what its buying public wants it to do. The result, the shaded area in Exhibit 7-3, represents your organization's core business. Anything outside the shaded area represents what you can't do, won't do, or no one wants or needs you to do.

Exhibit 7-3. The core business.

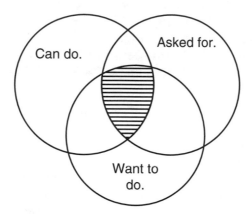

A successful organization literally exploits its core business. It maximizes what it can do best and wants to do, as long as a marketplace wants it to do it. But a successful organization can't remain successful unless it stretches itself beyond its initial core and responds to the changing demands of the market. Remember: Strategic thinking contains a high degree of anxiety about the future.

Notes

1. W. Edwards Deming, *Out of the Crisis* (Cambridge, Mass.: MIT Press, 1986).
2. Warren Bennis, *On Becoming a Leader* (Reading, Mass: Addison-Wesley, 1989).
3. Robert Krulwich, on ABC News' *Nightline*, April 9, 1996.
4. Genevieve Buck, "Stodgy Sears Turns Successfully Sassy," *Chicago Tribune* article reprinted in *St. Louis Post-Dispatch* (August 8, 1996), p. 7C.
5. C. K. Prahalad and Gary Hamel, "The Core Competence of the Corporation," *Harvard Business Review* (May-June 1990), p. 79.

8

Self-Management and Commitment

The quality of a person's life is in direct proportion to their commitment to excellence, regardless of their chosen field of endeavor.

—Vince Lombardi

Geese don't give halfhearted compliance or mere obedience to their goal. Every goose in the gaggle is dedicated to getting to where the whole group is headed. But, of course, bird *instinctive* dedication is for the birds, not for the human herd.

At no time, least of all in these times, could anyone expect from anyone else commitment without reservation. Loyalty is a learned behavior in human beings, and you have to earn another person's dedication to what *you* want. You can demand cooperation, and get compliance. You can demand obedience, especially if you hold another person's life in your hands, but that's hardly commitment. Consent in any of these cases does not imply *willingness*; people may go along with your demands, for whatever the reason, but danger lurks in how they respond to you.

> The care and feeding of self-management produces wholehearted commitment.

You can expect wholehearted commitment when you encourage and support self-management skills: wholeness, self-confidence, self-awareness, drive, self-respect/self-esteem, and respect for others. Without self-management, you can expect, at best, the lukewarm embrace of compliance from any and all your constituencies.

Self-Management Skills and Organizational Commitment

The tobacco industry has recently experienced the backlash you get when you treat people as pawns that you can manipulate at will. Let's give the industry's executives the benefit of the doubt and say they didn't lie to Congress and the world about how they manage the addictiveness of nicotine; they too were simply misinformed. Let's say that, anyway. Few people believed them, and that's the point. Even smokers turned on the industry. Many became malicious, even though they continue to smoke and buy tobacco products. That's what can happen to commitment.

Think of commitment as one end of a continuum, as in Exhibit 8-1. At the bottom of the scale you find malicious obedience, toward

Exhibit 8-1. The commitment continuum.

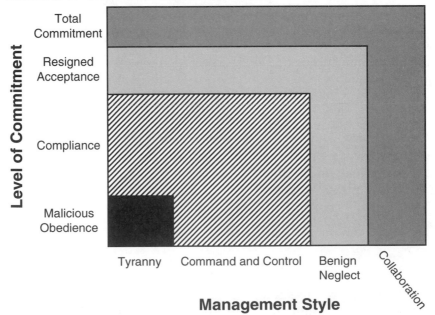

the middle is compliance, closer to the top is resigned acceptance, and at the top is total commitment. Each level of commitment is a response to a specific type of management style: tyranny, command-and-control, benign neglect, and collaboration (participative).

Malicious Obedience

This less than common type of conformity responds to demands made by harsh, punitive (tyrannical) management. "Do it or suffer the consequences."

Out-loud response: "Okay, I'll do it." Internal response: *But I'll get you in the end* (literally as well as figuratively).

The organizational result can be sabotage, slowdowns, walkouts, union organization, etc. On a personal level, watch your back and the people reporting to you.

Compliance

Compliance or acquiescence is not commitment; rather, it's a wishy-washy response to demands made by command-and-control managers, people who tell others what to do, when to do it, (often) how to do it, and (rarely) why to do it. "Do as I say or I'll punish you."

Out-loud response: "Okay." Internal response: *Yes, master.*

These most common behaviors shade off from tyranny and malicious obedience, the organizational result of which is a lack of enthusiasm and high turnover. Don't expect high productivity, creativity, or care for quality.

Resigned Acceptance

Whereas compliance is a wishy-washy response to command-and-control management, resigned acceptance is a wishy-washy response to wishy-washy management (often called laissez-faire management). "Do as you please; just don't rock the boat."

Out-loud response: "Okay." Internal response: *Somebody has to do it; I might as well.*

Total Commitment

Collaboration produces total commitment. When people feel they're linked together for mutual benefit, they also feel a wholehearted willingness to do something; only the personal desire to achieve a specific outcome or goal counts toward commitment. "Let's go there together."

Out-loud response: "Thanks for including me." Internal response: *This will be great for all of us.*

To get commitment you have to tap into the human desire to control the processes that affect their lives and to realize personal benefit or gain from doing something. Athletes drive themselves for personal fulfillment as well as for personal glory or wealth, not just for the success of the team. Ordinary people drive themselves for personal fulfillment, power, status, or wealth, not just for the good of the company.

That's not to suggest that people function only out of selfishness. Selfishness is not necessarily an ingredient of commitment. Still, ego satisfaction is an ingredient in the commitment recipe. Even the most altruistic of people want to derive some benefit from what they do, even if the benefit consists of no more than feeling good about themselves. To do other than good would make them feel bad about themselves; doing good prevents the pain of guilt or remorse.

Getting other people to commit themselves to goals you want to achieve requires that they want to achieve those goals too. The success of quality and productivity improvement comes not from demanding commitment to change from others, but rather from total commitment from both employees and managers. You have to earn their trust and confidence in what you do or believe before they will want to adopt your goals as their own. That ability to earn people's trust and confidence is part of leadership.

Look at getting commitment in terms of the six skills of self-management. When you collaborate with rather than dictate to other people, you treat them as whole people, which supports their self-confidence and their self-respect/self-esteem. You draw upon their inner mental and emotional strengths, you tap into their personal drive to satisfy their own needs by contributing to meeting organizational goals. Most of all, you treat them with the respect that they, as human beings, deserve. Now you can get their genuine commitment.

When you create an environment or climate in which each person (employees, vendors, customers, etc.) feels a stake in the process, you gain their loyalty. Organizational managers must find ways to "increase *stakeholder* value," not just "*shareowner* value."

Gaining commitment from all of your stakeholders requires coherent strategies that clearly enunciate your organization's vision, mission, goals and objectives, and implementation plans. Those strategies must spring from and mesh with the culture in which it exists, even if your organization has the foresight to extend its vision far into the future; get too removed from what your world understands and expects and you'll lose the world's commitment to your organization. In hindsight the world often laments, "They were ahead of their times."

Other Sources

Edosomwan, Johnson A. "Implementing Continuous Improvement Projects." *The Quality Observer* (June 1996), p. 4.

9

Core Competencies and Self-Management

People are always neglecting something they can do in trying to do something they can't do.

—Ed Howe, American poet (1853–1937)

Geese can fly—that's a no-brainer. But geese have to learn how to fly.

Most (not all) birds have the capacity to fly, but they all need to be pushed out of the nest and they all have to practice before they can become competent at flying. Likewise, we unfeathered friends have to learn how to do things for which we have a capacity.

> Regardless of your role or function in an organization, you need to develop the competencies appropriate to that role or function.

Increasing Group Power and Enlarging Core Competencies

Traditional organizational models, represented by the old Management 101, or command-and-control, model depicted in Exhibit 9-1, describe roles and functions hierarchically. Line employees learn and develop *operational, task-based skills* appropriate to specific and individual jobs. Supervisors and middle managers develop *process-related skills* for solving problems, for moving information and/or work through the organization, and for getting results through the efforts

Exhibit 9-1. The traditional management model.

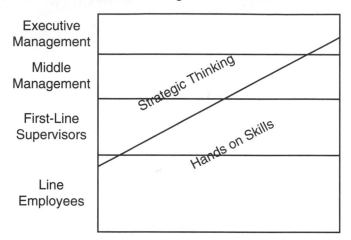

of other people (line employees). Executive managers learn and develop *leadership skills* for creating and communicating organizational goals and objectives and for steering the organization on the right course for satisfying the demands of its many constituencies. In short, managers *think* (plan, solve problems, design processes, etc.), line employees *do* (execute plans, make things, serve customers, etc.).

The spaces between horizontal lines in Exhibit 9-1 represent positions in the organization, the bottom space representing line employees, the next space first-line supervisors, and so on. The diagonal line divides the graph into two types of competencies: strategic thinking (planning, problem solving, decision making, etc.) and hands-on execution skills (making things, delivering services, etc.). The organization calls for less competence in strategic thinking at the lower levels and less competence in hands-on skills at the higher levels.

The newer model, shown in Exhibit 9-2, recognizes that technology and economics have put new pressures on organizations to evolve and to shift roles and functions into new or different hands. Economic and technological evolution, while flattening out organizations and shrinking layers of management, is driving responsibility for how the organization operates as well as what it produces or does down to line employee ranks. Line employees still have to do, and many of them now also have to think.

Information can flow through the organization via computer

Exhibit 9-2. The current management model.

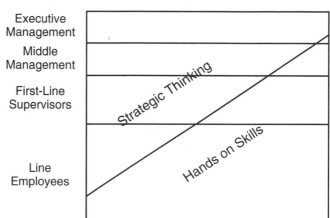

networks, bypassing the managers once responsible for its flow. Machines no longer need as many operators or tenders as they once did, thanks to computers and other nonhuman operators. Economies of scale that once demanded bigness now demand smallness: leaner, less centralized organizations and fewer managers. When giants like IBM and AT&T voluntarily split up into separate, smaller operating units, it's time to look at how we are making these changes.

Some financial analysts now measure organizational value in terms of the business's "knowledge bank" as well as on the basis of its tangible assets.[1] Many line employees are expected to develop competencies traditionally reserved to managers—thinking, solving problems, and making decisions—in addition to their hands-on skills. This has resulted in the creation of a new category of worker—the knowledge worker.

Self-Management and the New Worker

The demand for knowledge workers and others with strategic thinking skills has also dramatically changed businesses processes, such as "compensation strategies and programs [to a] competency-based approach."[2] According to a Towers Perrin survey of 150 mid- to large-size corporations reported by the Reuters News Service, the vast majority agree that "if you're not skilled and can't contribute to the team, to customer service and the organization's goals, you'll be paid less." A competency-based pay plan requires the company to "develop the critical behaviors and abilities employees need to achieve specific business results," and it provides "a mechanism for cross training people in different functional areas." In short, in the evolving business world, "mastery of specific competencies, the combination of skills, behaviors, and knowledge the organizational deems important to it success," *not* longevity, determines compensation.[3]

Therefore, the skills or competencies that serve the production level of business must make room for meeting new organizational demands for more and higher levels of knowledge and for more strategic skills. Those demands for more and higher levels of skills also demand greater self-management. At the same time, Donna Fein, editor of *Inc.*, points out, the gap between the need and the ability to satisfy that need increases, in part, because companies have scaled back their training efforts.[4] That raises three questions:

1. Are our line employees properly equipped and otherwise ready to take on strategic thinking responsibilities?
2. If our line employees *are* ready, are their managers emotionally ready to let them proceed?
3. Are our organizations properly designed to support and facilitate the new workers?

A negative answer to any of those questions suggests gaps not in technical skills but in self-management skills: readiness to learn and readiness to support learning. Unless those gaps are filled, the demand for strategic thinking will run into a major barrier: the lack of competence.

Increasing Group Power Through Coordination

Issues closely related to gaps in self-management skills concern the two strategic efforts that facilitate the coordination of activities and processes:

1. Identifying the nature of your core business and people's core competencies

2. Identifying common or shared goals toward which competent people can work together

Coordination without collaboration is possible, but ineffective. Both coordination and collaboration require the skills of self-management to make the organization successful.

The innate collaboration recognizable in the wild goose's V formation exists in all herd animals, including *Homo sapiens.* No Neanderthal or Cro-Magnon felled a woolly mammoth by himself. Teamwork, if not teams, is older than recorded history, yet in many operations managers feel obliged to *impose* it. (In some operations, managers actively inhibit it, imposing no-socializing—even no-talking—rules on their employees.)

Employees, for their part, find it hard to collaborate. Not only are they departmentalized and locked away in personal work spaces, cubicles, or offices, but many have no idea of what anyone else is doing. Some do not know what their organization's mission is, and many have no idea how they contribute to the organization's overriding goals. Some students of corporate culture have called this a "silo mentality."

Where that cultural mentality predominates, responsibility and authority are limited to specific jobs. Responsibility for the organization as a whole vaporizes as each siloed employee exclaims, "Not my job." Problems and blame become live grenades thrown from silo to silo. If complaints make it up to the CEO's or president's desk, she may mouth the words, "The buck stops here," but then she is sure to wend her way from one silo to another, looking for someone else to blame.

Teams don't always work, but teamwork always does. An organization doesn't need to be team-based to generate the synergy it needs for success. The power of synergy comes from turning competent, committed people loose to achieve common or shared goals. Effective management unabashedly requires teamwork and a *systems* or *process* orientation (not a task orientation) to coordinate between two or more people operating in the same process. Indeed, coordination of any kind requires taking a systems approach, which means to recognize that anything you do in one part of the organization will affect processes or people in another part of it. An organization is a complex system, more like a living organism that an inanimate object, and you bring a complicated system into harmony only by coordinating its activities.

By dividing the organization into functional levels (organization, operations, and individual), we can identify how a systems approach integrates what people do into a continuous process in which vision and resources are transformed into results. See Exhibit 9-3. Although we can take these "snapshots" of functional levels as an analytic model, in reality the lines blur; what writers Rummler and Brache call "white spaces" in the organizational chart don't really exist.[5] The feedback represented by the arrows at the bottom of the exhibit occurs at many points in the process.

Making the systems approach work requires three widespread dynamics that correspond to the three levels of organizational management illustrated in Exhibit 9-3:

1. *Organizational know-how* (the organization level): knowledge of how the whole organization works, how all the jobs contribute to the organization's success, and who does what or who gets things done
2. *Strategies know-how* (the operations level): knowledge of the company's strategies and how its processes contribute to the achievement of the strategies' goals
3. *Implementation know-how* (the individual level of management or of task performance): the ability to tie specific tasks or jobs into the organization's strategies and processes to ensure an effective flow of work upstream, downstream, or in whatever direction the work flows

Only for the purpose of analysis can we diagram these performance levels as in Exhibit 9-4. In practice, in a successful business, each level of performance must exercise all three forms of know-how. In the exhibit, the arrows represent the inputs each level of performance provides the others to transform those inputs into goods, services, or revenue. Each performance level affects the inputs of the other levels, each set of responsibilities contributes to producing the expected results, and the feedback the organization gets from stakeholders, customers, etc., about actual results closes the circuit; the system's processes are continuous and cyclical (i.e., spiraling toward continuous improvement).

Exhibit 9-3. Model of a systems, or self-management, approach to managing an organization.

Organization →→→	→→→ Operations →→→	→→→ Individual
1. Build organizational vision and mission out of input and feedback from all sources.	1. Produce operational plans to fulfill organizational vision and mission.	1. Know, understand, and contribute to process goals and objectives.
2. Communicate vision and mission.	2. Communicate goals and objectives vertically and horizontally.	2. Align personal goals and objectives with organization's.
3. Align goals and objectives throughout organization; make resources available.	3. Align goals and objectives vertically and horizontally; distribute resources.	3. Translate objectives into action (jobs, tasks,); transform resources into outputs.
4. Analyze organizational performance (results).	4. Analyze performance (process outcomes).	4. Manage work group or team activities.
5. Get and give feedback.	5. Get and give feedback horizontally and vertically.	5. Give and get feedback vertically and horizontally.
6. Revise organizational goals and objectives.	6. Improve performance.	6. Convert data into useful information; communicate it vertically and horizontally.

↑ ←←←←←←←←←←←←←←←←←←←←←←←←←←←←←←←←

This analytic model in Exhibit 9-4 has sharp boundaries (represented by the lines between the responsibilities). In today's reality, the boundaries between levels of responsibility tend to merge, fulfilling themselves in expected results that only coordinated efforts can produce. Feedback from various constituencies lets the organization

Exhibit 9-4. A systems approach to performance management.

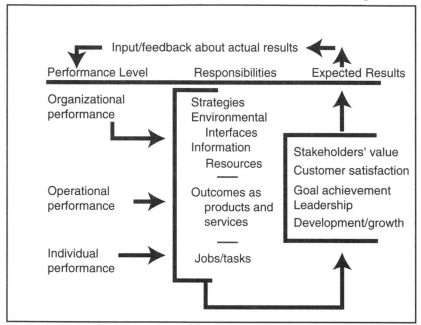

know whether expected results have been produced. Just as a gaggle of geese could not reach its destination if each goose did not fulfill its responsibility, an organization could not produce its expected results if each person did not fulfill his responsibility. (Nevertheless, a gaggle may adjust its speed for a weak bird until it can fly no more; likewise, an organization can carry along weak performers until their inadequate output begins to produce negative effects.)

By developing employee involvement or team-based approaches to planning, decision making, and problem solving, many companies blur the lines between managers and nonmanagers. In the now classic (i.e., successful) example of Johnsonville Foods, in Sheboygan Falls, Wisconsin, management has turned running the plant over to the employees.[6] Line employees get direction and boundaries from upper management, but the day-to-day operations of the plant, even some medium-range planning, has become their responsibility. The trend toward employee management of the organization can only accelerate as more companies downsize and flatten.

Any employee involvement demands greater openness. To ensure responsible employee freedom to participate in management decisions, Jack Stack, CEO of the Springfield Remanufacturing Corporation (SRC), has instituted (and has turned into moneymaking books and seminars) *open-book management.*[7] To help employees make decisions that have positive bottom-line effects, SRC trains them in budgeting and financial management. At any one time, any employee can tell you what the cash-flow picture looks like. Now twenty-five-cent bolts that used to wind up in the trash are picked up and replaced in their proper bins. Coordination requires competence in many aspects of the organization (e.g., nonaccountants must know basic accounting principles). Many managers have, in the past, reserved such competencies to themselves.

Notes

1. Joe McGowan, "The Coins in the Knowledge Bank," *Fortune* (February 19, 1996), pp. 101–102, citing Alan Benjamin, former director of SEMA Group.
2. Gail Grib and Susan O'Donnell, "Pay Plans That Reward Employee Achievement," *HRMagazine* (July 1995), pp. 49–50, citing a survey by Towers Perrin of 150 HR and compensation professionals. See also "Firms Seek to Revamp Employee Pay: Focus on One's Value to Bottom Line," *St. Louis Post-Dispatch* (August 24, 1996), p. 1C.
3. Grib and O'Donnell, p. 50.
4. Donna Fein, "What Drives the Skills Gap?" *Inc.* (May 1996), p. 111.
5. Geary A. Rummler and Alan P. Brache, *Improving Performance: How to Manage the White Space on the Organization Chart* (San Francisco: Jossey-Bass, 1990).
6. Chris Lee, "Beyond Teamwork," *Training* (June 1990), pp. 25–32.
7. Jack Stack with Bo Burlingham, *The Great Game of Business: Unlocking the Power and Profitability of Open-Book Management* (New York: Currency/Doubleday, 1992), passim.

Section 4

Management and Leadership: The Dual Functions of Managers

10

What Managers Manage and How They Manage It

Man who man would be,
Must rule the empire of himself!
    —Percy Bysshe Shelley, from "Political Greatness," 1821

A gaggle of wild geese couldn't make it home unless it made appropriate, economical use of all its resources, making the most of the contributions from each goose as it flies in formation. Smart managers, those geese, because smart organizational management consists of doing exactly the same things.

> The "meat and potatoes" of management consists of managing processes, things, and yourself—not other people.

As an organizational manager, you manage three dimensions: processes, things, and yourself. You plan and organize, solve problems, coach and counsel, enforce the rules, handle complaints, and manage performance. In short, you manage the processes through which resources are consumed and by which work gets done in an effort to produce desired (and desirable) results. Those are "meat and potatoes" functions of management.

Yet, managing has received some pretty bad press lately. Managers, we're told, should be leaders not managers.

What's that? Managers still have to manage the organization's core business and group and/or individual performance. How else will the business succeed? The *way* they manage is how they lead. Leadership is a *style*, a set of behaviors anyone, even managers, can learn.

The Management vs. Leadership Conundrum

Since Douglas McGregor described Theory X and Theory Y management attitudes in 1960,[1] management theorists have sought to replace one set of attitudes with another. Managers with Theory X attitudes, McGregor said, are hostile to workers, perceiving them as lazy, mindless, unworthy drones. Managers with Theory Y attitudes, contrarily, perceive workers as adult, thoughtful, energetic, creative partners in the work process. Theory X attitudes undermine the organization by reducing productivity, whereas Theory Y attitudes promote productivity by encouraging participation, empowerment, and partnership. Somehow, Theory X attitudes have become associated with management while Theory Y attitudes have become associated with leadership, although, as McGregor said, *good managers with Theory Y attitudes abound.*

In the rush to become leaders, managers often forget the importance of the meat and potatoes of their jobs. Craig R. Hickman, in *The Mind of a Manager, the Soul of a Leader,* goes so far as to distinguish managers from leaders by claiming that the words *manager* and *leader* are "metaphors representing two opposite ends of a continuum."[2] He finds managers at "the more analytical, structured, controlled, deliberate, and orderly end of the continuum": the *mental end.* He then locates leaders on the *soul end,* where they emphasize experimentation, vision, flexibility, freedom, and creativity. You can use "the tension between them," he says, to create a "management/ leadership environment." That's all very poetic, but it only serves to add to the confusion.

As a manager, why can't you also feel comfortable as a leader? Likewise, as a leader, why can't you feel comfortable as a manager? An old maxim declares that managers get their authority from their position (status power) while leaders get their authority from the people they lead. Why, then, couldn't anyone—even managers—be leaders (and, vice versa)? Only your skills and knowledge limit the roles you play in a group and the personal power (influence) you wield.

Practicing the skills and behaviors of self-management combines the skills of management and leadership (leading as you manage, managing as you lead) and guarantees that you do your job as a manager: use resources productively and achieve peak performance. Effective managers use self-management to raise their own performance as managers to the highest levels possible, and they teach self-management to their group members. They also use their management skills (their minds) and leadership skills (their souls) to encourage peak performance from others.

In fact, people usually do look to their managers to perform the dual responsibilities of management: to manage *and* to lead. In short, they don't want to choose between working for a manager or following a leader; *they want to work with an effective manager.* They look to their managers to give them clear statements of responsibility and acceptable performance standards, and to provide them with information and tools necessary for doing their jobs; they also look to their managers to give them support and recognition and feedback about areas in need of improvement. Those expectations form the basis of the *psychological contract*, the reciprocal (usually oral) set of relationships created when someone comes to work for you.

Exhibit 10-1 collapses Hickman's management-leadership dichotomy by linking the skills usually associated with leadership with those usually associated with effective management—both of which reflect Theory Y attitudes. The exhibit suggests that the skills of effective managers blend naturally with those of effective leaders into one supereffective role. A good manager uses:

➤ *Management skills* for making appropriate, productive, and profitable use of the organization's resources and processes in pursuit of desired and desirable results
➤ *Leadership skills* for encouraging employee competence (knowledge, talents, and skills), for improving coordination and collaboration among diverse individuals and groups, and for increasing everyone's commitment to the organization's vision and mission (core business)

Putting an End to the Conundrum

I use the comparisons in Exhibit 10-1 only to make analytic distinctions between management and leadership skills. This way we can

Exhibit 10-1. Functions and competencies traditionally associated with effective managers and effective leaders.

Traditional Leadership Skills	Traditional Managerial Skills
Communication	*Planning and organization*
⊤ Encouraging open discussion and dialogue ⊤ Providing information and feedback ⊤ Helping others communicate *Requires being open to other people, to their opinions, ideas, and feelings.* ⊤ Being flexible ⊤ Seeking out other people's ideas and opinions and learning from them	⊤ Setting goals and objectives ⊤ Pulling together human and material resources ⊤ Structuring activities ⊤ Assigning duties ⊤ Designing monitoring tools *Requires knowledge of organization's formal and informal structures and processes (how things get done); also requires developing networks of effective working relationships in the service of the work-group's success (see Sections 5 and 6).*
Motivation	*Problem solving*
⊤ Providing encouragement and incentives for people to give their best *Requires: (1) recognizing the diversity among people and the differences in what motivates them; (2) recognizing and accepting other people's achievements; and (3) providing leadership and guidance especially during tough times.*	⊤ Recognizing indicators of problems, and distinguishing between symptoms and real problems and their causes ⊤ Collaborating with others to develop creative solutions *Requires: (1) coping well with uncertainty and ambiguity; (2) managing or initiating change; (3) making decisive and timely decisions, but knowing when to seek help; (4) promoting new and original ideas for improving work group performance; and (5) taking an attitude of "If it ain't broke, make it better."*
Inspiration	*Coaching and counseling*
⊤ Taking the long view: looking beyond the present and beyond personal needs ⊤ Accepting the need for vision as well as for immediate results *Requires: (1) committing yourself to the tasks and goals of the business and of the work group; (2) respecting, appreciating, and valuing differences; and (3) promoting a spirit of collaboration with yourself and among others.*	⊤ Helping others to improve their performance or to develop as employees and as people ⊤ Seeking and effectively using feedback to help others ⊤ Providing both positive and negative feedback when helping others *Requires monitoring employee activities, recognizing strengths, and taking corrective action with regard to areas in need of improvement.*

Supporting employees	Training
ϯ Understanding and empathizing with how people think or feel about work in general and their work in particular ϯ Actively supporting people's development *Requires: (1) respecting, appreciating, valuing, and encouraging differences and diversity; (2) going to bat for people when they are right.*	ϯ Teaching people how to perform technical tasks and adding to their skills ϯ Teaching people how to solve their own problems *Requires having appropriate technical or functional skills or knowing where to find them.*
Team building	**Enforcing rules and handling complaints**
ϯ Encouraging cooperation, collaboration ϯ Building synergistic relationships ϯ Encouraging differences of opinion and open and direct communication to solve problems and achieve consensus *Requires involving others in making decisions that affect their lives (see Sections 5 and 6).*	ϯ Dealing fairly with others' concerns and issues ϯ Giving appropriate feedback and risking confrontation when necessary ϯ Being sensitive to people's needs and requirements ϯ Being helpful to people *Requires: (1) taking timely corrective action; (2) living by the rules you enforce; and (3) taking a customer focus (internal as well as external) and seeing to it that customer needs or requirements are satisfied.*

look here at the skills you need for combining management and leadership competencies. I'll save discussions of other leadership skills for the chapters in Sections 5 and 6.

Bottom line: To be effective, managers as well as leaders manage their own, the group's, and individual performance by taking a goal-oriented, needs-driven approach to daily activities. This requires attending to and completing urgent as well as important goals and preventing trivial and unproductive activities from getting in the way. Performance management is another form of self-management.

The ultimate goals of self-management and that of performance management are the same: performance—one's own, the group's, and each individual's. Likewise, each person in a group gets appropriate results by managing her own work. In a well-managed environment, the different people within a work group or team achieve group goals by tying their self-managed performances together. To maximize group power, D. Wayne Calloway, chairman of PepsiCo, wants eagles to become more like geese: "We take eagles and teach them to fly in formation."[3] Now, if you're the manager of this well-managed environment of gooselike eagles, what's your job?

Your concerns as an excellent manager are task-oriented, focused on achieving organizational, work group, individual, and team goals and objectives: helping the group achieve desired results through the resources, skills, and knowledge contributed by the people in your work group. Your competencies are no different today than they were for managers before you. But you need to apply them in a different way than do managers steeped in tradition, *with both the mind of a manager and the soul of a leader.*

Planning, Organizing, and Communicating

Planning and organizing, management skills, have little value to the group unless you listen to what the people doing the work say and watch what they do (leadership skills). Listening and watching make planning and organizing realistic. On the other hand, if you can't detail the plans to others, something both managers and leaders must do, they never get implemented. Communicating consists of both listening (and understanding) and telling (and being understood).

Individual planning is as important to your company's success as is organizational planning. In spite of the difficulties they have in planning the details of their own daily activities, managers in the traditional mode assume responsibility for planning everyone else's as well. You can often see workers sitting around waiting for work to be assigned to them rather than recognizing what has to be done and doing it.

If people don't know how to plan, teach them how. Teach them to read marketing and sales reports, or whatever business forecasts affect their jobs, and let them determine what has to be done to meet the demands the business makes on them. Teach them to take on the responsibility for their own lives and work.

Solving Problems, Making Decisions, and Motivation

You as a manager have to solve problems. Your problems, however, need not be the problems employees bring to you. That's what traditional managers do. Instead, *focus on your management problems*, one of which consists getting your employees to solve their own problems.

People respond to and commit themselves to managers who help them solve problems (a management skill). They respond even more to managers who teach them how to solve their own problems and then let them do it (a leadership skill). Collaboration and partnership are great motivators.

Train people how to recognize indicators (symptoms) of problems. Teach them to collect and use information for identifying leading indicators of the need to improve what they do. Show them the steps necessary for distinguishing symptoms from problems and causes of problems. If necessary, get training for everyone on basic tools for measuring actual results against plans and for weighing alternative solutions. If after all that, employees still insist on coming to you with their problems tell them, "If you must bring a problem to me, also bring with you three possible solutions we can discuss."

Problem solving always leads to decision making. Everyone has to make decisions, and everyone does. Traditional managers decide to let their employees delegate decisions up. The employees decide to let their managers make decisions for them. And, not making decisions becomes a decision as well.

Just as you have management problems to solve, you also have management decisions to make. Make decisions for everyone else and you might not get around to issues the company expects you to handle. To free yourself up for your job, let the employees make decisions appropriate to their work, to their level of expertise, and to their readiness to make decisions.

The mark of real empowerment is giving people the right, the opportunity, the skills, and the tools for making decisions and *letting them act on those decisions*—even if those decisions blow up on you. Responsible freedom is a learned behavior that companies like 3M and Hewlett-Packard encourage and nurture. Exercising a veto power prevents people from taking ownership of their responsibilities and denies them opportunities for learning from their mistakes and for growing. Anything that blocks growth, creativity, and innovation costs the company its competitive edge. Sometimes it hurts, but people learn more from their mistakes than they do from their successes.

Training, Supporting, Coaching, and Inspiring

Any manager worth her salary goes to bat for people when they're right and gives them support when they need it. Teaching them how to get the job done right supports them all of the time. It takes both positive and negative feedback to teach and support people. This is something effective managers have always done but that "leaders" are now taking credit for introducing into the workplace.

Whom do you remember most vividly and with greatest affection? The people who shouted slogans at you, or the people who taught and helped you succeed? Inspiration comes more from leading by example and doing "manager things" (coaching and counseling) than from booster posters on the walls.

Traditional managers complain that they spend all of their time "putting out fires" (either performance problems or behavior problems). *Workplace combustibles ignite mainly because traditional managers unwittingly start those fires themselves*, by failing to coach people on how to solve their own problems. If you don't have to be a police officer, you certainly need not be a firefighter either, not if people can take corrective action, which is the purpose of coaching, before you even know that anything has happened.

Problem solving and decision making should lead to taking corrective action. By encouraging people to work out problems, make decisions, and come to you afterward, they lift the burden of putting out those fires from your shoulders. Which of the two scenarios that follow makes more sense to you?

Scenario 1: The foreman of a unit downstream from yours comes to you one afternoon. "We've got a problem you have to handle. Fred, in your unit, is turning out defective parts. Too many of them. And, my people can't install them properly."

"Has anyone talked with Fred about this?"

"Naw. That's your job."

"Okay. I'll talk to him."

Scenario 2: An assembly worker downstream in the plant crosses the shop with a part in his hand. He stops at Fred's workstation and says, "Take a look at this part. It came with a bunch of others in a basket with your name on it. They won't fit in the assembly. What's happening?"

Fred turns off his machine. "Let me see that. What's it doing?" After the other worker explains the problem he's having, Fred answers. "I haven't changed the settings on the machine in a month. That shouldn't be the problem. Let's see how it's milling the part." And the two of them set about to identify and correct the problem.

Traditional managers, like those in Scenario 1, lament the burden they themselves have shouldered, but they've made themselves into the unit's chief cook and bottle washer—then they wonder why they come up short for performing their managerial duties. Instead, they should take seriously the way people in so-called primitive villages and tribes raise their children: The older children as well as the adults take responsibility for teaching the younger children the ways of their people.

No, we shouldn't call these people primitive, for they have learned what many traditional business owners and managers don't know: It really does take a whole village to raise a child. Each person in a group has his own skills, knowledge, or considered opinions to pass on to other people. This is an essential value underlying diversity in the workplace. Further, cross-training works best when experienced people show less experienced people what to do and how to do it.

Look again at the second scenario. People working together can solve problems even if you don't know they're doing it. You have to train them to take on these roles because traditional managers have trained traditional employees to refer all problems to the manager.

Recruiting, Hiring, and Removing People

This traditional management activity also remains an essential function of management performance. But, where's it written that you have to do this work all by yourself?

Here's where the village idea can also help you. New employees have to work with the whole group, not just with the supervisor. Ask the people doing the work to write the task and job descriptions. Give group members a chance to talk with the three most likely candidates, and get their feedback before making the final hiring decision. Involving everyone in this process improves the likelihood that you'll select the right person for the job and create a cohesive group. Still, if you do have to fire or transfer someone out of the group, get help in making that decision from people who have daily, close contact with the offending employee. Taking other people's opinions into consideration helps protect you from the slings and arrows arising from an unconscious bias.

Enforcing the Rules, Handling Complaints, and Building Teams

Appropriate policies and procedures (rules) encourage collaboration between coworkers and between employees and customers. Without rules (also called "constitutions"), teams will collapse. Without rules (e.g., customer service standards), customers' needs can't be met. Managers with Theory X attitudes enforce rules, handle complaints, and build teams. What distinguishes them from leaders (managers with Theory Y attitudes) is not so much what they do as how they do it.

Traditional managers usually resent being thrust into the role of police officer, enforcing company policies, but it's a role they've taken on themselves. Rules serve a purpose and must be followed, and, yes, there will be those who flout or break the rules, but you need not be a police officer if everyone knows what the rules are and takes responsibility for living within them.

Once more the "village" can come to the rescue. Companies can avoid costly lawsuits, e.g., for sexual harassment, if everyone takes responsibility for living up to the highest behavior standards as well as work standards. You can expect everyone to enforce company policies without turning them into "stoolies" by taking a tip from the so-called neighborhood watch, in which people are trained to watch out for one another and help one another live together in their work community. Peer counseling is something new in business, but it has worked well in high schools all over the United States for many years.

Likewise, you need not do all the record keeping or write all the reports. You enrich people's jobs and prepare them for supervisory responsibilities by asking them to write their own reports or proposals as well as to keep records of their own and their work group's performance. You review them, to be sure, but that's mainly to keep yourself well informed.

Managing Performance

When you act to ensure that everyone pulls together to meet organizational goals, no one can tell when your management skills leave off and your leadership skills begin (and vice versa). The processes by which goals are achieved are the performances you, as a manager, must monitor and correct when they go off course. The process by which you encourage synergy within the group to achieve the goals, you as a leader, must create, monitor, and adjust when relationships break down.

Managing Performance, Not Just Paying for It

Paying for performance has been around forever (paying good workers better than poor workers), but some managers have often raised the theory to the level of a panacea, believing that paying for performance will improve productivity all the way around. Don't count on it. It takes a lot more than pay to ensure peak performance.

In theory, merit pay has merit. In practice, the road is filled with potholes. For example, when one company set up a system to pay buyers bonuses to keep down cost of purchases the buyers relied " 'on second-tier sources, [accepting] poor-quality materials.' "[4] Pay for performance can encourage workers to improve their work, but it falls flat on its face unless you determine first "What's a meaningful thing to measure? What's [a] reasonable [standard]?"[5] Pay for performance, yes, but a system for *managing* performance is required to get desired results.

The system for managing performance depends on how you define your organization's core business, a definition that flows from the company's vision. Only by clearly understanding the core business can you manage a work group's performance, which means to use all your resources and make the most of the contributions of each person in the group. Individual or group performance improves the more you involve employees in moving information and setting standards, in distributing productive resources, in coordinating work flows, and in monitoring progress. This way everyone takes responsibility for and works at achieving the goals that flow from the company's vision.

Managing a work group's performance requires taking the vision for your organization to a practical level in which you identify just what it is your organization does and what it has to do to maximize the core competencies of its people. Only then can you use all your resources and make the most of the contributions of each person in the group to achieve desired (and desirable) results.

Supporting Core Competencies to Fulfill the Core Business

Managing performance by supporting core competencies applies the organizational model described by Exhibit 7-2 (the flow of energy from vision through action) to individual performance, placing the company's vision and mission, as well as group and individual goals, at the base of a series of activity spirals, as in Exhibit 10-2.

The model represents change and growth over time as upward flow and expanding image. The series of loops in which one loop begins where another leaves off represent managing performance by working toward new goals. (The time measurement is your choice.) From the organization's perspective, what the individual does to implement the plan (the third loop from the bottom) serves the organization's core business.

Managing Performance: Fulfilling Vision and Mission

Once the business's vision and mission are communicated throughout the organization, you and other people, working together, interpret them in terms of what the group or the individual can contribute to achieving organizational goals and objectives. The performance management spiral begins for you and your employees when you apply the organization's goals and objectives to individual, work group, and team action plans.

Within a work group or a team, responsibility for specific tasks is assigned or delegated to individuals. In a well-managed environment, the authority for making appropriate decisions or taking appropriate action goes along with the accountability for success or failure. Each loop in the spiral in Exhibit 10-2 represents one aspect of the performance management process.

1. *Set goals.* At the "Now" corner of the horizontal/vertical junction, identify organizational goals to which the desired perform-

Exhibit 10-2. The performance management spiral.

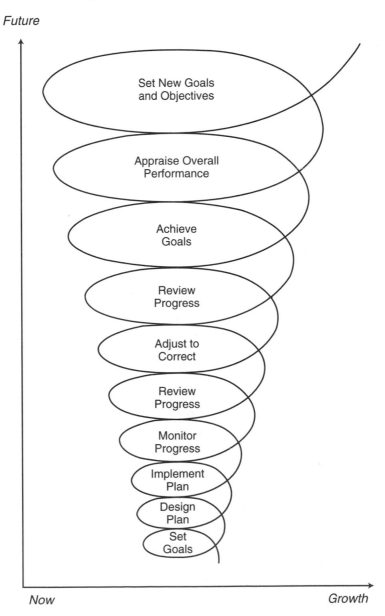

Source: Adapted from Donald H. Weiss, *Achieving Excellence: The Performance Appraisal Process,* 2d ed., rev. (Watertown, Mass.: American Management Association, 1994), p. 6.

ance will contribute and the results you expect from working together with your work group or with individual employees during the performance period. Identify observable or measurable outcomes in the "Future" (upper end of the vertical, or time, axis).

2. *Design plan.* Identify realistic objectives (milestones) that have to be reached to achieve the goals. Establish and agree upon methods for monitoring and reviewing progress.

3. *Implement plan.* Let the work group or individual employees do their jobs. Encourage them to assume responsibility for reaching objectives.

4. *Monitor progress.* Use established and agreed-upon methods for keeping track of what is happening. Without riding herd, stay close enough to the work to keep problems from becoming crises. Regularly monitoring work and assessing performance ensure that quantitative and qualitative goals and objectives are met. SBC Communications, Inc., has systematized "coaching by walking around" for its managers.

5. *Review progress.* Meet regularly with the work group or individual employees to look over production or other records, "sitdowns" they call them at SBC. Recognize good work and identify slippage in production or in quality. Design plans for taking corrective action, e.g., additional training, where necessary.

6. *Adjust to correct.* Give the work group or individuals the opportunity to take corrective action before taking any drastic measures, such as disciplinary procedures.

7. *Review progress.* Continue to meet regularly to discuss how things are going. Recognize good work and identify areas still in need of corrective action.

8. *Achieve goals.* Reach the end of the performance period with goals achieved or *exceeded.*

9. *Appraise overall performance.* Summarize the period's progress and performance and how it contributed to reaching organizational objectives. Recognize work done well; make recommendations for future development (the "Growth" end of the horizontal axis).

10. *Set new goals and objectives.* A new spiral begins when current goals and objectives are met and reviewed. You and your work group or you and individual employees identify the organizational

goals to which this performance will contribute and the results you expect of them or him during this performance period. The organizational results may be new or different, and the performance must reflect those changes as well. Identify observable, if not measurable, outcomes.

To make managing the performance management spiral useful to the employees as well as to you, encourage them to manage the spiral themselves.

Everyone a (Self-)Manager

Traditional managers' best practices and self-management have a great deal in common. Self-management *is* management, from which both the individual and the organization can benefit. Managers' best practices ensure personal success for an individual; they help him shore up his value to the organization and ensure his employability, no matter what happens to his job security. Dana Mead, chairman and CEO of Tenneco Corporation, cautions us to change our thinking "about job security to . . . [thinking] about *employment security.*"[6] For the organization, the success of the group as a whole depends on how well individuals manage their lives and their work. Through self-management, they manage their own performance and take responsibility for their own success and for the success of the group.

You can expect a person to take responsibility for her own success and for the success of the group only if you give her that responsibility and authority and hold her accountable for what she's supposed to do. The more she manages her own performance through the entire spiral, the more accountable she is.

You can hold a person accountable for his actions only if you relinquish your total control over what he does. When you're calling all the shots, making all the decisions, ordering all the actions, you're responsible for all the results, not the other person. Even if your calls are right on the mark but *he* performs poorly, you must take the hit; you're the one to whom your boss will look when things go wrong.

Furthermore, you can expect people to make a commitment to something only if they have a sense of ownership of it. Yes, you can achieve compliance, but not the real commitment described in Chapter 8. Unless people feel in control of the missions in their lives, they can't feel a genuine commitment to them.

Still, self-management (the way I described it) is only the beginning. Teamwork and teams can help prevent goal conflicts and improve the coordination of work by sharing and comparing goal statements in various dimensions in which individuals or groups are working. See Sections 5 and 6. Applying self-management to performance management allows a group to manage the goals and processes that affect other people and their work either downstream or upstream from them.

Notes

1. Douglas McGregor, *The Human Side of Enterprise* (New York: McGraw-Hill, 1960).
2. Craig Hickman, *The Mind of a Manager, the Soul of a Leader* (New York: Wiley, 1990), pp. 7–13.
3. Quoted in Louis E. Boone, ed., *Quotable Business* (New York: Random House, 1992), p. 35.
4. According to Craig Schneier, a Princeton, N.J., consultant quoted by Amanda Bennett, in "Paying Workers to Meet Goals Spreads, but Gauging Performance Proves Tough," *Wall Street Journal* (October 11, 1991), p. B6.
5. Citing Bonnie Milliman, manager of customer services and logistics at Corning Inc. See also "Performance for Profit," *Personnel* (April 1990), pp. 6–7, citing a survey of 3,052 companies by The Wyatt Company: 49 percent of companies with strong performance management procedures exceed their financial goals, whereas only 11 percent of companies with a poor grasp of them exceed theirs.
6. Dana Mead, on *ABC News Nightline* with Ted Koppel (American Broadcasting Corporation, April 9, 1996). Italics added.

Other Sources

Brassard, Michael, and Diane Ritter. *The Memory Jogger II: A Pocket Guide of Tools for Continuous Improvement and Effective Planning.* Methuen, Mass.: GOAL/QPC, 1994.
English, Gary. "Tuning Up for Performance Management." *Training and Development Journal* (April 1991).

Kotter, John P. *A Force for Change: How Leadership Differs From Management.* New York: Free Press, 1990, pp. 3–18.

Mangelsdorf, Martha E. "Plan of Attack." *Inc.* (January 1996), pp. 41–43.

Prahalad, C. K., and Gary Hamel. "The Core Competence of the Corporation." *Harvard Business Review* (May-June 1990), pp. 79ff.

Weiss, Donald H. *Why Didn't I Say That?! What to Say and How to Say It in Tough Situations on the Job.* New York: AMACOM, 1994. Several chapters (especially Chapter 11, "Managing Differences") offer helpful methods for engaging in peer counseling.

11

Managers as Leaders

Great minds must be ready not only to take opportunities,
but to make them.
                    —Charles C. Colton, British author (1780–1832)

The familiar **V**-formation of wild geese seems to undulate as the gaggle flies. No flight leaders and squadron leaders head the formation and keep the alignments in place. Instead, the birds shift positions and exchange places at will but always in a rhythmic dance that advances the flock toward its goal. As wild geese make their way home, they not only manage their resources well; they each also lead. The result is *shared leadership* within the group.

> Managers, like anyone else, can adopt leadership values and practice leadership roles.

Most managers can manage as I described managing in the last chapter. They're good at handling task-related problems that bottom-line outcomes measure.[1] Yet, it takes more than good management to inspire great performance. It also requires leadership, which includes:

- Seeing the wholeness of the organization and where it can possibly go
- Seeing the wholeness of each employee
- Treating each employee with dignity
- Flexing with the real needs of the organization and the real needs of people
- Sharing leadership with nonmanagers as well as other managers

Does anything in that list of behaviors prevent anyone, or everyone, from accepting leadership values and practicing leadership roles? Managers appointed by their managers can also be elected leaders by their followers.

You can't always quantitatively measure the results of leadership; while you can trace bottom-line results back to efficient management with relative ease, backtracking from the bottom line to effective leadership poses some major problems. How many dollars can you attribute, for example, to understanding workers' personal problems? Managers at Merck, Inc. sum up the matter with, "You just have to believe it."[2] That doesn't mean you can't trace *any* bottom line results back to effective leadership.

After nearly ten years of hiring employees, Connie Swartz, president of Creative Courseware, in Kansas City, Missouri, still doesn't offer a formal benefits package. That's because *Inc.* magazine says "employees have voted consistently for increases in hourly wages as opposed to, say, health insurance." Flexible hours, relaxed company rules, and a high level of communication have attracted invigorated, committed employees she needs in her business, and apparently she's doing something right. "For the past five years her turnover has been zero."[3]

Separating managing and leading from each other satisfies the unfortunate reality that most managers feel threatened by the possibility of letting go of the traditional status power that comes with their position. Yet, effective leaders don't wield power; they share it—and sharing leadership with group members takes chutzpah.

Many managers find it risky to communicate openly and freely, to open themselves up to needs, ideas, thoughts, and opinions of other people, and to take on long-term challenges. Taking the word *manager* as just a title, not a mandate to control everything that happens, is unthinkable to traditional managers. But, think like a Canada goose. Each bird has a place in the pecking order, while the whole gaggle takes responsibility for flying to its destinations.

Measuring Leadership

Executives use bottom-line results to measure the effectiveness of managers reporting to them. Followers decide whether or not their leaders are effective, and they usually appraise leadership performance with their feet. When employees believe they have a stake in the organization's success, that they aren't being exploited by managers who don't reward employee performance, they'll exceed their manager's expectations and that in turn will make their managers look good to those measuring their performance.

Those premises drove the turnaround at Corning Inc. in 1990, when the company moved from the brink of bankruptcy to industry leadership.[4] Train your people, form partnerships with people (including labor unions), promote diversity, and improve the quality of life at work and in the community that supports your business. You might not quantify all the results, but you can't always reduce facts of life to mathematical equations.

According to George Schenk, director of People Strategies, Monsanto measures the success of its Global Learning Centers in terms of *"the value its internal consultants add to what their clients are doing."* A problem would not have been solved but for the information supplied by a design team member. The project would have taken longer and have been more discouraging had it not been for the energy and enthusiasm of a subject-matter expert. Such nonmeasurable leadership values count heavily in the Global Learning Center's activities.

While balance sheets and cash-flow statements may not pinpoint the contributions of value-added leadership, other tools can uncover them. Multirating systems for measuring the "effectiveness of leadership" (two-way appraisals, 360-degree feedback) at companies like Massachusetts Mutual Life Insurance and Monsanto foster partnerships between employees and managers.[5] But what do people want from their leaders? What do you measure?

Characteristics and Behaviors of Leaders

A sweeping generalization: Leaders get commitment through effective communication, by encouraging individual participation and contribution, and by developing collaboration and cooperation. Leadership behaviors reduce turnover, lost days, tardiness, conflicts, while they increase individual and group productivity. You can quantify all these results and trace them back to the quality of organizational leadership often associated with the following list of best leadership practices.

As you read this list, pick out the similarities between it and the six competencies of self-management:

☛ *See the whole picture and create a vision of what could be.* Effective managers lead by dreaming—realistic dreams, to be sure. They see their job as making the future happen by thinking strategically, organically, organizationally. Yet they also grasp the details that move processes and resources into desired and desirable outcomes. (They *understand* them, even if they can't do them.)

☛ *Communicate the whole picture and the vision to other people.* Effective managers' dreams end up on other people's drawing boards and in their machines because they can translate them into practical mission statements that other people can understand and that stimulate other people to action. Through direct contact, newsletters, video presentations, they let other people know where they think the organization should go. They leave it to the whole organization to determine where it has been.

☛ *Respect, show concern for, understand, interpret, and articulate the needs, aspirations, and feelings of the group and of individual members.* Effective managers hire people because they respect the abilities their employees bring with them: their skills, their knowledge, or their teachability. From respect for abilities comes respect for employees' needs, and aspirations, and the desire to see to it that their needs are met, their aspirations are fulfilled, and their feelings acknowledged.

One reason managers' dreams resonate for other people is that the vision reflects their needs and aspirations. Effective managers draw on them to form their dreams. They listen to what people say and read what they write. They convert the "I-Them" schism that has characterized labor-management relations into "We," which in turn helps them understand what people need or want for themselves. "They are me." They want to see the fruits of their labor in any number of forms, including money. A great leader, a follower would be.

☛ *Communicate group needs, aspirations, and feelings for, to, and outside the group.* Listening to what employees value or believe is important, and enabling the organization to provide adequate and fair compensation plans and to enact career paths and career opportunities for all employees, converts employees from merely "hands and backs" into people. At the middle level of the organization, in particular, effective managers stand up for the people who look to them to do so, and eliminate the "I-Them" schism that has held back productivity and organizational success. Whether you provide capital and other resources, whether you manage capital and other resources, or whether you transform capital and other resources into finished goods or services, *you are all in this together.*

➤ *Provide people with direction,* focusing their energies on specific goals and, all the while, maintaining a high group morale. Commitment comes from ownership. Effective managers dream, and when they translate those dreams and communicate them to other people, they lay out broad goals they want "Us" to achieve. Others translate the broad goals into individual, specific goals that take into account their needs, aspirations, and feelings.

➤ *Demonstrate enthusiasm for the group's mission, objectives and standards.* No one can accuse effective managers of desultory moping about. If anything, they sometimes go to the extremes of cheerleading and have to have their exuberance restrained by realities. Why would anyone go into the fires of hell for you unless you rushed into them first?

➤ *Demonstrate an avid desire for change, growth, or improvement.* How hollow dreaming about the future is unless you want to make that future happen. The group's mission, objectives, and standards mean nothing unless they look beyond the now to the moment when the goods or services are delivered, the checks are in the bank, and the warranty period is over. At that point effective managers move beyond the now to the next moment.

➤ *Have the energy and inner security necessary for conducting the business of the group.* Dreaming, driving change, making things happen exhaust even the strongest of effective managers. It requires constant renewal to make a manager successful. Never underestimate the importance of diet, exercise, and rest as ingredients of organizational success. Workaholics, addicts all, not only do not produce desirable results, but they drain resources and burn out before you can get the full benefit of their skills or knowledge. Effective managers make opportunities for themselves and other people to rest and to play.

➤ *Harmonize the various dimensions of your own life.* A quote I've seen attributed to novelist and dramatist James Barrie reads, "Nothing is really work unless you would rather be doing something else." A life full of dissonance is a life full of conflict. Both exhaust you more than does fulfilling work. Know what's important to you before doing what's important to someone else. It's a matter of emphasis, not of balance.

➤ *Help others to harmonize the various dimensions of their lives.* Effective managers allow others the same luxury of doing what's important to him. Flextime, comp time, family days at the office help people focus on what's important.

These leadership practices among all levels of management have been positively correlated with bottom-line measures. Employees look to all the managers of the organization to lead the charge. As a manager, if by default or neglect you delegate leadership roles to other people, you risk losing your importance to and influence in the group. Should that happen the company would lose the synergy it needs for reaching its goals.

Flexibility and Leadership

When people talk about flexibility in business, they usually refer to relationships with people: understanding employees and managers, empathizing with their concerns, and helping them harmonize their work and their personal lives. However, besides *personal flexibility,* you need *organizational flexibility*—not just to support making change happen but also to initiate it. You also need flexible managers capable of sparking creativity and innovation as well as committing themselves to strategy-powered evolution or revolution.

Organizational Flexibility

Supervisors get themselves in trouble if they give employees room to maneuver around company policies and procedures when the company doesn't sanction granting employees that freedom. Most companies, still structured hierarchically, are managed through command-and-control. In the words of one CEO's exaggerated boast, "Eighteen hundred decisions are made every day in this company, and every damn one of them had better cross my desk."

The movement toward horizontal organizations, self-managed employees, and cross-functional teams still struggles against organizational and human inertia. Removing the time clock doesn't stop managers from checking their watches when employees come to work, and not all employees embrace the new order either. In the words of the treetop publisher/editor in the comic strip "Shoe," continuous feedback, for example, means "nodding your head more when [he's] talking."[6]

The weakness in U.S. business and industry lies in its lack of people skills, according to a number of surveys, including one in the 1996 *World Competitive Yearbook,* published by the Swiss company International Institute for Management and Development. This "truth" is what makes business satires such as "Shoe" and Scott Adams's "Dilbert" so popular. In the real world, the sharks still devour the good guys, or at least force managers to find subtle or disguised ways to practice their principles. The organization must provide the platform for doing self-management or it's just back to business-as-usual.

Individual leadership flourishes only when its executives have a strong vision of where the organization is going and open themselves to new ideas about ways to encourage employees to:

➤ Participate in process improvement or change.
➤ Hone their skills, improve their competencies, and increase their knowledge.
➤ Maintain high levels of performance.
➤ Engage in creativity and innovation.

Effective management, then, means (1) grounding the organization in a strong sense of a core business (which is based in part on the organization's core competencies), and (2) opening up the environment by providing incentives that increase productivity.

Giving People a Stake in the Future

Many managers still don't believe that money is not the prime or only driver of productivity, and yet it hasn't been for over twenty years.

According to Steven Berglas, in *Inc.* magazine, "over time intrinsic rewards are far more likely to motivate . . . the people who work for them."[7] Employees respond to many kinds of incentives (intrinsic and extrinsic), and they especially respond to organizations that allow them to participate in the decisions that affect both the life of the organization and their own lives. They take command of and commit themselves to change, continuous improvement, and growth when they have ownership in the organization and in their own responsibilities. Combining participation and ownership generates the kind of coordination and commitment that turns a so-so company into a dynamo, a lesson well learned by the Atlanta-based fast-food chain Chick-Fil-A.

Chick-Fil-A has grown to 600 stores without seeking investors from the stock market. Instead, the company splits its profits fifty-fifty with its operators, a large number of them with $100,000-a-year incomes. Employee turnover averages 5 percent a year. Operators earn 50 percent more than their competitors, and their competitors suffer 35 percent turnover.[8] *The combination of participation and ownership truly matters.*

Participation without ownership is shallow. Ownership without participation is hollow. Many employee-stock-ownership-plan (ESOP) companies struggle because they don't fairly share the wealth with the employee-owners, they don't encourage self-management, and they don't communicate effectively. In short, they haven't learned from the examples of Monsanto Chemical Company, Pfizer, Continental Air, and many high-tech companies: Only a combination of (1) sharing the wealth with rank-and-file employees through a well-designed and well-managed plan (including stock options, bonuses, etc.) *and* (2) enhancing communication will excite employees about what happens in or to the company.[9]

ESOPs run into trouble when the worker/owners don't see gains commensurate with sacrifices. When people are permitted to make decisions and take responsibility for implementing them but are not rewarded directly for their increased participation, they believe they are being exploited in the Marxist sense: To the bosses go the profits. At the same time, giving people a piece of the action but denying them control over their own property, sends the message that all they really own is stock. As Dana Mead, CEO of Tenneco, said during an interview on ABC's *Nightline* television program, you can't buy loyalty with stock ownership alone.[10] ESOPs fail when traditional managers rule, where only few employees own a majority of stock, and where shareholder influence dominates.

Systems to Promote Organizational Flexibility

The simple answer to the issue of organizational flexibility seems to be: Offer all employees ownership of the company and let them run the show. To this, managers and shareholders usually say, "No way," protesting that this is tantamount to "letting the inmates run the asylum." (Who says Theory X management is dead?) Both positions— turning companies over to their employees, and "No way"—are extremes, but you hear both of them on the street.

The more pragmatic answer falls short of the revolution: systems that promote and support flexibility among *all the employees.* One way to encourage flexibility is to open all-way communication through easy-to-access channels, such as:

- Open-space offices where people can talk freely and openly with one another
- Open-door policies that enable people to talk freely and openly with their managers without fear for reprisal for honesty
- "War rooms" in which free-for-all brainstorming and arguments over tactics can take place
- Transition teams made up of both management and nonmanagement employees, and transition meetings in which change can be planned and managed
- Tiger Teams that have the freedom to attack problems and proactively create new processes or products

Another method for promoting flexibility is to *develop as-needed real-time training programs.* Tie skill training to solving specific and local problems, but also lay down a foundation through training for attacking future challenges.

Third, cutting-edge tools for networking and team building promote flexibility. Use electronic performance-support systems such as Lotus Notes or Self-Management Communications, Inc.'s Get Organized! The Workgroup and Personal Performance Manager.

Finally, lead from the top to encourage flexibility everywhere. Take the "Pepsi Challenge" promoted by PepsiCo's chairman and CEO, Roger Enrico. In a program he calls "Building the Business," he personally works at developing other leaders by spending over 100 days a year conducting small-group workshops for all senior executives of the company.[11] Without this kind of leadership from the top and systemic changes, your flock winds up short on wing power.

Making the Organization Flexible

Nothing happens until people make it happen. Organizational flexibility is just a concept until managers *make* the organization flexible. The results of organizational synergy may be more than the sum of its parts, but the organization itself is nothing more than the sum total of what people *do.* Your job title—manager—doesn't ensure flexibility; indeed, few job descriptions of managers even mention "being flexible" as an important job function. Most descriptions canonize the old (and wrongheaded) distinction that separates management and leadership, which makes it difficult for managers to assimilate leadership notions.

Managers, by the nature of their jobs, must attend to task-oriented, administrative details. However, in the realities of today's business world, neither managing nor leading by itself generates the overall results we're looking for. Managers must be leaders as well, and vice versa. They have to attend to their details, but they also must make a difference in the lives of the people around them.

As the old notion of management says, getting desirable results through the efforts of others is a manager's responsibility, but only by recognizing that people have to have a say in how they achieve those results can you become their leader. Leaders create teamwork and build a cooperative and collaborative as well as a productive environment. They support people's efforts in whatever they do. They encourage, coach, mentor, and guide other people. They cheerlead on occasion, and they always take a realistic but enthusiastic perspective on the challenges ahead. Their vision becomes their driving force and the force that pulls other people to them. An effective manager has to blend the best of both management and leadership competencies to keep the work group on the *process track* as well as on the *task track.*

Contrary to the Hickman metaphors that I described in Chapter

10, management and leadership are not mutually exclusive. Every successful organization, large or small, requires both management and leadership from top to bottom. Carrying self-management to its logical conclusion makes the combination possible among nonmanagement employees as well. Effective managers recognize that not only do goals have to be achieved (the task orientation of managers) but human needs must be served (the process orientation of leaders). It's a matter of harmonizing the demands of different dimensions of the workplace (the Japanese principle of *wa*), and here's where flexibility comes into play again.

Other Ways for Managers to Lead

Whatever your position in your organization, you can and should lead. At organizational levels, the details themselves don't concern you; rather you focus on the strategies for defining and growing the company. Call it the "vision thing," if you wish. At process levels, you lead by laying out the plans for executing the strategies and by developing the resources and by supporting the people who make things happen. At task levels, your attention to continuous improvement gets the right things done the right way. Only when everyone takes responsibility for leading in their own way can the whole organization arrive safely at its destination.

The future, no matter how unpredictable, is every manager's concern, particularly at the organizational levels of a business. To make that future happen in desired and desirable ways, open yourself to the possibility of reinventing your core business and your role in it. Shifting paradigms in change management guru Joel Barker's sense of the phrase (i.e., replacing one model of reality with another) carries flexibility to an extreme.[12] Flex your mind, expand the boundaries of where you are at any given time, explore new ways of doing the same things or doing new things with the resources you have: That's more practical or pragmatic.

People like Bill Gates (of Microsoft fame) and James R. Houghton (CEO of Corning, Inc.) add the dimension of time to Exhibit 7-3, the Venn diagram that describes a core business. Managers of their ilk look at "what we can do," "what the buying public asks us to do," and "what we want to do" *along a time line stretching from the present into any number of possible futures.* The model shown in Exhibit 11-1 represents the future as "what we can do in the future," "what the buying public will ask us to do," and "what we will want to do."

Exhibit 11-1. Core business over time.

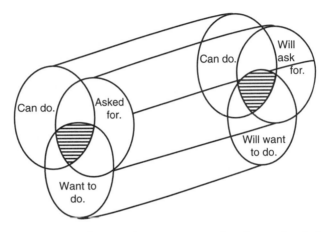

New iterations of inventing your core business don't have to replace older images. Instead, they should extend the reach of your questions:

➤ What can we do best and how can we expand the skills, knowledge, and technology into other areas?
➤ What other products or services does the buying public want (or might it want) that we can satisfy with the resources we have or can reasonably acquire?
➤ What do we want to do with the resources we have or can reasonably acquire that will satisfy what the buying public wants (or might want)?

The risk comes from trying to predict "what the buying public will ask us to do." This is where making the future happen comes into play. Don't forget, for geese to fly from "here" to "there," they must stretch their necks out—without the benefit of reports about the weather ahead.

The same risk attends defining your own role in an ever changing business environment. You can't lead unless you fly out of the head of the formation. To redefine yourself and what you do regularly ensures your place in organizations where you know "what [your] 'work' is."[13] Your work is different from your job, and knowing the difference can, at least, ensure your employability somewhere else, your economic survival.

Leading to Empowerment

Effective managers care about individual and group task goals *and* about getting the best from other people, managing differences, and resolving conflicts. The role of manager-leader and how it contributes to team power is clearly illustrated in the V-formation used by migrating geese. Every goose is "empowered" to be the leader whenever needed to take the lead.

Empowering individuals and groups (i.e., giving them the right, the opportunity, the skills, and the tools for *acting* on the basis of their decisions as well as for making them) means involving people in the decision-making process, allowing them to influence each other, and then recognizing them as influencers who act without fear of reprimand or of being overruled by an executive decision. Managers who don't *redefine themselves* as facilitators instead of bosses, enablers instead of doers, feel threatened by this degree of empowering.

Empowerment in a group happens only when leadership is shared. Therefore, only the person in charge can create the environment in which group members:

➤ Contribute to and influence the group in a way appropriate to their individual abilities, skills, and preferences.
➤ Share vision and mission, looking forward, seeking challenges, initiating change.
➤ Share responsibility for the group's results; everyone is willing to act on group decisions.
➤ Share responsiveness; the entire group is willing to seek out ways to help one another and to find opportunities for growth.

In short, manager-leaders apply self-management to practical daily life and model the self-management they expect from other people.

Notes

1. According to a Wyatt Company poll cited in Mark Golin et al., *Secrets of Executive Success: How Anyone Can Handle the Human Side of Work and Grow Their Career* (Emmaus, Penn.: Rodale Press, 1991), p. 30.
2. Sue Shellenbarger's "Work and Family" column, "Enter the 'New Hero'; A Boss Who Knows You Have a Life," *Wall Street Journal* (May 8, 1996), p. B1. Shellenbarger has written extensively along those lines, e.g., "Managers Find Out How to Be Flexible," *Wall Street Journal* (December 11, 1991), p. B1, and "Some Workers Find Bosses Don't Share Their Family Values" *Wall Street Journal* (July 12, 1995), p. B1.
3. "Workplace: The Value of Flexibility," *Inc.* (April 1996), p. 114. See also Baxter W. Graham, "The Business Argument for Flexibility," *HRMagazine* (May 1996), pp. 104–110.
4. See "Corning's Class Act," *Business Week* (May 13, 1991), pp. 68–76.
5. Robert Hoffman, "Ten Reasons You Should Be Using 360-Degree Feedback," *HRMagazine* (April 1995), pp. 82–85. See also "Performance Reviews: Can the Boss Make the Grade?" *Inc.* (May 1996), p. 114.
6. Jeff MacNelly, "Shoe," *St. Louis Post-Dispatch* (December 3, 1994).
7. Steven Berglas, "When Money Talks, People Walk," *Inc.* (May 1996), pp. 25–26.
8. Frederick F. Reichheld, "Solving the Productivity Puzzle," *Wall Street Journal* (March 4, 1996), p. A10.
9. Robert Steyer, "Monsanto Puts Bucks Behind the Buzzwords," *St. Louis Post-Dispatch* (May 19, 1996), pp. 1E, 7E; Scott McCartney, "Back on Course: Piloted by Bethune, Continental Air Lifts Its Workers' Morale," *Wall Street Journal* (May 15, 1996), pp. A1, A8. See also Susan Chandler, "United We Own," *Business Week* (March 18, 1996), pp. 96–100.
10. Dana Mead, ABC Television Network's *Nightline,* April 9, 1996.
11. Noel M. Tichy and Christopher DeRose, "The Pepsi Challenge: Building a Leader-Driven Organization," *Training and Development* (May 1996), pp. 58–66.
12. Joel Arthur Barker, *Paradigms: The Business of Discovering the Future* (New York: Harper Business, 1992), p. 37.
13. Danny G. Langdon and Kathleen S. Whiteside, "Redefining Jobs and Work in Changing Organizations," *HRMagazine* (May 1996), p. 97.

Other Sources

Bernstein, Aaron. "Should Avis Try Harder—For Its Employees?" *Business Week* (August 12, 1996).

Brooks, Susan Sonnesyn. "Managing a Horizontal Revolution." *HRMagazine* (June 1995).

Chandler, Susan. "Northwest: The Turnaround Bill Arrives: An ESOP Saves the Airline. Now Labor Wants Its Due." *Business Week* (August 19, 1996).

Hequet, Marc. "Beyond Dollars." *Training* (March 1996).

Moore, James. *The Death of Competition: Leadership and Strategy in the Age of Business Ecosystems.* New York: HarperCollins, 1996. See also excerpt in *Fortune* (April 15, 1996).

Stamps, David. "A Piece of the Action." *Training* (March 1996).

"What Can You Really Do About Productivity." *Training/HRD* (March 1981).

For just a sampling of reports, see: Grib, Gail, and Susan O'Donnell. "Pay Plans that Reward Employee Achievement." *HRMagazine* (July 1995); Amos, Denise Smith. "Perks Pay Off for Companies and Workers." *St. Louis Post-Dispatch* (September 4, 1995); Rose, Robert L. "Hard Driving: A Productivity Push at Wabash National Puts Firm on a Roll." *Wall Street Journal* (September 7, 1995). The laundry list of books and articles is too long to include more here, but any bibliography should include books and articles by and about James MacGregor Burns, Warren Bennis, and John Kotter.

12

Managing the WIIFM: Recognition and Rewards

Leadership is an action, not a word.
—Richard P. Cooley, bank president (1923–   )

Wild geese in flight do more than manage their resources and make the most of flock members' contributions. They each also perform a leadership action to increase both individual and group power: They honk loudly to cheer one another on. Without both management and leadership, how else would geese ever reach their destination?

Good leaders are just as concerned as are good managers about bottom-line results (reaching their destination), which shows up in Exhibit 10-1 under the leadership skill set called "Support Employees." Effective managers understand how people think or feel about work in general and their work in particular; they actively support people's development, and they go to bat for others when they are right. This skill also requires respecting, appreciating, valuing, and encouraging differences and diversity.

> Effective manager-leaders find ways to support the task-oriented activities for which they're responsible, and they're concerned about how the work gets done, about the morale of the group, about the way the group gets along, and about ways of inspiring the group toward excellence.

In the role of manager, you have to help employees do their jobs and get the results expected of them. You have to find ways to support the task-oriented activities for which you, as a manager, are responsible. At the same time, as a leader, you have to be concerned about how the work gets done, about the morale of the group, about the way the group gets along, and about ways of inspring the group toward excellence. Only by practicing both sets of skills can you hope to increase individual and group power. And, make no mistake about it, supporting employees calls for a complex interweaving of both sets of skills.

I call one aspect of supporting employees "Managing the WIIFM," the topic of this chapter. I call a second aspect "Vision Skills," the topic of Chapter 13. Which side of management-leadership you display at any given time depends entirely upon the circumstances.

Why Leaders Need to Manage the WIIFM

WIIFM = What's in it for me? That simple formula expresses a common value: Most people expect something in return for their efforts when they come to work. Motivation depends on that expectation, and it forms a major clause in the psychological contract between employers and employees.

You expect people to come to work and, with a minimum of supervision, produce the outcomes for which you hired them. Employees then expect to be compensated for their work, and they expect guidance and support from you. That basic, usually oral understanding carries as much psychological importance as does a written document. (Additionally, if it ever comes down to a "he said–she said" debate in front of a jury, you could be found liable for creating an oral contract just as binding as a written contract.)

Some employees expect and want little more than guidance and support from their supervisors. Self-managed, they come to work energized and satisfied by what they do, rewarding themselves with *intrinsic satisfactions* (e.g., doing their jobs well, or growth, or self-fulfillment). But that's not the rule. Most employees expect and want some kind of payoff from their employers—an *extrinsic reward*. That's where WIIFM leadership comes in.

WIIFM Leadership and Managing Incentives or Rewards

The ability to use extrinsic rewards (in addition to pay for performance) as incentives to encourage people to be more productive marks the WIIFM leader. Pay for performance has its limits, namely that people need more than cash compensation to feel good about what they do (especially when it comes to doing the extras). That something more takes different forms, some tangible, others intangible, and as the list below suggests, it takes certain abilities to support employees with extrinsic rewards:

☛ To relate well with others and to get to know them
☛ To plan a system of rewards that is fair and consistent
☛ To prevent conflicts over rewards
☛ To match rewards to organizational goals and to the individuals receiving the rewards
☛ To get commitment
☛ To prevent diminishing returns
☛ To encourage others to seek out ways for self-rewarding activities

Relate to and Get to Know People

Everyone wants some kind of extrinsic payoff from their efforts, whether it be tangible or intangible. Effective managers recognize in themselves that they need extrinsic payoffs for their efforts as much as everyone else does. The exercise in Appendix C, "What Drives Me?" showed you that extrinsic rewards hold some value for you regardless of where on the scale of importance they fall. (If you haven't done that exercise, I suggest you do it now before going on. The results will help you understand what this chapter's about.)

Experience with "What Drives Me?" shows that only on rare occasions do different people rank all the payoffs the same way. As a result, you need to know what drives each person reporting to you. One employee, driven by a desire for knowledge, feels rewarded by challenging assignments. Another employee, driven by a need to exercise power, responds to freedom to make decisions and to act on them. How you reward people depends upon two-way communication about their drives, their likes and dislikes, their aspirations—whatever reward system you create. The more you know about individuals, the more you can tailor rewards that will enable them to see for themselves "What's in it for me."

Getting to know other people means to balance friendly relations with goals and standards that, when achieved, form a basis on

---

which rewards are given. Your intention here is not to become friends and let subjective factors determine rewards. Letting everyone know you'll reward them only for objective results prevents a lot of unnecessary game playing.

In short, know what turns on other people and the reasons for giving rewards; don't guess. In general, *base compensation* meets people's basic needs for food, clothing, and shelter. *Incentives* for asking for more than minimum levels of productivity, on the other hand, have to meet people's higher-level needs: social relationships, recognition, integrity, self-satisfaction, feelings of personal power, growth, advancement, a sense of fairness or equity. These needs are like fingerprints: No two people express them or find satisfaction for them in the same way. So, you see, you do need to find out what drives other people to work.

Plan a Fair and Consistent System of Rewards

Ask employees to produce only at minimum levels and they'll give you what you ask for in return for their base compensation. Ask for an extra inch beyond the minimum only if you plan ways to give in return recognition and rewards over and above base compensation. Plan to give a great deal more in return for asking employees to go an extra mile. Mitchell Fein, productivity improvement consultant, expresses this in stronger terms: "If you want people's attitudes [toward productivity] to change, you've got to change the conditions under which they work."[1] The very least required for earning employee commitment is a positive, productive climate.

Planning the kinds of rewards to offer, when to offer them, whom to offer them to, and how to deliver them is just as important as planning how and when to invest in capital goods.

Set Reward Objectives

Don't be surprised if people look for recognition or reward at each bend of the performance management spiral described in Chapter 11. Little successes breed big successes; typically people feel successful only if their effort is recognized by other people, especially by their supervisors. You see it on the home front all the time, among most men who do something ordinarily called housework: "See, honey, I washed the dishes tonight." They expect a pat on the back, at least. Therefore, when planning a system of rewards, base them on these six criteria:

1. What people do to contribute to achieving organizational goals and objectives
2. Productivity standards that stretch people above minimum requirements
3. Employee drivers, i.e., what each employee thinks is:

    ➤ Valuable (perceived value)
    ➤ Fair (equitable in proportion to effort and to what other people receive)

4. Realistic estimates of the group's and individual's abilities to achieve task-oriented goals
5. Realistic estimates of the company's ability to provide the payoffs (based on budgetary constraints and previous experience with the company's willingness to extend itself)
6. Short-term rewards that provide immediate reinforcement ("good job" pats on the back) and long-term rewards that encourage creativity, innovation, and growth

Once more, don't guess. Talk with the people in your group, talk with HR professionals, and talk with the executives who have to approve what you want to do. All of them have to be on board if you expect your reward system to work.

Time Line

Sometimes time pressures generate extra effort. Identify specific, reasonable target dates for achieving goals and receiving rewards. Frequent or unnecessarily tight deadlines punish people and act as demotivators. Another reason for getting to know people: Some people relish the stress of time pressures, while others, when faced with them, spin into "a panic mode," the result of which is failure.

Prevent Conflicts Over Rewards and Cheating

The Dallas-based personnel agency that "refused to join the recession" encouraged cutthroat employee competitions. Every month, for example, the employees struggled to reach outlandish goals for writing "job orders" (agreements with employers for seeking job candidates) set by the owner and the EVP. If the agencies met their monthly overall goals on or before the last day of the month, they would get a half day off (after a lunch feast at company expense). Individuals, in their turn, vied for tickets to concerts, shows, movies, or ball games. The most consistent individual winners, it turned out, also lied and cheated the most consistently: mainly by writing fake, unverifiable job orders that they reported into the agency figures.

Competition between members in a group usually forces people to become adversaries rather than partners. People can be greedy. Some will cheat and lie to earn just an extra half day off or to win two tickets to a concert. So, take into account each person in the group, seeing to it that there's something for everyone. One way is to have people compete only against their own performance standards to produce verifiable results tied to organizational goals. "Earn two tickets to the ball game by exceeding your production of last month by 10 percent."

Encouraging teamwork also creates opportunities for cooperation among individuals or among departments; cooperation, in turn, increases productivity as well as commitment to the organization and its mission. You can avoid competition for basic rewards by offering rewards for cooperation. Think small, whenever you can, because it doesn't take much to make people feel important. Consider the moment of fame Advanced Micro Devices of Sunnyvale, California, gives employees.[2] Group photos in the company publication give recognition and encourage the ongoing spirit of cooperation and collaboration, which is then reflected in bottom-line results.

Match Rewards to Organizational Goals

Goals that lead to organizational and individual fulfillment almost always demand that people stretch beyond minimum expectations. Yet, since their base pay almost always compensates for minimum effort, you get what you pay for.

Big achievements merit big incentives. Provide exemplary rewards for exemplary performance, and strive for equity in relation to expectations by making the reward equal to the effort it takes to get it. "Gee, thanks. Can you spare it?" is an appropriate response to a $10 prize for a $50,000 savings.

Strive for equity between people, also, by being fair in the distribution of rewards relative to what individuals achieve. "That's mighty big of you" is also an appropriate response from someone who produces 20 percent over minimum, if she gets the same-size reward as someone who produces 2 percent over minimum.

Create competition for rewards for exemplary performance only where it won't interfere with teamwork and cooperation. Competition *between* teams sometimes influences productivity and encourages teamwork (e.g., when two teams, working on independent projects vie for beating deadlines), but competition between individuals hardly ever does. Cal Snap & Tab, in the City of Industry, California, sets targets for spoilage, and the team with the lowest scores wins a cash prize that is then distributed among all the members of the team. The outcome has been a dramatic drop in spoilage and waste, while increasing cooperation and collaboration.[3]

Match Rewards to People's Values

The moral of another tale from the personnel agency in Dallas points out the importance of knowing what turns other people on (or off). It also shows how important it is to honor an individual's wishes and needs.

The high-tech recruiting division had a bona fide star I'll call Frank. A born-again Christian, Frank dedicated his life to building a church, and he had told everyone that for him the job was merely a means to an end (which he quit after earning and saving the money he needed). His every act satisfied only his need to fulfill his own life vision.

Frank's consistently outstanding performance was also a source of embarrassment because the company insisted, in spite of his frequent protests, on publicly citing his figures and giving him plaques, medals, and statues during monthly breakfast meetings, which he almost always failed to attend. For Frank, making him the role model for everyone else was only a hypocritical manipulation. What he did served a high purpose that for him was his just reward; he didn't want medals or to be a role model for making money. The company's extrinsic incentives were just a symbol of the sinful greed and hubris he decried. Only dedication to his calling kept him at the agency, and the only inspiration he ever offered to his coworkers was spiritual, not material.

In their turn, the other employees spurned the company's efforts. Everyone knew what drove the man and his feelings about being put on display, and they felt embarrassed for him. They also knew how different Frank was from them and didn't believe it possible to achieve his stature in the agency business. Instead of being inspired by his performance, they were turned off by the company's shameless mishandling of the motivation process. Whereas Frank served his God, the company only served its owner, while each person served himself.

When Frank left the company, employee performance didn't change for the worse (or for the better, for that matter), although the loss of his revenue severely shocked the bottom line. The employees lost nothing, but both Frank and his employer suffered the agonies of rejection and resentment. Talk about failing to understand employee motivation.

Provide Value

The value of specific performance motivators varies by race, gender, and age—but, mere increases in base income, as study after study demonstrates, mean less than job security, challenging problems to solve, exciting work, being treated like adults, working in a positive social environment, and opportunities to grow.

Recognition programs need to be "as sophisticated and well planned as any other business process." The most effective programs "are communication-based, performance-focused, and [driven by their] symbolism" more than by their tangible payoffs.[4]

Rewards symbolize what they *mean* to the organization and to the people receiving them. Do the incentives your company offer have value to both the organization and the individual? Not only do people have to perceive the rewards' value to them; they have to perceive the rewards' value to the company. To be blunt: If incentives cost the company nothing in terms of cost, time, opportunity, or power, why should anyone care about them?

Provide Opportunities for Self-Rewarding Activities

Self-management calls for self-rewarding. The more you encourage *intrinsic* motivation, the more people learn to respond to intrinsic rewards. Indeed, change in the business environment I described in Chapter 1 (a workplace that demands employee flexibility and adaptability, more teamwork, more independence and initiative, greater competency), often doesn't work because many managers don't see the value of empowering people to make decisions and to act on them as an incentive. They fail to see the emotional as well as economic value of empowerment for self-managed people *in terms of self-esteem*. In turn, empowered employees fail to understand the emotional cost to managers to give up autocratic power or the ability to micromanage everyone's work. What both managers and nonmanagement employees have to learn is that empowering people provides opportunities for self-rewarding behavior by giving something of value to both the giver and the receiver—self-esteem for the employees, greater effectiveness for the managers.

Prevent Diminishing Returns

A sales group in a St. Louis-based printing firm does what most sales firms do: It rotates a monthly reward from one month's highest producer to the next. The gold-plated loving cup gleams on the winner's desk for all to see—but no one really cares. Getting the cup has become a group joke, an extrinsic recognition that has, in large part, lost its gleam.

Repetition usually does breed contempt. Unless you vary incentives, the trite and cliché ones produce diminishing returns. People get tired of chasing the same rainbows.

Get Commitment to Rewards and Incentives

People have condemned WIIFM leadership for turning managers into animal trainers, offering treats to employees in return for learning tricks. That could be true in command-and-control environments where only the managers draw up all the plans and hold out all the carrots (while hiding the sticks behind their backs). Employees may

yearn for the carrot and fear the stick, but they feel no commitment
to their jobs or to the company.

On the other hand, the manipulative aura vanishes when the reward system incorporates suggestions from employees involved in the
design and delivery of rewards. Employee-designed recognition programs can excite their designers, and companies get commitment
from their employees because they don't feel that anything is
" 'forced on [them]. . . . [T]hey're a part of the decision-making process.' "[5] If you have to reject someone's idea, explain why. Asking for
and then ignoring employees' input demotivates them and breeds resentment and contempt for any reward system you install.

Five Ground Rules for Making Rewards
Fair and Consistent

*1. Make your reward system consistent with the values expressed in
your vision.* Vision statements espouse values that often don't match
values-in-practice. The more flagrant violations of espoused values
often make headlines, e.g., Texaco, Avis-Rent-a-Car, Denny's, where
management practices in the past made a mockery of well-intentioned
antiracism policies. If your vision statement says, as many do, "We
aspire to treating each person as an individual, with respect for his or
her dignity and self-esteem," your reward system must reflect that
vision statement (which many do not). Effective managers make every
effort to put espoused values into practice. The greater the divergence
between them, the less respect employees feel toward the company
and its executives.

If your vision statement values exceptional or excellent performance, respond in kind. To be sure, merely acknowledge work that
meets minimum standards (ho-hum work rates a ho-hum response);
that's what you pay people to do. However, you *reward* people for
exceeding the minimum standards of the job; that's how you improve
individual as well as group productivity and help employees stretch
themselves.

2. Treat everyone as an individual. Don't try to reward everyone
the same way. Everyone is different in some way, and individuals
prefer to think of themselves as unique (not just different). Basing

rewards on both goals or standards and on individual differences
helps you tailor specific rewards to specific needs. For recipients to
perceive rewards as fair, i.e., of having at least equal value to their
effort and to the rewards given other people, they must:

➤ Perceive the value of the rewards to themselves and to the company.
➤ Perceive the rewards as proportional to the effort they expend or
the outcomes they produce.

Many employers have found ways to reward people that satisfy
the recipients' personal needs and aspirations while also serving the
company. Employee-friendly companies such as 3M and Hewlett-
Packard also tend to be highly successful. It takes a little more effort
to individualize rewards, but the payoffs to the recipients and to you
are worth it, as these five examples show:

1. The Advanta Corporation, a financial services company in
Atlanta, Georgia, rewards peak performers by asking them to assist
in training new hires and temporary employees. It gives the "stars"
feelings of self-esteem, a sense of pride, and the feeling they've
stretched mentally. They are doing more than what they see as mundane or dull or menial tasks. More interesting work (not just more of
the same) rewards them.[6]

2. In other cases, recognition or praise from supervisors will do.
A computer manufacturer in Massachusetts, Cognex Corp., "gives
. . . special time with . . . manager[s] over dinner or lunch."[7] A pat
on the back *and a little something more* builds strong bonds with
employees.

3. Yet, for others, praise from their supervisor is not enough.
They need social recognition and feel rewarded when they're recognized by the group or, at least, when recognized in front of it. You
don't have to have a meeting to do it, either. H. J. Heinz publishes
information about employees at all levels in its house organ and annual reports.[8] However, take care; some people, like the recruiter in
Dallas, feel uneasy when held up as a model to others.

4. Nonmanagers have few chances to take on obvious leadership
roles. Yet, many people see such roles as a way to express themselves
as adult, useful human beings. Assigning them to head a committee

or a task force to improve productivity or the quality of work or work life rewards them and encourages self-management practices. Outstanding performers at Shimadza Scientific Instruments, in Eldersburg, Maryland, are "promoted to special assistant to the president for two weeks," during which time they increase their understanding of the business and its demands as well as feeling highly rewarded.[9] Practicing self-management produces self-managed people.

5. People feel a strong need for control over their lives and respond well to anything employers will do to help them get it. A study of worker preferences "offers some clues . . . about how to increase productivity while improving employee morale." Paid time-off banks, flexible work schedules, and the ability to work compressed workweeks rank among the top-five nontraditional benefits to which employees respond most favorably. Control doesn't totally replace cash or cash substitutes (e.g., insurance coverage, including prevention and wellness coverage) in importance, but it ranks high in employees' lists of preferences.[10]

Genuine drivers are only those payoffs that meet the individual's own needs or goals. Therefore, to meet these needs or goals, promised rewards must satisfy at least four criteria:

1. Rewards should be given only for successfully completing a task that meets real needs of the organization, of the manager, and of the individual.
2. Rewards must be deliverable.
3. Rewards have to be accessible and immediate, not vague promises.
4. Rewards should fit with the previous experience people have had with the organization.

3. Encourage autonomy. Tell people what they can do to get rewards. Then, let them decide whether or not to go for the specific brass ring that satisfies their needs—and how. You might even let them decide what they want, after discussing what is available or within reason. Companies like TWA have used a bonus-point system in which teams and their members can earn points for exceeding specific standards or achieving high-performance goals; they can then trade in those points for prizes listed in a picture catalogue. Many companies also find that performance review or career planning sessions are a perfect time and place for discussing individual desirable payoffs. Why guess at what turns on another person, when all you have to do is ask?

4. Respond to either positive or negative results in a timely manner. People expect you to reward them at the time they do something they believe is noteworthy. They also expect you to withhold rewards and take corrective action when something goes awry. A quick response signals interest and confidence in the other person. Employees become hostile when supervisors fail to respond appropriately or promptly to negative results. Failure to respond on time or at all signals either that you think the other person's doing okay or you don't care what he does. Either behavior reinforces poor performance and extinguishes good performance.

People also become hostile when their supervisors respond only to problems, a phenomenon called crisis management and often a favorite form of management behavior. Early in my own management career, an employee made it quite clear that I undermined myself when I told her, "It's obvious I appreciate what you're doing. If not, I'd be on your case." Her eyes sprang open wide and she retorted, "How about recognizing the good I do, too?"

5. Take corrective action in a positive and supportive manner. Employees expect this from you also. Taking positive corrective action is in itself a form of reward; it gives people the attention and supervision their contract with you requires. That attention helps them see that you want them to succeed and to get the rewards they know now are in reach (if they'll make the effort to reach for them). Knowing that you will not reward poor performance, but rather that you'll take steps to improve it, makes rewards even more valuable.

Rewards have more meaning when you withhold them if performance doesn't meet or exceed standards. In fact, withholding rewards is the best-known form of punishment there is, and it's the easiest to apply. However, punishment poses an important management problem: What constitutes effective punishment? Promise to fire someone and the motivation lasts only as long as the threat hangs over her head. Managing through fear produces compliance, at best.

There are no immutable rules for taking corrective action, just a few guidelines:

➤ Take corrective action in a private, confidential place. In public it will backfire. In today's open-space workplace, it's becoming harder to find a closeable door, which places another responsibility on you to treat people with dignity. Not only should you help people earn their rewards, you also need to protect them from embarrassment.

➤ Express appreciation for cooperation in changing the behavior or performance in question. Demanding, punitive behavior or abusive language creates resistance. When taking corrective action, you're supposedly helping people to improve, not tearing them down. People respond in kind to kindness, and in this age of incivility every little kindness is itself a reward.

➤ Give credit for good work. Not everything a person does is bad, no matter how poor that person's performance. Find something, anything, to commend. Mary Poppins's spoonful of sugar does help the medicine go down.

➤ Be honest and forthright. Honesty and directness informs people that you consider them to be adults, mature enough to take negative feedback. Treating them as adults rewards them.

➤ Turn the discussion into a problem-solving session and involve the other person in making the decisions. "Constructive criticism"? It's an oxymoron. Criticism, by definition, is destructive. However, together you can build plans for change with objective feedback about poor performance or unacceptable behavior.

➤ Discuss both positive consequences for change and negative consequences of not changing. Positive consequences are the rewards people want in return for changing. Negative consequences spell out how rewards will be withheld, a process that could lead, in the last resort, to dismissal if change doesn't happen.

➤ Get commitment from the other person to making the change and make a commitment to help her. You can't get a commitment unless the other person sees the reward that's in it for her. No benefit, no effort. Likewise, if you're not willing to make an effort to help her make the change, why should she make the effort to please you? You reward her; she'll reward you.

The Right and the Why of WIIFM Leadership

Where do you get the right or the power to offer all these marvelous rewards? The source of power inherent in WIIFM leadership comes from the authority you get from your position or status as a manager. Managers, by virtue of their position, have the authority to make decisions about what their work groups do and how, when, and where they do it. Cascading down from key managers, status gives managers control. If you exercise that control too lightly, people suffer from neglect. If you exercise it too seriously (coercive power), people suffer from tyranny. More important than the amount of power you have is how you use your power. Successful managers harmonize their status power with their personal power (which I describe in Chapter 13) and elicit positive responses from other people.

Status power gives managers the right and the ability to offer rewards in return for effort; it gives them the ability to do something good for other people. Doing something good for someone in return for his doing something for you (quid pro quo), the principle underlying WIIFM, gives you a tool for transacting daily business with other people.[11] In fact, it's the basis on which all bilateral contracts are formed.

Let's turn over the coin. Why bother? Why should you, as a manager, concern yourself with WIIFM leadership? People come to work, they do what you tell them to do, and you pay them. Isn't that the way it's supposed to be?

Maybe that was the way once upon a time, but our society has moved on from there. Reengineering today must focus on growth, and employees, for a while paralyzed by the fear of downsizing, are emboldened once more to ask for raises, bonuses, and incentives of many kinds. They want rewards for taking on the burdens imposed by downsizing on the survivors, as well as promises of incentives for what they do in the future. Your choices as a manager come down to these: Stagnate or grow, revert to the management style of the past (overseer and paymaster for hired hands) or recognize the realities of global competition and the demands of the new workforce. By offering to share the wealth produced by growth, you create a positive, productive environment in which employees (and you) can increase personal and group power on the jobs. That increase in power feeds on itself and produces more wealth to share.

The bad rap WIIFM leadership gets from many people results from their misconception that it's manipulation or bribery, but there's nothing inherently wrong with repaying people's efforts with prizes, bonuses, plaques, and recognition—in addition to pay for performance. Therefore, don't count on seeing the task-oriented results for which your managers hold you accountable unless you transact business and develop "contracts" with people doing the work of your own work group. Only an *ideal* world of totally self-managed people can dispense with WIIFM as a motivating force.

Notes

1. "What Can You Really Do About Productivity," *Training/HRD* (March 1981), p. 27.
2. Bob Nelson, *1001 Ways to Reward Employees* (New York: Workman Publishing, 1994), p. 148.
3. Nelson, pp. 149–150.
4. B. Jackson Wixon, Jr., "Recognizing People in a World of Change," *HRMagazine* (June 1995), pp. 65–68.
5. Nelson, p. 142, citing Darrell Mell, VP of Telemarketing, Covenant House.
6. Nelson, p. 198.
7. Item in "Work Week" column of *Wall Street Journal* (April 2, 1996), p. A1.
8. Nelson, p. 38.
9. Nelson, p. 198. See also "Congratulations! In recognition of your fine work, you can meet the boss," "Work Week" column, *Wall Street Journal* (April 2, 1996), p. A1.
10. Results of a telephone survey of 1,000 employees nationwide conducted by Godwin Booke & Dickenson and HRStrategies (Aon Corp., Chicago) are cited in Ellen Joan Pollack, "Workers Want More Money, but They Also Want to Control Their Own Time," *Wall Street Journal* (November 28, 1995), pp. B1, B12. See also Sue Shellenbarger, "Managers Find Out How to Be Flexible," *Wall Street Journal* (December 11, 1991), p. B1; Shellenbarger, "Some Workers Find Bosses Don't Share Their Family Values," *Wall Street Journal* (July 12, 1995), p. B1; Shellenbarger, "Enter the 'New Hero': A Boss Who Knows You Have a Life," *Wall Street Journal* (May 8, 1996), p. B1.
11. Steven Kerr, "Risky Business: The New Pay Game," *Fortune* (July

1996), pp. 94–95; Donna Fenn, "Goal-Driven Incentives," *Inc.* (August 1996), p. 91.

Other Sources

Berglas, Steven. "When Money Talks, People Walk: Why Cash Rewards Miss the Point." *Inc.* (May 1996).

Burns, James MacGregor. *Leadership.* New York: Wiley, 1978.

Reinemer, Michael. "Work Happy." *American Demographics* (July 1995).

Weiss, Donald H. *How to Get the Best Out of People.* New York: AMA-COM, 1988.

Wilson, Thomas B. *Innovative Reward Systems for the Changing Workplace.* New York: McGraw-Hill, 1995.

13

Vision Leadership

It is time for a new generation of leadership, to cope with new problems and new opportunities.

—John F. Kennedy (1961)

Lest we be guilty of attributing too much intelligence to wild geese, let's remember that much of what we admire is instinctive and not consciously developed. They go where they go because they have to go there, not because they choose to. Credit human beings with raising leadership behavior to an art form through conscious, deliberate, learned behavior.

When you think of vision leaders whose names spring to mind? John Kennedy, Martin Luther King, Jr., Cesar Chavez, Golda Meir, Mohandas K. Gandhi? These people not only had vision, but they also used a *charismatic* style of personal power rather than status power to influence huge numbers of people. Theirs was vision leadership on the large scale.

> Vision leadership consists of touching people's lives and moving them down paths they would not otherwise have taken had it not been for the inspiration the Vision Leader provides.

However, charging the air with a charismatic personality doesn't define vision leadership. Rather, touching people's lives and moving them down paths they would not otherwise have taken had it not been for the inspiration the vision leader provided mark this style of leadership. Whereas WIIFM leadership depends in part on status power (the right and the ability to make decisions that affect other people's lives), vision leadership has nothing to do with status power. It derives its energy strictly from personal power, the ability to influence other people. By believing in themselves and in the abilities of other people, by setting the example of excellence, they shape lives, processes, and events—regardless of their position in the organization. If Joe in the mailroom has a vision of the workplace that improves the quality of work or the quality of work life of the people who execute his vision, he too is a vision leader on the small scale of daily life.

Personal Power and Vision Leadership

Anyone can be a vision leader because people (even people you don't know) who see you as worthy, in some way, confer that status on you. You can be a knowledge leader, a skill leader, a social leader, a morale leader, a group process leader. You need only act in ways other leadership admire and wish to emulate. That said, you can see that managers can also be vision leaders.

Vision leadership by definition gets its energy from personal power. Everyone has personal power: the ability to take control of your own life. Whether or not you exercise that power determines your level or degree of self-management. Everything I've said about self-management reflects having the self-control and self-discipline to use personal power, and just by being self-managed, you influence other people. They see you as a role model, someone to admire and emulate.

Indeed, a prerequisite of being a leader boils down to the fact that people see you as one. A Don Quixote may have a vision and decide to make a stab at influencing people, but unless people admire rather than laugh at him, he fails in his quest. Contrarily, a person whom others follow is by definition a leader.

At the extreme, people give up their personal power to someone whom they see as in control of her own life and of things, processes, and events. They become followers and many turn their leader into an idol, even if she doesn't ask for the adoration, doesn't know it's happening, or doesn't want it to happen. What the idol does or says is enough for these people to give themselves up to the leader, and they trust the leader to live up to the standards of the vision.

That other people don't have the same feelings toward the leader that his followers do doesn't negate his leadership. The Jim Joneses, Joseph Stalins, and Adolf Hitlers of the world live up the definition of leadership in spite of their evil ways and horrendous results. No one can deny that they touched people's lives and moved them down paths they would not otherwise have taken.

The extent to which the vision leader honors the trust people put in him and treats his followers fairly and justly distinguishes him from a tyrannical leader in the mold of Jones, Stalin, and Hitler. A vision leader worthy of universal admiration enhances the power people entrusts in him and gives it back to them, encouraging them to take control over the events that affect their lives. Isn't that what "empowering others" means?

In the world of business, vision leaders believe truly that employees are "our most important asset." When managers make insincere claims, workers can see through the smoke to the facts. Facts such as these:

- ➤ In 1995 and 1996 stocks boomed and market indices piled up records, while layoffs continued.
- ➤ "Income statements bloomed with rosy-cheeked health," while ordinary incomes remained stagnant.
- ➤ In 1996, employers (86 percent of major corporations) continued to outsource work to cheaper labor markets, with over 400,000 layoffs in 1995 (the most conservative estimate recorded).
- ➤ The chasm between CEO and line workers salaries continues to widen.[1]

Employees see the hypocrisy in their CEO's sentiment when she says, "We deeply appreciate the accomplishments of thousands of dedicated employees" while cutting off 2,000 of them. Vision manager-leaders inspire people rather than con and manipulate them.

A Source of Inspiration

WIIFM and vision leadership aren't mutually exclusive. You can use both in the service of your organization and its employees. Vision leaders manage the WIIFM when the occasion arises, but their greatest virtue is their ability to inspire other people to seek success as its own reward. Under the leadership of Jim Riggleman, the players on (and the fans of) the Chicago Cubs (perennial losers in baseball's National League) celebrate every victory as if they had just won the championship. No doubt they would like to win that championship, but to them to win *a game* is a success to cheer about. The win is its own reward. And what is true on the diamond is true in the workplace.

Pride of craftsmanship lives. Pride of ownership, too. The employees at GM's Saturn plant in Springhill, Tennessee, are typical of a large body of workers in the United States who strive to be the best and take pride in their responsible roles in the company. By personally taking responsibility for turning out excellent products, each Saturn employee not only contributes to the final output but also puts himself in a position to lead when the occasion arises.[2] The Saturn workers are not alone. In the words of cellist Sado Harada of the Tokyo String Quartet, "We don't think about who gets to show off their great sound, their great technique. We must project as one and put forth the quartet's musical personality."[3] Yet, have no doubt about this: Without inspiration from leadership at all levels of the organization, self-management in business would not exist.

Inspiration can come from something as simple as cheerleading or from something as lofty as a farsighted vision. You inspire people when you think and talk health, happiness, and optimism, not in a sappy, Pollyannaish way, but with a sincerity tempered by realism: realistic optimism. All things considered, it really isn't a bad world, but bad things do happen—bad things you have to be willing to accept and then *manage*. Taking control of events, rather than letting them control you, separates you from self-defeatists. Helping other people work past or around those bad things separates you from uncompromising fanatics.

Vision leaders also inspire other people by how they prepare for future threats. They can become anxious about the future, but they use healthy concerns to prepare themselves for whatever the challenges. They can get angry, but they use the energy of their anger to mobilize constructive forces to confront the danger. In short, they recognize that in the presence of trouble, self-managed people have the knowledge, the talent or skill, and the strength to overcome the obstacles to their success. Their inspiration infects the whole environment with excitement and enthusiasm about challenges they and others in the group face and about the successes everyone achieves.

Here's what a realistic optimist believes: If you think that you and other people can achieve anything you set your mind on achieving, you probably will achieve it; think that you can't do it and you won't. You have to be the sort of person who will sacrifice and do whatever you have to do (short of trampling on other people's lives) to get to where you need and want to go.

Inspiration also comes from emphasizing the positive possibilities of what people do. Vision leaders see the value of moving people toward success and excellence, and they invest themselves in helping their followers reach organizational and individual goals. Spending 100 days a year developing the leadership capabilities of his managers makes Roger Enrico, PepsiCo's chairman and CEO, a vision leader, and he's not the only CEO doing it. Jack Welch (General Electric), Lawrence Bossidy (AlliedSignal Inc.), Michael Lock (General Signal Corp), and Bill Brandt (American Woodmark Corp.)—just to name a few—contribute their knowledge, wisdom, and skill in classrooms on a regular basis.[4] Unless these successful CEOs believed that opportunities to lead and to inspire others to do the same added value to the bottom line, they wouldn't be doing it.

Leading by Example

No classroom performance can replace shirtsleeve leadership by example, which affects people's lives far more than does preaching or cheerleading. "Do as I say, not as I do" doesn't fly well in today's workplace. If you want other people to be informed, you have to inform yourself and then *pass on that information* to them. If you want other people to be skilled, you have to develop your skills as well, and then *use those skills for the benefit of the group* as well as for yourself. If you want other people to feel motivated and committed to the group, you have to be motivated and make a commitment to the group, then *demonstrate motivation and commitment by what you do.* If you want other people to be self-managed, you have to be self-managed as well and then *use that self-management as a constructive and positive force.*

Most sports fans find it much easier to sit on the sidelines and get pumped up by the exploits of other people than to get out on the playing field and do it themselves. In turn, their cheerleading pumps up the athletes as well and reinforces their desire to do well for their fans. On the other hand, the athletes resent it when those same fans play armchair coaches and second-guess them on miscues or bad calls. Likewise, foot soldiers don't really get fired up when their commanding officers give them a rousing pep talk before a major battle and then stay behind to direct them from the safety of bunkers miles behind the front lines while the soldiers are getting shot at. The second-guessing and the cheerleading are both easier to take and are more reinforcing when you know the cheerleaders and the second-guessers are also out there doing it (or at least have been there and have done that).

Positive Pygmalions

What do the ancient Greeks, poet-playwright Johann Wolfgang von Goethe, playwright George Bernard Shaw, social psychologists Robert K. Merton and Robert Rosenthal, and educator Marva Collins all have in common? They all believe in the power of the self-fulfilling prophecy, also known as the Pygmalion Effect, to reinforce a person's willingness and ability to succeed.[5] Vision leaders are "Positive Pygmalions," a common outcome of self-management.

The idea found its first expression in the Greek myth about Pygmalion, the sculptor who believed in the beauty of his statue so profoundly that he fell passionately in love with it; the goddess Athena, deeply moved by Pygmalion's love for his creation, granted his wish and brought the statue to life. You may have read Shaw's dramatic version of that story, *Pygmalion*, or seen it dramatized on the stage or on film; or you may be familiar with the musical version of the play, *My Fair Lady*. The moral of the Pygmalion story is that if you believe in your own abilities to lead other people and in their ability to fulfill their potential, the possibilities are wide open. Professor Henry Higgins, in Shaw's version, reflects the real-life Pygmalion you, as a Vision Leader, can become (although the arrogant character of the good professor hardly commends itself as a role model).

Positive Pygmalions are people who believe in and act on the following four principles:

1. *Positive Pygmalions believe in their ability to lead.* Buoyed by self-confidence and self-esteem, they take on and vigorously pursue

difficult challenges without much regard for satisfying immediate personal needs. Legends are born of military heroes, sports figures, and community icons who have overcome great adversity and sacrificed much to do great things—because they believed they could in spite of barriers and personal handicaps that stood in their way. They believed in themselves, and that's all that mattered to them.

2. *Positive Pygmalions also believe in the people they lead.* Robert Rosenthal's research demonstrated the truth in Robert Merton's theory of the power of the self-fulfilling prophecy: that when teachers believed that some children in their classrooms were brighter than others, they gave them more attention. The more they believed in their charges' abilities, the more they saw to it that the children succeeded. In Goethe's words, "Treat people as if they were what they ought to be and you help them to become what they are capable of being." These studies have been replicated over and over, and they have become a classroom staple of social psychology, but living testimony to the power of the Pygmalion Effect comes from the heart of Chicago, Illinois.

Educator Marva Collins, supported by anecdotal evidence and statistical probabilities, states convincingly that simply believing in every child's potential, and *letting him or her know it,* can raise that child from failure to success. Her approach supports children's self-esteem and steeps them in classical education and the classics. As she says, "If children can understand Rap, they can understand Shakespeare."[6] Not only do Vision Leaders believe in themselves, the way Marva Collins does; they believe in the value and the potential of the people around them.

3. *Positive Pygmalions guide as well as support other people's efforts, even in failure.* This third principle rests on the foundation of the other two. Vision Leaders encourage people to take the initiative, to take risks, to learn from the mistakes they make. Taking risks and managing for the long term by themselves don't make Jamie Houghton, chairman and CEO of Corning Inc., a Vision Leader; his leadership comes from encouraging and inspiring others to do the same—even if the risks don't always produce acceptable payoffs. Positive Pygmalions hang on to their faith in you long after others have let go, but only as long as they see you're making an effort on your own behalf to grow and to succeed.

You know that life's not a series of safe bets; rather, it's full of challenges and risks, some of which are likely to backfire on you. Airlines, especially after a serious accident in which, say, 200 people have lost their lives, usually proudly proclaim that you take a greater risk driving your car on the freeway than in flying at 35,000 feet. Even eating a rare hamburger has become risky business. And, people don't always overcome every challenge or survive every risk, but successful people nurture their success by learning from every failure, which is why quotation books are filled with bits of self-management wisdom from Vision Leaders, such as these:

"Failure is success if we learn from it."
        —Malcolm Forbes (publisher, 1919–1990)

"When in doubt, risk it."
        —Holbrook Jackson (journalist, 1874–1948)

"We learn wisdom from failure much more than from success . . . and probably he who never made a mistake never made a discovery."
        —Samuel Smiles (author, 1812–1904)

"The two hardest things to handle in life are failure and success."
                                —Anonymous

"He who has never failed somewhere, that man cannot be great."
        —Herman Melville (author, 1819–1891)

Those homilies all express the support vision leaders give to the people who follow them: that failure and success are two sides of the same coin; that if you risk nothing you gain nothing—that even if you fail at what you do, you gain the wisdom (you hope) not to do the same thing the same way again. Not too many executives recognize the value of risk funding the way 3M does. That company's outstanding success comes in large part from the corporate culture of Vision Leadership that encourages everyone to "think outside the box" and to make every effort to enhance the company's research and development.

4. *Positive Pygmalions make resources available to other people to help develop them.* As Vision Leaders, they see things others don't see, or they see them in a different way. They possess information, equipment, or skills they don't hoard for themselves; hoarding prevents the organization from pulling together the knowledge and skills of everyone in the group. You achieve your own and your organization's potential and shared goals by sharing all the resources everyone needs.

Today, information has the power to alter a business fundamentally and profoundly, and information flows from so many different sources at such a rapid pace that few people can ever hope to comprehend it all. No CEO can succeed by telling people what to do without also listening to what they think he or she ought to be doing as well. Former U.S. president Gerald Ford, it is said, has attributed his success to having "a lot of experience with people smarter than I am."[7] Communication networks, interpersonal as well as electronic, must be open in all directions, and Vision Leaders see to it that they not only inform others, but that others inform them as well. In a well-managed organization, truly powerful visions are created out of the experiences of many people.

Notes

1. Data and quotations (Ira Stepanian and Charles Gifford, Bank of Boston) come from Ani Hadjian, "Watch What We Did, Not What We Said," *Fortune* (April 15, 1996), p. 140; see also daily newspapers, e.g., Jim Gallagher, "Sending It Out, Taking Heat," *St. Louis Post-Dispatch* (June 16, 1996), pp. E1, E8.
2. David Woodruff, "At Saturn, What Workers Want Is . . . Fewer Defects," *Business Week* (December 2, 1991), pp. 117–118.
3. Kenneth Labich, "Elite Teams Get the Job Done," *Fortune* (February 19, 1996), p. 93.
4. Keith H. Hammonds, "Corning's Class Act: How Jamie Houghton Reinvented the Company," *Business Week* (May 13, 1991), pp. 68–76; Noel M. Tichy and Christopher DeRose, "The Pepsi Challenge: Building a Leader-Driven Organization," *Training and Development* (May 1996), pp. 58–65; Bob Filipczak, "CEOs Who Train," *Training Magazine* (June 1996), pp. 57–64.
5. Robert Merton, *Social Theory and Social Structure* (New York: Free Press,

1968), pp. 128–129, 421–436; Robert Rosenthal, "Teacher Expectations and Pupil Learning," in R. D. Strom, ed., *Teachers and the Learning Process* (Englewood Cliffs, N.J.: Prentice-Hall, 1970); Rosenthal, "The Pygmalion Effect Lives," *Psychology Today* (September 1973).
6. "Too Good to Be True," *60 Minutes*, CBS News (September 24, 1995).
7. Quoted in Louis E. Boone, ed., *Quotable Business* (New York: Random House, 1992), p. 239.

Other Sources

Frigon, Norman L., and Harry K. Jackson. *The Leader: Developing the Skills and Personal Qualities You Need to Lead Effectively.* New York: AMACOM, 1996.
Sabbagh, Kurt. *Twenty-First Century Jet: The Making and Marketing of the Boeing 777.* New York: Scribner, 1996.

Section 5

Collaboration, Teamwork, the Experiences of Groups, and Managing the Storms

14

Creating a Collaborative Environment

The valuable person in business is the individual who can
and will cooperate with others.
                    —Elbert Hubbard (author, 1856–1915)

When they migrate, wild geese get where they're going only because
they enthusiastically collaborate with each other to get there; they're
all committed to the same goal. Ever see a "lone goose"?

Independence and self-reliance, great virtues in anyone's opinion, can become liabilities when carried to extremes. Compounding
the problem, a great many people have turned loners into legends, the
"Grizzly Adamses" of the twentieth century. Instead of their being
willing collaborators, you have to drag them kicking and screaming
into meetings and other group activities.

Hermits and lone eagles become legends *just because* what they
do and how they live fly in the face of normal human instincts. Like
it or not, people are social beings, herd animals, and most of them
work best when collaborating with other people. No, that doesn't
contradict the principles of self-management. Self-managed people
are self-reliant, but they're not loners. They work comfortably with
others, they collaborate, exchange ideas and opinions, give and accept
feedback—in short, they're team players who can also get along on
their own.

> Collaboration consists of three basic processes to which the whole group
> must be committed: contributing, influencing others, and being influenced
> by others.

Collaboration

Since independence and self-reliance have been nurtured in a competitive culture, collaboration doesn't just happen by wishing it so. Adults, in the main, have to be trained to commit themselves to three basic processes: contributing, influencing others, and being influenced by others. The quality of group problem solving, group decisions, group planning, and the execution of plans depends on the quality of contributions and the way in which people influence one another.

Contributing

Making a contribution consists of providing other people with dependable information, skills, talents, or other resources they all can use to succeed in their efforts. Look at what happens when people *don't* contribute to one another's efforts.

A while back, several people in a training unit of an international financial institution played the common corporate game of undermining a peer's efforts. They deliberately didn't tell a hapless program manager that they saw fatal flaws in a program he was designing. Why? Because they despised their business manager, the man who had recruited the program manager. As a result, the seminar crashed in its first pilot and never did get properly repaired. The failure of that program was then cited by at least one executive as a reason to regard the unit as superfluous. So, who, if not everyone, was hurt by a lack of collaboration?

No one person, not even the best managers, can fulfill all the demands of a work unit. Managers find this out the hard way whenever they have to fill in for workers on strike. Sharing information, skills, talents, and resources gives the whole work group the substance and depth it needs to achieve its goals or, better, to exceed expectations. To make individual contributions worthwhile to the group, they have to be reliable, trustworthy, useful, and productive. Just talking for its own sake, stretching the truth, sailing opinions on a draft of hot air may seem like contributions, but on closer inspection such "contributions" lose their value.

Influencing Others

Contribution plays a large role in group decision making, but without influence, good ideas can arrive stillborn. The quality of the contribution *plus* the quality of influence within the group determines the quality of decisions and outcomes the group produces. Don't look for high levels of performance from yourself or from the group unless you and others allow yourselves to be influenced through encouragement, differences, and disagreement.

Influence, a major aspect of leadership, consists of moving other people to think and to do what they would not have thought or done otherwise. Some people, although they make little or no substantive contribution, have great influence, while others who make important contributions have no influence at all. You can find many examples of them both right in your own offices: allies for advancing ideas and people who generate them.

Sometimes how an idea is advanced is as important as the idea itself. That's the lesson an engineer at Monsanto Chemical Company learned during a presentation skills workshop. She had developed a novel, inexpensive way of processing a chemical but couldn't sell her ideas to management. During the two-day workshop, feedback from her peers and instructor helped her turn her idea into what she called "a killer presentation."

Every organization has its own politicians: people who can advance the ideas of others, people who have an "in" with the decision makers. They often don't have many original ideas of their own, and they often don't like being thrust into the role of idea creator or of problem solver. Enthusiastic supporters of their more creative allies, they can become Vision Leaders in their own right, *championing* novel ideas or solutions.

People often confuse con artists with Vision Leaders. Masters of sham have mastered the skills of influence, despite our low regard for them, and we can learn from them:

➤ How to position a proposition to show off its advantages
➤ How to make the deal so exciting that other people see the beauty of the idea for themselves

Con artists focus on results and what their proposition means to you. They emphasize the benefits of those results to you without ever calling attention to themselves or to the benefit of the proposition to them. *Ensuring that the benefits really do flow to other people as well as to themselves separates Vision Leaders from lowlife con artists.*

Especially in a corporate setting, it's impossible to influence people for long unless you recognize their needs and feelings when you stand up for your own interests, express your own views or opinions, or give constructive feedback. When you manage the WIIFM, you can rely on appropriate quid pro quo arrangements to influence people and bargain for results. You influence people with Vision Leadership by using openness and kindness toward them, thereby modeling the positive behavior you expect them to exhibit toward you and toward each other. Both forms of leadership can be applied at the same time. A Vision Leader collects points for who he is as well as for the returns he offers.

Being Influenced by Others

You can't collaborate with other people unless you're willing to be influenced by them when they offer something of value to you and/ or the group. Allowing yourself to be influenced contributes to your ability to influence other people. Chuck Knight, CEO of St. Louis-based Emerson Electric, has said the company "shines" by making planning a "line job" rather than a staff job. He and his executives require their line managers to develop and submit the plans the company will pursue. Implementing the plans that emerge from the task and process level of the organization keeps the company at the top of its global market.[1]

Listening may be the most valuable collaborative skill you can develop. People respond positively when they know their ideas and opinions are valued by their leadership. However, in a study reported in *American Demographics,* only one third of 4,300 respondents "say their companies do a good job of listening to or acting on their suggestions."[2] Flattening the organization helps the communication process by eliminating barriers between departments and layers of employees. Flattening also helps by eliminating the competition for artificial promotions (a notorious practice in banks). You reward people appropriately for their contributions with recognition, pay for performance, and bonuses.

Failure to listen and to be influenced creates resistance to your attempts at persuading others. People throw up barriers against you when they feel you're twisting their arm all the time but not listening to them. Resistance fades in proportion to the level at which people see their own ideas put into place. Involving employees in decisions that affect their lives actually *increases your level of influence over them.*

Encouragement as Influence

No one can motivate anyone else. Since motivation comes from within, the word *self-motivation* is redundant. Therefore, you can't say manager-leaders motivate other people any more than you can say they manage people. Regardless of style, manager-leaders provide proper incentives that help others sustain their motivation, and in so doing influence them to contribute to the success of the organization.

Either WIFFM or Vision Leadership (or a mix) encourages people to give their best. Which style you use is a *response* to what sustains a person's motivation: either tangible rewards (e.g., cash) or other kinds of rewards (e.g., recognition). Vision Leaders, as Positive Pygmalions, succeed only if other people understand and consent to what they are attempting to accomplish; at the end of his play *Pygmalion,* Shaw wisely turns Eliza Doolittle against Henry Higgins because her mentor wasn't honest with her and because he used her to promote his own ends.

How do you, as a manager-leader, influence people through encouragement?

- ☛ Coaching/counseling encourages commitment.
- ☛ Supporting other people's efforts, even in failure, encourages initiative and creativity.
- ☛ Open, frequent communication encourages collaboration.
- ☛ Sharing organizational know-how encourages people to try out new ideas or solutions with upper management.

By treating each employee as a whole person and recognizing that individuals as well as organizations have to harmonize competing values and goals, you'll encourage people to solve their own problems and to work toward the solution of organizational problems. You can't ask for more influence than that.

Differences and Disagreements as Influence

Whereas necessity is the mother of invention, disagreement is its father. Conflict, on the other hand, is its scourge. Not all disagreements or differences involve conflict, but all conflict involves disagreements or differences.

Conflict occurs when someone believes someone else is depriving him or her of the right to satisfy his or her own needs or interests. Inside a business, competing for limited rewards breeds stronger conflicts, which in turn can destroy the organization by fostering distrust and resistance to influence. Whatever its intensity, competition makes "one person's success depend on another's failure."[3] Corporate infighting between individuals and between work groups is inappropriate.

Studies dating back to 1954, by Peter Blau of Columbia University, show that competition inside a business prevents growth and progress. And studies by Robert Helmreich of the University of Texas show that the most successful people, rather than scoring high on competitiveness, score highest on *cooperation.* Save competition for besting the real "enemy," the companies vying for your customers, but also recognize that excessive business competition can lead to irresponsibility and unethical business practices.

Deliberately initiating disagreements contributes to business growth and progress. It's like deliberately setting back fires to control a forest fire. You might say, if it ain't broke, make it better. Then, appropriate management of those differences and disagreements prevents conflict from emerging from them.

With guidance from Jamie Houghton, the unionized, self-managed employees at Corning, Inc., in Blacksburg, Virginia, work with each other and with management, engaging in dialogue (problem solving) and resolving disagreements or reconciling differences by reaching consensus. Working twelve and a half–hour shifts, alternating three- and four-day weeks, they "make managerial decisions, impose discipline on fellow workers, and [require of themselves that they] learn three skill 'modules'—or families of skills—within two years or lose their jobs." Rather than fight with one another, they save their competitiveness for, in the words of one of their nonmanagement employees, "beating the Japanese."[4]

You should start fires that encourage disagreement, differences, and debate. Differences of opinions, backgrounds, methods and values drive the organization's ability to change, to grow, to create, and to innovate. Diversity in the workplace ensures the differences that bring the varying opinions, information storehouses, skills, and personal learning or decision-making styles to bear on company processes, challenges, and problems. This convergence of perspectives prevents what author Irving Janis called "Group Think" (agreements that prevent differences from emerging that might possibly hurt someone's feelings or possibly cause you political harm).[5] Only civility and trust can guarantee that disagreement and debate remain healthy and not degenerate into conflict.

You personally can help sustain the health of disagreement by:

➤ Emphasizing collaboration
➤ Creating as many possibilities for creative group problem solving as you can
➤ Creating other possibilities for positive social as well as work-related interactions

Consensus Decision Making: The Apex of Collaboration

Under some conditions—when time is of the essence, when only one person has the needed skill or knowledge, when organizational demands make it imperative, etc.—flying on your own makes sense. However, the success of a group depends on flying together whenever possible, on the contributions each member makes and the influence the members have on one another.

Since the quality of a group decision is proportional to the quality of contribution and influence from all its members, the highest form of collaboration (the method that makes the most of contribution and influence) is problem solving and decision making by consensus. *The goal of consensus is not a perfect solution or one right answer, but a decision with which everyone can live.* To reach that goal, the group must rely on everyone's making valuable contributions, building a case for their own points of view, and listening with an open mind to everyone else's. In short, civility and trust make consensus-seeking work.

The process can occur at any point during a group problem-solving or decision-making activity. Sometimes, when people fail to agree on the specific nature or cause of a problem, they have to accept a conclusion that makes the most sense to the whole group. When they examine alternative solutions to a problem, they may have to accept the most reasonable one. Nothing kills problem solving quicker than saying, "Let the majority rule." The majority can be wrong, as demonstrated in the extreme by the *Challenger* disaster, when the majority overruled the lone dissenting, but correct, opinion.

When asking your group to use consensus as a decision-making process, lay down the following ground rules for reaching personally satisfying as well as profitable decisions:

1. Require that everyone come to the meeting prepared to work on the problem or to make the decision and prepared to work on it together; preparation includes gathering relevant information and formulating useful ideas or suggestions to offer at the meeting.

2. Identify what the group is trying to do; set a goal (e.g., "find the causes of customer dissatisfaction").

3. Give *each* person an opportunity to express his opinion. Encourage shy people to contribute by asking the group to write anonymous opinions the facilitator will read (or that can be reduced to a Post-it note and stuck to a sheet of butcher paper).

4. Teach people to think through and document their opinions, and to keep them brief and to the point. When someone rambles, help her focus on her main points by asking her to state them as "bullet points." You could even have her write them as such on a flip chart.

5. Mediate heated disagreements and help everyone remain calm and focused on the task at hand, no matter how intense the session gets. Emotional outbursts may satisfy the "outburster's" needs, but they disrupt the group.

6. Encourage the group to debate but to keep an open mind about one another's ideas or opinions. You may have to teach people to listen without bias, to make a sincere effort to understand, and to show respect for other people's opinions. Sometimes the most outrageous ideas solve the most difficult problems.

7. Keep the group focused on the central issues and on the group process. Bring forward side arguments; any idea important enough to discuss during a meeting belongs on the table for everyone to discuss.

8. Uncover personal agendas. Get contributors to make their intentions clear as they promote ideas. Hidden agendas destroy trust and the group's ability to function at peak levels.

9. When many ideas flow in the discussion, have the group narrow alternative decisions down to the most workable two or three. Give each person an opportunity to express his opinion on these ideas.

10. Debate differences of opinion in open forum and resolve them in a like manner.

11. Make decisions that are for the good of the group or for the good of the organization as a whole, even if they seem unpopular to some people. Few problems can withstand the assault of people of goodwill.[6]

Hard decisions are not popularity contests. The failure of engineers to agree on the unpopular decision (to scrub the launch) cost the *Challenger* astronauts their lives. Consensus decision making does not require unanimous agreement that an idea or an opinion is absolutely correct or the only possible answer to a problem. Rather, it requires unanimous agreement to *try out* an idea or an opinion to see if it works. Contrary ideas or opinions can then be developed as *backup plans.* Moving toward a goal, therefore, may not always be in a linear progression; you may have to take one step forward and one step sideways to get to where you want to go.

How Manager-Leaders Support Collaboration

Effective manager-leaders help people collaborate by coordinating and aligning various goals and objectives into a single, albeit very intricate, system of processes. They follow magazine publisher Carol A. Tabor's advice: "Hire the best people and then delegate." They use WIFFM and Vision Leadership (whichever is appropriate to the circumstances) to sustain the group's motivation, especially in times of crisis. They encourage differences and discourage conflicts. They rely on group consensus, when appropriate. They live the basic principle behind teamwork: They build relationships with other people and help other people build relationships with one another.

Hire the Best and Delegate

If managers could, by themselves, fulfill all the responsibilities assigned to them, they'd never have to hire anyone else to do work for them. Even self-employed people don't do everything they have to do by themselves. Most hire professional help on contract: a CPA, an attorney, an advertiser, etc. One-person companies, such as consultants, hire secretarial services for some things. Executive suites, "Call Notes," the Worldwide Net, and other overhead-reducing services or products can turn a basement mom-and-pop operation into a major, global player. What you can't do yourself, you get other people to do for you.

On the other hand, when people do things for you, especially in a large organization, they might find it difficult to feel a sense of ownership of their work or of the outcomes they produce. Ownership in most organizations (traditional or modern) flows with the level of authority, accountability, and responsibility: from the top to the bottom. The degree of ownership also parallels the flow of vision to action: the greater the involvement in deciding what the company will or will not do, the greater the ownership of the organization's mission people feel. The process seems so simple that it appears mundane when seen in print; yet many people don't realize the simplicity of the process until they read it in a book like this.

The Downward Flow of Delegation

When a CEO in a closely held or family-owned business reports to his board, the buck does stop at his desk. The people to whom he reports hold him personally accountable and responsible for the organization's success or failure. In larger, publicly owned companies, the situation varies insofar as the executive reports to a board of directions (many of whom are paid "outsiders") that shareholders hold responsible for the fortunes of their investments.

Regardless of the structure of ownership, in a company of any appreciable size, the executive hires middle-level managers to whom she assigns some of her authority, accountabilities, and responsibilities. Managers hire other people to whom they assign some of the authority, accountabilities, and responsibilities given to them. In larger organizations, they may hire supervisors, lower-level managers, who then hire other people to carry out tasks needed for implementing the processes planned by managers. Still, the managers are ultimately accountable and responsible for what they assign to supervisors and/or to line employees.

WIIFM and Vision Leadership in the Service of Collaboration

The whole organizational edifice crumbles without coordination and collaboration. Manager-leaders, themselves self-managed, deliberately hire or develop self-managed people who will take ownership over everything they do by setting their own goals and designing their own action plans. Hence, the classified ads that read: "Wanted, Self-Starters!" To create and maintain a collaborative environment, manager-leaders must use both WIIFM Leadership and Vision Leadership.

Managing the WIIFM builds a strong bridge between you and the people carrying out the assignments you give them. Still, you can't *buy* loyalty, no matter how well you manage incentives and other satisfiers. Although short-term organizational success does rely on it, the commitment under WIIFM Leadership lasts for only as long as the promise of reward dangles from the end of the stick. Vision Leadership, on the other hand, builds the strong bond between you and other people you need for long-term success. The psychological contract makes both forms of leadership necessary.

The Role of the Psychological Contract in Supporting Collaboration

An important part of the psychological contract consists of the employees' basic expectation of supervisory guidance and support. These mostly *tacit* expectations consist of culturally transmitted, unexpressed understandings between employees and supervisors, expectations that spell out the relationships that should bind them together. The basics also include base compensation, a safe and productive environment, and general benefits. These keep the organization and employee/management relationships healthy. Adding to them really doesn't do much for jacking up employee motivation. Take them away, however, and see how fast your employees become *de*motivated (dissatisfied).

Today's psychological contract expands employee expectations to include the right and the opportunity to manage their own work, to participate in important decisions that affect their lives, and to be afforded opportunities for challenging or interesting work, recognition, and self-satisfaction. People get "turned on" by being treated as adults, by being informed, and by being asked to take part in major decisions. They likewise respond to warm social relationships on the job and by opportunities for taking leadership roles. These mostly self-rewarding WIIFMs deliver genuine incentives or motivators. Pile these on in appropriate ways, and you'll spin up employee morale and motivation.

All the expectations created by the psychological contract set the stage for collaboration. The contract itself, because it is a bilateral agreement, commits both the employees and their supervisors to performing their functions cooperatively. Spelling out those functions creates a clear understanding of how they will work together. Creating the expectation that employees will work collaboratively rather than competitively and setting up the appropriate reward systems to encourage collaboration moves the contract into the stream of the group's processes.

While living up to the terms of the contract supports collaboration, violating them destroys collaboration. When an employee violates it, the supervisor loses confidence in that person and might fire her. When a supervisor violates it, the employee loses confidence in the *organization*, becomes demotivated, and quits (even if she doesn't leave the organization). As with any living organism, the parts have to work together in order for the whole to sustain itself, to grow, and to prosper.

Civility in the Workplace and Collaboration

Both short-term and long-term organizational success depend on the conscious willingness on the part of everyone to work together in a friendly cooperative manner, to collaborate. Unfortunately, some people find this becoming more difficult today.

While no one expects everyone to be friends with everyone else, they do expect a modicum of civility in their dealings, a friendly manner. However, says *U.S. News and World Report*, civility has reached a low point in the society of the United States. A survey it conducted with Bozell Worldwide "reveals [that] a vast majority of Americans feel their country has reached an ill-mannered watershed."[7] It's common to hear managers scream at and dress down employees in public. The following examples come from actual meetings: "You're a yellow-bellied defeatist [because you don't agree with my growth plans]," "Your report's full of errors and is total s---!" "You dumb f---! Do it over until you get it right.") It's rare to hear of managers actually "reward[ing] interdependence and the collective result."[8] So rare, in fact, the situation has prompted business ethicists Thomas Michaud and Andrew Cullen to publish an "Employee Bill of Rights" that urges "managers to remind employees of their workplace rights and obligations."[9]

Managers at some companies, such as Johnsonsville Foods and Textron Inc.'s Defense Systems subsidiary, do champion civility and collaboration. It makes good business sense. Never underestimate the power of civility and trust. "Please" and "Thank you" may seem ritualistic, but they symbolize your respect for other people. And who has never been infected by a smile? The same goes for reliability, for steadiness, and for doing things for others without expecting anything in return. They're powerful tools for encouraging contribution and mutual influence. Collaborators must want to contribute to each other's efforts, to be influenced by others, and to exercise their personal power in influencing others. Civility and the trust it produces encourages willingness to collaborate. In this regard, *anyone* can be a Vision Leader.

Notes

1. Cynthia Hutton, "Companies That Compete Best," *Fortune* (May 22, 1989), p. 10.
2. Michael Reinemer, "Work Happy," summary of a survey conducted by Watson Wyatt Worldwide (a consulting firm in Washington, D.C.) in *American Demographics* (July 1995), p. 28.
3. Alfie Kohn, "How to Succeed Without Even Vying," *Psychology Today* (September 1986), p. 22.
4. John Hoerr, "Sharpening Minds for a Competitive Edge," *Business Week* (December 17, 1990), p. 74.
5. Irving L. Janis, *Group Think* (Boston: Houghton, Mifflin, 1982); see also Janis, *Victims of Group Think* (Boston: Houghton Press, 1972).

6. Paraphrasing Voltaire, "No problem can stand the assault of sustained thinking."
7. John Marks, "The American Uncivil Wars," *U.S. News and World Report* (April 22, 1996), p. 67.
8. Thomas Angster, human resources director for the book group at R. R. Donnelley & Sons, quoted in Joann S. Lublin, "My Colleague, My Boss," *Wall Street Journal* (April 12, 1995), p. R4.
9. In *Business Ethics* (September/October 1995) and reproduced in *ASTD's Management Report* (Fall 1995), p. 4.

Other Sources

Byrne, John. "And You Thought CEOs Were Overpaid: Outside Directors Are Catching Up Fast," *Business Week* (August 26, 1996).
Herzberg, Frederick. *Work and the Nature of Man.* New York: World Publishing Company, 1966. "One more time: How do you motivate employees? Not by improving work conditions, raising salaries, or shuffling tasks." *Harvard Business Review,* January-February 1968 (reprint order no. 69108).
Marshall, Edward M. *Transforming the Way We Work: The Power of the Collaborative Workplace.* New York: AMACOM, 1995.

15

Teamwork and Work Groups

Sacrifice makes [teammates] comrades.
> —Phil Jackson, head coach of the Chicago Bulls[1]

I don't for a second suppose that a gaggle of wild geese in V-formation constitutes a team. However, migrating geese do exhibit *teamwork*.

Teamwork is characterized by collaboration and getting the best from other people. Note that I didn't say that teamwork is an essential characteristic of teams. The reason I didn't is that a formal team—a work team, a baseball team, etc.—can be deficient in teamwork and still be considered a team, even when it's so dysfunctional that it discourages collaboration and gets the worst from other people.

> Teamwork is characterized by collaboration and getting the best from other people regardless of how they're organized.

Teamwork Without Teams

Although teams don't always work, teamwork always accomplishes the goals expected of it. Employees usually collaborate with one another without any specially designed subunits, and they don't feel betrayed at all if the company doesn't redesign itself into teams.

According to the surprising results of a 1995 *Inc.*/Gallup survey (repeated with almost identical results in 1996), most workers in small to medium-size companies are satisfied with the status quo.[2] Ninety-one percent of the employees surveyed say they were anywhere from satisfied to extremely satisfied and quite comfortable with their work lives, even if they aren't organized into Johnsonville Foods– or Corning Inc.–style work teams.

In the survey, over 70 percent of the 803 respondents agreed that management does what is necessary to make their company "a great place to work" and "a good workplace for all the people [not just] for . . . the privileged few." The majority said that they have opportunities to do what they do best in work that contributes to the company's mission, that they know what's expected of them, and that they receive recognition or praise for good work. They also reported their belief that their opinions count and that people in the company care about their growth and development. The group also said they are committed to doing quality work, and believed that their coworkers are similarly committed. Indeed, that's quite common; at the Saturn plant in Springhill, Tennessee, for example, the workers *demanded* that management not sacrifice quality for the sake of increasing output.[3]

Teamwork, which by any definition means subordinating personal interests to those of the group, works. You can have cooperation, collaboration, and commitment to a shared or common goal; you can have ongoing learning and continuous improvement; you can have productive meetings; you can have all that *without* creating formal teams. Indeed, the suggestion that "we're going to create teams here" often strikes fear in the hearts of both supervisors and nonmanagers.

The Fear of Teams

In the minds of many people in organizations, the word *team* often evokes fears of loss: loss of authority, of identity, of recognition, of independence, and even loss of jobs. The only common fear that doesn't involve loss is the fear of having more work with fewer people to do it and no reward. Teams often fail as a result of the self-fulfilling prophecy created when people believe the old joke that a camel is a horse designed by an overworked, underpaid, unappreciated committee. It doesn't have to be true. Many effective committees have produced magnificent results, including the Mars exploration of 1997.

Employees want identifiable roles, they want their opinions to count for something, they want managers who care about their growth and development, and they want everyone to make a commitment to doing quality work. That, to them, is the meaning of *teamwork*. The point? Organizational success doesn't always depend on teams, but it almost depends on teamwork.

Three Rules of Organizational Behavior

That a gaggle of wild geese unerringly gets to where it's supposed to go suggests three rules of successful organizational behavior that supports teamwork:

1. The organization's leaders need to know where the organization is going and how it's supposed to get there. Their vision gives direction to the core business. They then pass that vision on to the organization.
2. Everyone else needs to know where the organization's going and how it's supposed to get there. With a grasp of the leaders' vision, the employees execute the mission to make the core business into what it can be. They then lead within the sphere of their own action and influence.
3. Everything everyone does must be directed toward where the organization is going and how it's supposed to get there. To focus all this energy (to create synergy) requires developing individual competence, coordinating business processes, and getting commitment from the entire organization.

Jack Stack said essentially the same thing in a short magazine article: "To be successful in business, you have to be going somewhere, and everyone involved in getting you there has to know where it is. . . . [Y]ou have a much better chance of winning if everyone knows what it takes to win."[4]

In Support of Ordinary Work Groups

Although high-performance teams have been getting all the glory these days, teams aren't always the appropriate way to organize work groups. In a good many cases, when unit goals and objectives can be met through individual effort, individual effort is what we need.

Case in point. Many years ago, I worked in a storm window factory in Philadelphia as one of two glass cutters. Our foreman distributed work orders to us. We cut the glass to order, we passed the glass to the framers, and we rarely talked to one another about anything. We didn't need to.

The same thing happened when I was "promoted" to frame cutting. The foreman there distributed work orders to us cutters, we cut the aluminum frames to order, and we passed the frames to the framers. We rarely talked to one another there, either. We had closer bonds with units downstream, the framers, than we did with one another in the unit. Management had to support everything we did with a place to work, orders, raw materials (glass or aluminum), equipment (cutting tools), and compensation and benefits, and reward individual effort with individual returns. But in ordinary work groups like those in the factory, all that matters is achieving or exceeding unit outcome objectives through individual effort. Communication and teams are unnecessary and can interfere with productivity when they require taking time away from production.

We didn't have a lot of productivity incentives in those days, just the reassurance that we'd get a paycheck and periodic raises, but we did our jobs, took pride in our work, and almost always exceeded expectations (beating deadlines, completing more orders in one day than we did the previous, and the like). Ordinary work groups may look the same today, but many of the demands of both them and management have changed, requiring more teamwork and more productivity incentives.

Indentifiable Roles for Work Groups and Their Members

Every person in the organization should have identifiable roles designed to satisfy demands of the organization and the work groups to which he or she is assigned. (The work groups themselves should similarly have identifiable roles.) But, those assignments form only the baseline for working in and with a group.

People in groups play more subtle roles related to two types of group dynamics: (1) task and (2) process.

Task Dynamic and Roles in a Collaborative Work Group

Every work group has a purpose, goals, and objectives. These constitute the business of the team, the dynamic that provides the "what" and the "why" for which the group was formed and that informs (drives) the work of the group. Everything the group and individual members do should contribute to fulfilling that purpose, to achieving its goals and objectives. It needs information, skills, talents, aptitudes, and abilities that get the job done. Fail to pay sufficient attention to task, and the group fails. In a work group where collaboration or teamwork is needed for reaching task goals, the responsibilities for achieving them fall on the group as a whole as well as on its individual members.

Insofar as the task dynamic consists of the drive to get things done, to achieve goals, it generates activities that drive a group towards its work-related objectives. Since sometimes the goals imposed by the larger organization are often vague, sometimes ambiguous (e.g., "make a profit," "develop systems that support growth," "expand the organization's market share"), the group may have to define or articulate its own vision or goals, as well as its tactical objectives (how it intends to fulfill its mission). You can help the group either by creating the vision and defining the tactics or by encouraging the group to generate both the vision and the tactics. Effective manager-leaders usually create the vision, and, in Warren Bennis's phrase, "manage the dream."[5] The more you allow the group to elaborate on the vision and to define the tactics, the closer to effective teamwork you'll move.

When you manage the dream, you focus the group on the mission and lead it to generate desired outcomes. You rely on the drive of the self-managed people to achieve them. By delegating task responsibilities to the group and encouraging it to fulfill them with little or no supervision from you, you create a climate in which group members encourage and influence one another to take on task behaviors.

Task behaviors described in Exhibits 15-1 and 15-2 contribute to fulfilling the group's mission. Performed properly, they produce the information, processes, and individual activities that are necessary for the group to succeed. Different group members must play one or more of these roles because some roles are easier to perform for some

Exhibit 15-1. Task behaviors individuals must perform.

Individual Task Behaviors	Descriptions
Activity management	Chairing, coordinating, resource management, meeting management
Initiating	Making suggestions or proposing new ideas, getting things started
Information seeking	Asking questions for clarification or accuracy
Information giving	Offering data or authoritative information
Opinion seeking	Asking for views as to values or to the relative merits of ideas or generalizations
Giving opinions	Stating views as to values or to the relative merits of ideas or generalizations
Elaborating	Interpreting, explaining, or explicating facts or opinions; drawing conclusions
Shaping or orienting	Identifying progress toward goals, defining positions, organizing activity
Consensus seeking	Polling the group for its readiness to make decisions or to resolve disagreements
Consensus taking	Making decisions or resolving issues; formulating a position; agreeing to abide by group decisions
Summarizing	Pulling together related ideas, opinions, or suggestions; restating them; coordinating activities of subgroups or members
Reporting	Taking minutes or recording discussions, decisions, etc.
Representing	Communicating the group's progress or decisions or actions to the external environment
Maintaining	Providing materials and performing routine tasks, such as distributing agenda, timekeeping, etc.

Exhibit 15-2. Task behaviors groups must perform.

Group Task Behaviors	Descriptions
Brainstorming	Generating new or different ideas; facilitating creativity and innovation
Setting standards	Establishing criteria for evaluating ideas, opinions, decisions, products, or services
Evaluating	Measuring group ideas or activities by the group's standards
Producing	Executing tasks, doing the group's work (product or service) that achieves its mission

people than they are for others. Some people are more creative than others, some are better at articulating ideas than others, and some are more adept at executing the details. Everyone's best skill or aptitude is needed.[6]

Process Dynamic and Roles

People don't work well in groups by concentrating only on the tasks they have to perform. In fact, a heavy emphasis on task can turn a work group into a bunch of galley slaves.

Process consists of the manner in which the group arrives at its goals. The process dynamic sometimes exercises on its members a more potent force toward success than does the task dynamic. It derives its power from the reality that everyone has personal and social needs to meet: e.g., the need to depend on others, the need to be involved, the need to be committed to something larger than oneself, or the need to experience cohesion. The respect for others that self-managed people have shows up in interpersonal relationships, communications, feelings, and social dynamics (including leadership) within the group. These constitute the process dynamic, and in a successful group, everyone plays one or more process roles described in Exhibit 15-3.

Harmonizing Task and Process Dynamics

The task dynamic of a collaborative group creates interdependence, a dependency on others for information or skills required for achieving

Exhibit 15-3. Process roles.

Process Behaviors	Descriptions
Gatekeeping	☛ Taking interest in other people's opinions or feelings ☛ Opening channels of communication
Listening	☛ Paying attention to what other people are saying
Expediting	☛ Keeping discussions on track yet encouraging everyone to contribute ("Let's take a minute to hear everyone's opinion on this subject.")
Encouraging	☛ Praising, rewarding, reinforcing ☛ Being open to other opinions or feelings (even if they differ from the majority's)
Harmonizing	☛ Negotiating (reconciling disagreements, mediating) ☛ Relieving tension (including appropriate humor)
Yielding	☛ Giving up an unpopular viewpoint ☛ Forgoing status ☛ Admitting mistakes ☛ Meeting other people halfway
Observing	☛ Heeding the group's process ☛ Calling attention to possible damage to effective functioning ☛ Expressing feelings present in the group ☛ Calling attention to group reactions to what is going on ☛ Diagnosing problems
Accepting	☛ Respecting people's rights to express themselves and to meet their own needs ☛ Respecting or promoting differences among people ☛ Using differences between people as starting points for rational problem solving
Cheerleading	☛ Encouraging the group to feel good about what it is and does, how it functions, or its successes

goals. Sometimes you have to rely on others to help you achieve your own objectives. You often also have to share responsibilities when doing the group's or your own work.

Feeling involved in the group's activities supports the process dynamic, and involvement can take many forms. Sometimes that simple feeling that your opinion counts for something means a lot, as we saw in the *Inc.*/Gallup survey. Sometimes taking a leadership role means a great deal to people, but for many people believing that the organization relies on them to carry out orders is the kind of involvement they want. Without the feeling that "they depend on me," parenthood, loyalty, or patriotism would find few takers.

Involvement can also mean disagreeing with others, confronting issues—sometimes confronting people if they seem to be overstepping their bounds or trampling on someone's rights or needs. Being heard and having their ideas count for something are for some people the only incentives they have for staying employed in your organization.

Working together to accomplish the group's mission means a lot to group members. The shared responsibility supplies a basis for getting commitment from the group's members to feel at one with the group's mission and tactics and at one with other group members. At the same time, the members also need to feel a commitment from the group to helping them to succeed individually. That sense of cohesion with kindred spirits enhances involvement and makes a group member feel that he or she is an important contributor to the group.

When people feel committed to the group's work-related outcomes and believe that all the group members are equally committed, they feel they are a part of something larger than themselves. They recognize their own need for help in accomplishing their goals, and they recognize the reality that the group will fail unless everyone pulls his own weight within the group.

Building an effective group hinges on how well you or the group harmonizes all these relationships between the task and the process dynamics—knowing when to accommodate or emphasize one rather than the other. Everyone, not just you, has to recognize and satisfy both sets of needs and not diminish the importance of one or another. You, as manager-leader, have the special responsibility of showing the group—by how you act within the group—how these two dynamics work and how to control them to everyone's and the group's advantage. Fail to manage either dynamic, the group may very well crash and burn.

Notes

1. Quoted in Edward O. Welles, "Phil Jackson," *Inc.* (September 1996), p. 36.
2. Jeffrey L. Seglin, "The Happiest Workers in the World," *Inc.* (June 1996), pp. 62–76: satisfied (20%), very satisfied (35%), or extremely satisfied (36%). See also Michael Hopins and Jeffrey L. Seglin, "Americans @ Work," *Inc.* (June 1997), pp. 77–85.
3. David Woodruff, "At Saturn, What Workers Want Is . . . Fewer Defects," *Business Week* (December 2, 1991), pp. 117–118.
4. Jack Stack, "That Championship Season," *Inc.* (July 1996), p. 27.
5. Warren Bennis, *On Becoming a Leader* (Reading, Mass.: Addison-Wesley, 1989), p. 192. See also Warren Bennis with Burt Nanus, *Leaders: The Strategies for Taking Charge* (New York: Harper & Row, 1985).
6. Dick McCann and Charles Margerison distinguish among eight work-style preferences in "Managing High Performance Teams," *Training and Development Journal* (November 1989), p. 52.

16

Six Experiences of Groups

Good will doesn't happen; it grows.

—Anonymous

Geese don't choose the gaggles into which they're born, and they don't have to learn how to live within a variety of groups the way you do when you change jobs or are assigned to different groups within the organization. Whereas one generation of geese follows another into the normal life of a gaggle, groups of any kind (e.g., work groups, interdepartmental groups, teams, etc.) undergo six common experiences, depending on how and why they're formed: introducing, stage setting, probing/testing, creating, producing, and maintaining, as described in Exhibit 16-1.

> The better a group manages its six common experiences, the smaller are the chances it will engage in destructive conflicts and the greater its effectiveness as a group.

Different groups experience the realities of group life in different ways, in different sequences, and in a variety of tempos, which is why I shy away from calling these processes a life cycle and I won't refer to these experiences as stages. The common model of "Forming, Norming, Storming, and Performing" does refer to these experiences as a set of predictable stages in the life cycle of a team and oversimplifies team development. Since few teams, if any, go through this process in its ideal form, why use the model?

Likewise, rather than treat Storming (i.e., turmoil, struggling to adapt) as a separate stage of group development, as people usually do,

Exhibit 16-1. Six common group experiences.

Experience	Description
Introducing	Coming together as a group; adding or changing personnel; gathering information about one another.
Stage Setting	Laying out the ground rules; creating the climate.
Probing/Testing	Getting to know one another; positioning within the group; developing trust, candor.
Creating	Identifying objectives; solving problems; designing methods for doing business; establishing a climate for innovation and productivity.
Producing	Executing the group's functions.
Maintaining	Taking care of continuation needs.

it makes more sense to me to see it as a possible consequence of *any* relationship. People can hassle with one another at any time, during any aspect of the group's development or functioning, and often those hassles can be very productive. I'll talk about storms, how to prevent them, and how to manage them in the next chapter.

Introducing

Whenever strangers get together, they gather information about each other: backgrounds, values, skills, and interests. They engage in polite, superficial (usually work-related) conversations, mainly about their backgrounds and other items that satisfy their curiosities about one another and the roles they might play within the group. When a new person comes into an established group, the process repeats itself. When a group is formed, the amount of time the introducing process consumes depends on how well or poorly the people already know one another.

Stage Setting

Usually the group leader or someone higher up explains both the group's objectives or mandate or other business requirements and the ground rules for how the group will function. Stage Setting establishes the mission and the climate for the group and may last only a few minutes, if people have worked together before or work together presently. (When a new person enters the group, she has to be oriented to the mission and climate of the group.)

If the mission is clear and immediate, you might say little more than what Gene Kranz told his White Team at Houston's Mission Control: "I'm pulling you men off console. . . . [You] will be coming up with the protocols [the people in the control room are] going to be executing. From now on, what I want from every one of you is simple—options and plenty of them."[1] Everyone knew each other and had worked together as a team, but since their objectives had changed, Kranz needed to set the new stage in his terse but precise way. Under other conditions, you may have to set the stage in a little more detail.

When creating the climate for the group, you often do it by modeling behavior (acting in the manner in which you expect group members to act) rather than by telling people what to do. During meetings, for example, if you sit at the head of the table in the conference room, you send the message "I'm in charge." On the other hand, if you ask the group to create the agenda, you send the message "We'll all collaborate here." By word or by deed, whether the group's vision and mission are mandated or the group is free to create its own, you (the leader) structure its behavior.

Mandated Vision and Mission

You should consider the issues in this section whenever you lead a group, but if you intend to create and lead a high-performance team, you particularly need to ensure that the members know what the company expects of the team, and the expectations should be written. When setting the stage, review the three mandates that give the group direction:

1. The group's business goals (long-term as well as short-term), the results to which management expects it to contribute
2. The group's vision of itself (what it should be and how it should achieve its mission)
3. The group's mission (what it should achieve, its task roles in relation to business goals)

Laying down more than these three basic strategic requirements leads to micromanaging and could endanger a group's creative processes.

A Degree of Self-Management

Work groups and semiautonomous teams (i.e., teams that report to a manager with veto power) should make some decisions as to how they organize themselves and operate, what results they will produce, who will produce them, and when and how they will be produced—as long as they acknowledge the group's business goals and elaborate on its vision and its mission. These group-driven stage-setting activities include:

- Organizing group structures (e.g., to be semiautonomous, to enlist outside meeting facilitators or rotate the role among the members, to elect a team leader and a team administrator)
- Defining and assigning task roles (who does what to achieve the group's mission, including activity management, research, record keeping, etc., as well as specific jobs)
- Planning regular meetings and producing meeting guidelines (e.g., agendas, preparation, on-time rules)
- Establishing quality measures with regard to the group's outputs (no defects, no customer complaints, etc.) and success (no turnover, meeting all deadlines, etc.)
- Planning group training activities (problem solving skills, team facilitation skills, etc.)

The goal of setting the stage is to give the team an identity as well as an organizational purpose. That identity helps members suppress personal interests in the service of the greater good, and it helps them see how their personal success contributes to the success of the team as a whole.

Probing/Testing

Usually, when a group first assembles, after the preliminary and perfunctory introductions, people tentatively experiment with their dynamics and structures. They don't always know they're doing it, but they spend a lot of time finding out who is in the group, how the group will work together, how people relate to each other, and who will influence whom (and how). Turnover or change in membership affects groups the same way. To facilitate the process, you may have to openly identify what's happening and why. That helps the group prevent problems that could get out of hand.

The Probing/Testing process could go on throughout the full life of a group and may be the most important experience a group has. The degree to which people get to know each other below the level of introduction and understand each other's values, needs, and interests colors all of the other experiences in group life. It can also determine the group's level of success. Contrarily, if probing or testing goes on as an undertone rather than as an overt activity, it could generate unhealthy conflict.

Probing/Testing can take minutes, days, or weeks. Astronaut Jim Lovell took only a few minutes to accept Jack Swigert as Tom Mattingly's replacement because Swigert was trained to the same standards as the man he replaced. The screenwriters for *Apollo 13* made a bigger issue of the process not only for dramatic effect, but also because, for most of us living in a less rarefied atmosphere than NASA's, extensive Probing/Testing of new team members does take place, and we can relate to the film's version of the incident. You rarely find the kind of backup or cross-training NASA does in the mundane world where most people work.

Trust and candor (essential aspects of the group's climate) vary from group to group or from time to time. Self-managed group members rarely experience interpersonal conflict. They express opinions openly and honestly, and no one gets upset or disturbed. The positive and productive feelings the people share are genuine and sincere. According to a number of people at the Spring Hill Saturn plant, that kind of positive climate occurred right from the start. Only later, in late 1992 and early 1993, did difficulties occur when some union members felt that management was taking advantage of the nonmanagement personnel.

Other groups struggle continuously, especially if self-management hasn't been prized or developed by the organization. Poorly managed groups that suppress bad feelings rarely accomplish their task objectives, and those bad feelings linger on among the members long after the group is disbanded. How a group comes to grips with these facts of group life often depends on how well you set the stage and the way in which the probing and testing in the group is conducted. The more open the process the better, and, in some cases, the more time you can afford to give to the process the better as well.

People need to probe below the level of introductions to find out what they expect to get out of the group and out of one another, and how they personally will benefit from the group's success. They need to know each other's strengths and weaknesses, as well as each other's dedication to group goals and objectives. Comfort and trust levels emerge depending on how the group members perceive each other or how they mesh.

Since probing and testing goes on all the time (whether people realize it or not), this behavior gets beneath the surface or veneer of sociality and can make even self-managed people feel uncomfortable. Most people resist efforts to get "too close." They erect self-protective barriers and guarded behavior that blocks group growth. In short, candor and openness don't come easily; you have to encourage and nurture them.

Making all this interpersonal sizing-up and testing open and aboveboard helps people become linked more intimately than they would through having only their basic group needs met (i.e., by leadership and subject-matter experts). They form friendships and separate themselves from others, and they often take sides. They make those linkages because it's easier to trust and be candid with one person than it is to open yourself up to a whole group. Those linkages, however, can create a "we-them" situation within the group, causing the group to stumble over its own member relations and preventing group growth. Anything that blocks group growth, if ignored or left to work itself out, can tear apart a group, and individuals and the organization alike suffer.

Linkages often also produce a need for people to test each other's ability or willingness to dominate or to influence, to identify whom they can influence and whom they're willing to let influence them. People prefer to acquiesce to others who seem to have knowledge, skills, or experience the group can use, but sometimes, in spite of themselves, they acquiesce to someone who just wears down the group with the force of his personality or opinions.

Whenever you form a new group, reinforcing the importance of candid feedback should take place as soon as possible. Nevertheless, since probing and testing goes on all of the time, you can introduce the feedback instrument in Exhibit 16-2 at any time. It brings the

Exhibit 16-2. Group processing feedback from a group member.

Instructions: Using a separate form for each person, rate each member's behavior in the group. Circle one number in each category (1 = poor; 5 = superior). Write a comment on two in the space available; identifying specific instances, including what you thought was effective as well as what you thought was not. Give the form to the person whose name you wrote in below.

Desirable Behaviors	Ratings	Comments
Helps create trust as well as a positive climate	1 2 3 4 5	
Communicates high personal standards	1 2 3 4 5	
Demonstrates commitment to the group's efforts	1 2 3 4 5	
Actively listens to other members of the group	1 2 3 4 5	
Gives others opportunities to influence him or her	1 2 3 4 5	
Makes contributions (adds value to the discussions)	1 2 3 4 5	
Influences others	1 2 3 4 5	
Seeks consensus	1 2 3 4 5	
Facilitates discussions; encourages others to join in	1 2 3 4 5	
Other issues	1 2 3 4 5	
Group Member's Name	Date	

ordinary (often covert) experiences of probing and testing to the surface and helps prevent the storms discussed later (Chapter 17).

Use Exhibit 16-2 to give the individual named (at the bottom of the form) feedback from group members. The list in the left-hand column identifies behaviors that help the group. The rating scale in the center scores the person's behavior as poor (i.e., 1 = doesn't help the group at all, and 2 = doesn't help very much) to superior (i.e., 4 = helps or 5 = helps greatly). The third column gives you room to cite specific instances of behavior you found effective as well as what you thought was ineffective or detrimental to the group, whether the behavior had been directed at you, another person, or the group as a whole. You're not looking for the person to defend himself or apologize, but you want him to know what you're thinking or feeling, and the more feedback the person gets the easier it is for him to decide what to do (if anything) about the situation.

The goals of this process check? Surfacing both good and bad feelings about each other and helping each other function more effectively in the group. Given the weight or importance of this activity, the discussion should be well thought out and planned as a separate meeting, with feedback as its sole purpose and an agenda published in advance. Don't tack it on at the end of a regular meeting. Since issues can become sensitive and you too may be a target of negative feedback, you may want to enlist the help of an outside, trained facilitator to walk the group through the feedback discussions. It's also best to begin this process *before* storms erupt; afterward, people don't sit still easily when they get this kind of feedback.

Why bother? Work groups that take an individual focus don't worry much about probing and testing between people. Each person has her own job to do. As a group, members of a work group may produce the unit's objectives, but they don't have to work together to do it. The circumstances of the group may never call for a process check like this. The situation is different when you take a group focus. Unless people feel comfortable with one another (which is the goal of all that probing and testing), both group creativity and productivity are jeopardized.

Creating

Groups exhibit their creativity—the Creating phenomenon—in two ways: creating the character of the group and creating new ways to achieve goals and objectives. Forming a new group or confronting a group with new objectives calls for creative thinking and even innovation.

Creating the Group's Character

Some groups jump from the experiences of Introducing to those of Creating quickly, sometimes in a matter of hours—and never consciously experience Stage Setting and Probing/Testing. This is particularly true of what I call an ad hoc voluntary team, one in which people volunteer to work together to solve a specific problem and then go their separate ways. As such a group sets its stage, it forms its character quickly and the members can attack their goals and objectives creatively.

Other times, as in a new, long-lived work unit, getting the preliminaries out of the way can take days. In such groups, change happens every time a new person or a new objective is introduced into the group, and the group may have to go through Introducing, Stage Setting, and Probing/Testing all over again. The conditions in which the group exists determine just how quickly the group can create its own personality and begin attacking its goals and objectives creatively.

In the Apollo emergency, Gene Kranz imposed his own values on the Tiger Team and mandated the team's charter. In a crunch, that might work just fine. However, under normal conditions, imposing your values on the team ("This is what our team will be like and how it will go about achieving its goals and objectives") will probably meet with rejection or rebellion. People are more inclined to feel committed to the group's goals and objectives if they have a hand in creating the group's character (or culture). The group becomes theirs, the goals and objectives (even if imposed by upper management) become easier to accept, and the results and rewards become a source of pride. Corning, Inc. "offers a model of how [businesses] can reinvent themselves" when they give everyone some voice in the changes that affect them.[2]

Task-Related Creativity

The character of a group also affects how the group manages the creativity it brings to its task-related activities. How the group manages its creativity then affects how individuals identify their tasks and the obstacles on their way to success. Should you, as a group leader, dictate to the group or make outrageous demands before the group has had a chance to engage in creative activities, you'll encourage compliance rather than commitment to problem solving or to achieving the group's goals. Opening the door to innovation encourages the group to work at being innovative and to take risks. Give the group opportunities to solve its own production problems, and the group will work at being more productive.

What makes Johnsonville Foods the classic case of team management is the way the company allows the group to work out solutions to major problems. Typically, top executives reserve to themselves the right to decide whether or not to take on a major contract that could have significant consequences for the company as a whole. Yet, here, top executives have confidence in the abilities of the employees they hire to let them make the go/no-go decisions as well as design the how-to action plans. While this is not business-as-usual for most companies, the movement, especially in the service of continuous improvement, is gaining momentum.[3]

An "if it ain't broke don't fix it" mentality still infects many companies, and that mentality produces stagnation rather than continuous improvement. An "if it ain't broke *improve on it*" mentality dominates the thinking of high-performance teams at IBM, 3M, and Hewlett Packard (as well as Japanese companies, such as Toyota). Only freeing people and their groups to achieve their potential can drive organizations toward creativity and risk taking. Without this mentality, the status quo norms (the explicit or implicit rules or understandings) inherent in the Producing and Maintaining aspects of team life, below, anchor the organization and drag it back against the tide of change.

Producing

Effective groups establish the norms that make their work possible and that prescribe who does what, when, and where. The norms become the foundation that make it possible for a group to repetitively get out its work (until another demand for change comes about). No matter how creative and energetic a group may be, it can never forget that its task-related objectives are the reasons for its existence. After all the testing, planning, and creativity comes the time to produce or go away.

Without an "if it ain't broke improve it" mentality, the routine of producing can dull a high-performance team's cutting edge. Unless everyone, whether on a formal team or not, remains alert to problems or to better ways of doing things, the organization can't fulfill its mandates. When General Mills created its self-managed production teams, the change was newsworthy, not because the teams didn't have "bosses" but because without bosses they still improved productivity and were successful at doing what they were called upon to do.[4]

Customer Tests of Productivity

Satisfaction of internal or external customers has become the litmus test of group productivity. Therefore regular polling of customer feelings measures how well the group is doing. By assigning one person the role of "customer liaison," the group manages its performance against standards of acceptability. (This role also can be split and assigned to two people: one for internal customers and the other for external.) That person stays in regular contact with the customer to ensure that the group is in fact meeting standards, and maintains all documentation relative to the product or service delivery plan (defects, delivery deadlines, etc.).

The final outcome of productivity testing should be improvements in the group's outputs and the reduction of operating costs.

Maintaining

Any group performs for you only if you take care of it. You have to support the team's production with *task maintenance* (administrative details, production needs, delivery needs, etc.) and *process maintenance* (group dynamics, communication needs, etc.). Maintenance requires that everyone watch over what is happening within the group and take action to adjust or fine-tune it. You are ultimately responsible for what the group does and how it does it. This is particularly important with regard to the storms that could possibly swamp even the most creative of groups.

Notes

1. Jim Lovell and Jeffrey Kluger, *Lost Moon: The Perilous Voyage of Apollo 13* (Boston and New York: Houghton Mifflin, 1994), p. 159.
2. Keith H. Hammonds, "Corning's Class Act: How Jamie Houghton Reinvented the Company," *Business Week* (May 13, 1991), p. 68.
3. Chris Lee, "Beyond Teamwork," *Training* (June 1990), pp. 25–32; Brian Dumaine, "Who Needs a Boss," *Fortune* (May 7, 1990), pp. 52–53. See also John Hillkirk, "Kodak Develops New Way of Managing," *USA TODAY* (August 8, 1990), p. 4B.
4. Dumaine.

Other Sources

Weiss, Donald H. *How to Build High Performance Teams.* Watertown, Mass.: American Management Association, 1991, Chapter 2.

17

Managing the Storms

There is nothing so annoying as to have two people go right
on talking when you're interrupting.

—Mark Twain (1835–1910)

Geese don't always get along with one another. Spend an afternoon
by the pond and watch them scrap over food and mates. After a few
hours of listening to them honk threats at one another, you'll marvel
that they can ever coordinate their migratory patterns. The trick?
They don't let personal feelings interfere with their semiannual treks.

Likewise, while "arguments, battles of wit, and issues of right
and wrong are behaviors that deviate from harmony" (according to
Bob Messing's interpretation of the Taoist notion of "contention"),[1]
they ought not destroy relationships within a group. Indeed, differences of opinion and disagreements ought to lead to harmonizing
contrary opinions, to synthesizing competing ideas, or to creating
new beliefs—all of which can help the group grow. Storming affects
group life no matter how well people manage themselves or their
group; the trick here is in how well the group brings harmony back
into the group to prevent the storm from doing permanent damage.

> Conflicts occur when at least one involved party believes, rightly or
> wrongly, that his right to satisfy his needs or interests has been denied—
> that someone is blocking his way to reaching some goal or objective.

Storming

Any group worth its salt goes through some kind of storming at one
time or another. The probing/testing behavior I described in the pre-

vious chapter produces storms. Effective group members, when probing one another, test their own limits within the group. They push
other people past their limits. They argue, they debate. They use
storms to help one another grow.

On occasion, less effective group members fight and jockey for
influence or power. At any time, in any group, a member may
struggle to satisfy his own interests at the expense of the group. When
that seems to be the case, process feedback (with a tool such as the
one I provide in Chapter 14) can help bring the offending group
member back into line.

Sometimes the storm is mild, hardly worth noticing. Sometimes
it's tempestuous, a genuine conflict. All conflicts involve differences
of opinions, values, goals, or desires, but not all differences produce,
or need to produce, conflict. Conflicts occur when at least one involved party believes, rightly or wrongly, that her right to satisfy her
needs or interests has been denied—that someone is blocking her way
to reaching some goal or objective. Frustrated, the person feels the
need to win some payoff at the expense of others. The situation's
made all the more difficult if the person's right *has* been denied and
the offender is not aware of it.

Any two people in the same room can produce differences of
opinion, disagreements about anything, or conflicts over minutia.
Most storms, however, come from six identifiable situations: (1) disagreements of belief, (2) disagreements of attitude and values, (3) semantic disagreements, (4) power playing, (5) neurotic game playing,
and (6) ineffective management or leadership.

Disagreements of Belief

Disagreements about facts or perceptions can lead to conflicts when
the differences stay unresolved and one or all of the parties feel frustrated. They come to an end only when everyone involved accepts
direct or indirect evidence in support of one belief or the other.

The relativity of perspectives complicates any effort to resolve
disagreements of beliefs: The so-called "same facts" don't always appear the same way to each person. In a once failed approach to forming marketing teams, Allied Signal set up account teams for each
major customer that "included key people from each product division
. . . that did business with that customer." Headquarters saw these

teams as a coordinated effort to market to key accounts; the divisions "saw the teams as just another way [in which headquarters was] trying to control the divisions"[2] by co-opting them. Whether you're talking about the weather or about market share statistics, no two people see the world the same way. Each person interprets "the same experience" in different ways depending on their personal perspective at any given time or place.

Your *perspective* (your way of taking in and processing information about the world and your way of reacting to what you take in and process) shapes what you call "reality." What makes your perspective unique to you includes how you feel at the moment, what happened earlier in the day, what experiences you have had over the history of your life. Attitudes, values, self-concepts, previously held beliefs all round out your perspective. To make sense of your present experience, your mind organizes the data it takes in to fit into its perspective. It uses paradigms or models to filter experiences and to interpret those experiences as a belief. Given that you and other people see things differently, the people in your group need to take time to check out your beliefs with one another to determine if they are alike or in need of reconciliation. To prevent or to resolve conflicts of beliefs requires that people agree to talk about their experiences and form a consensus about the facts involved.

Disagreements of Attitude and Values

Two or more people may agree on the facts but apply different values to those facts or take different attitudes toward them. If their values or attitudes remain unreconciled, they can wind up in a very severe storm. Disagreements of attitude in the workplace include:

- Differences between organizational goals and personal goals
- Differences of needs and different ways of meeting them
- Differences based on culture (including morality or ethical values), ethnicity, race, religion, gender, or age

Differences between organizational goals and personal goals are reflected primarily in expectations or standards and attitudes toward work. When creating the psychological contract, you and the employee should agree on specific responsibilities in support of one another's goals and organizational functions. A proper new employee orientation based on the psychological contract prevents failed expectations from leading to unbridled shouting matches. To deal effectively with differences of attitudes in groups, when setting the stage (early in a group's life), talk about expectations and discuss them thoroughly.

Additionally, even if you and another person agree on what the goals are, you also have to take a similar attitude toward them. People come to work with unique expectations and attitudes toward their work, but enough similaritites exist to permit the group to function collectively and to agree on what the group's goals are. Disputes usually focus on whether those are the right goals or if you're using the right methods for achieving them. These debates concern values that you must reconcile right from the start. Poorly thought out expectations—unrealistically high or low—can produce frustration, resentment, and anger.

When creating a team, selecting team members for the compatibility of work attitudes helps, but often a person's real values and attitudes don't emerge until a crisis happens; then he may act in surprising and nonproductive ways.

Likewise, you always have to stay alert to the possibilities that values and attitudes can change with changing circumstances. Political-party leaders are painfully aware of how difficult it is to predict how people will feel about anything and everything in their lives at any given moment.

Differences in the way different people meet their own needs often give rise to conflicts. Power, self-esteem, and security are only a few of the needs that people meet through their work. When the organization or other people frustrate those needs and wishes, anger and resentment turn little irritations into major incidents.

Differences of needs also signal differences in attitude. And, it's quite possible that the immediate issues may be masking a conflict of attitudes in which your needs or those of others are not being met or in which your way of meeting your needs and the ways other people are meeting theirs aren't meshing. Likewise, the perspective through which you take in and process information contains values and attitudes you derive from the influences of your origins and other life experiences. Unless they are resolved at the outset, differences in values and attitudes based on culture, race, ethnicity, religion, gender, or age can lead to conflicts.

Hiring "for diversity" can backfire if you do not properly prepare for the differences that define diversity. Those differences emerge from life experiences that range from simple things, such as foods, to deep social-psychological issues imbedded in race relations. Attitudes and values arise from those life experiences and color everything we do. Many white people, as a result of their upbringing and cultural education, see African-Americans as threats to their financial and social well-being; many African-Americans, because of their experiences in and with the systems created and run by white people, see whites as obstacles to their opportunities for satisfying lives. People can't truly know what coworkers from different backgrounds feel, but they can understand that everyone has reasons for believing and feeling the way they do.

Sensitivity to those differences can come about only through open dialogue and by recognizing the dignity of all human beings. Cartoonist Mort Walker may be talking to all of us by sending General Halftrack of his comic strip "Beetle Bailey" to sensitivity training. Walker is really addressing all the attitudes attending relationships among people, not just gender issues (the General's weak spot). Sexual harassment is only one of the many flashpoints endangering business relations. Affirmative action is another.

Author/consultant Terry Eastland, writing in *The Wall Street Journal*, sees affirmative action, especially set-asides, as a form of discrimination against the white majority in which the rights of white-owned companies and employees are trampled.[3] In his mind they are onerous preferences based solely on race, a practice he thinks must stop; and he seems to speak for a large percentage of white people. On the other side, most minority people (covering the whole spectrum from African-Americans to Southeast Asian immigrants) and females see affirmative action, including set-asides, as a means for preventing the white, male economic/political "majority" from awarding jobs and contracts to white males only, preferences that have occurred throughout the history of the United States; they know that their rights have been trampled upon in the past and believe that affirmative action is the only way they can gain an economic foothold. These are genuine conflicts of attitudes and values that will not change quickly or merely by the force of legislation. It takes reeducation and rethinking on the part of all parties involved to resolve these conflicts.

Mort Walker's comic strip gives us something else to think about regarding issues of business and workplace discrimination. We can see that in his attempt to "civilize" the General, Mort Walker also runs the risk that many people will mistakenly think he places all the ills of society in general and of the workplace in particular on the backs of the General Halftracks of the world. I don't think that's what Walker has in mind. It's true that insensitive people can often be obnoxious; on the other hand, a person may find it too easy to blame such Halftracks for difficulties that he has brought on himself; that shifts responsibility from the individual to other people, which makes a sham of praise as well as of blame. If you insist on blaming other people for your failures, you have difficulty accepting praise for your successes.

Semantic Disagreements

Groups sometimes run into storms created when what seems to be a disagreement of belief, fact, or attitude masks a simple matter of semantics. However, those semantic disagreements can blow up into horrendous conflicts when the words you use to convey beliefs and attitudes cause confusion that no one bothers to eliminate. Words with more than one meaning—ambiguous words—especially can become the basis for trouble. Especially important are so-called relative terms such as *tall, small, far, better than, good*, and *bad*. When labor and management sit down to negotiate pay increases, the words *small* and *large* won't do. Is a 5 percent a year pay increase "too small" or "too large"? Is CEO compensation "too small" or "too large"? The answers depend on your perspective. Supplying precise definitions resolves disagreements derived from different meanings of the same words. Most of the time.

Cross-functional teams often suffer from slinging around jargon and coined words—words with specialized meanings or that have been made up to refer to new or previously unidentified events or things. When specialists use arcane language that people from other fields don't understand, they create confusion that can lead to conflict. Here's a "techie versus nontechie" storm story. In a cross-functional team in a training unit, two IS people got into a discussion no one else could follow. The team leader, a computer-phobe, became so agitated and angry that he called off the meeting and stalked into his boss's office to demand that the techies be removed from the team or he would quit it. This whole affair could have been prevented if everyone had followed this simple rule: A cross-functional team needs a common language that everyone can understand and that matches its common purpose; when deciding on such a language, team members need to take into consideration other people's areas of expertise.

Language creates additional problems insofar as it evolves over time, with words disappearing or changing in meaning. And, since words are often emotionally loaded, semantic differences can hide a disagreement in attitudes about the word itself. The simplest example I can think of is the word *gay*. Once upon a time, calling someone gay meant that she enjoyed life. Today it means that she's a lesbian. At a meeting, I said, "We'll have a gay old time when this project's done," to which a much younger person vehemently responded, "I don't think so." He truly didn't know the older meaning of the word.

Semantic disagreements that explode into conflict can be avoided by heeding the simple rule above: Everyone in a group has the responsibility to ensure that people talk with one another in a mutually acceptable, common language. Introducing, probing, and testing all include getting to know that different people use language differently, that specific ethnic or racial characteristics affect speech and manner, that ethnic or racial symbols (a form of language) give them a sense of pride, while others hold those same symbols in contempt.

Semantic disagreements often mask real disagreements in belief or real disagreements in attitudes. Take the word *downsizing*. What the word means to you depends on your perspective. Whether you're the manager doing the downsizing or the employee being downsized, *downsizing* has the same meaning ("letting people go"). But the emotional overtones and the value loading for the manager bring a promise of reward, while for the employee they bring fear and trembling. For the one, it means "cost effectiveness," for the other it means "being fired." The moral? People in positions of power (i.e., managers) have to become sensitive to the differences created by emotional overtones or value loadings of words.

Power Playing

Power playing consists of taking advantage of other people for your own benefit. Using status power to command people to obey rather than personal power to influence behavior, and stealing ideas or using employees as shields against other managers are forms of managerial power playing. Send an employee to participate in a cross-functional team but don't give her decision-making authority and watch what happens. The situation humiliates the employee and interferes with the team's effectiveness. Unless you give the person the authority she needs, you should participate in the team, not she. Another version of this power play is to send someone into a situation with other people, let him make decisions, and then blame him if things don't go the way you want them to. In either case, you hurt the employee's credibility with other people and your own credibility with everyone.

Sometimes the organization's system itself breeds power plays, especially if management creates teams but continues to reward individual employees for personal accomplishments. Then team members begin competing among themselves for rewards rather than cooperating with one another. One member may try to cozy up to you, the manager, to curry favor (sandbagging information the team needs). Another may try to organize a subgroup to take control of the team to support his bid for advancement.

Other power plays are closely associated with poorly controlled competition. They thrive in an environment where resources or rewards are limited or access to them is restricted. Tight budgets, limited opportunities for promotion, constrained scope of authority among managers, and rewards through favoritism discourage teamwork between individuals or between work groups. A group invites conflict when it fails to control or misuses competition or operates with poorly defined goals, objectives, and roles or with poorly engineered workflow between members. Only by carefully setting the stage and regularly probing and testing the group for feelings and opinions can power playing be prevented from blowing up into major storms.

Neurotic Game Playing

Neurotic games are a form of power playing, an effort to control other people for personal (emotional) gain. A while back, transactional analysis, a popular brand of psychology and management tool, said that everyone plays some type of game or encourages others to play games. If a person is playing a game rather than just defending himself from games other people are playing, he will behave as follows:

- He will feign a benign appearance, which makes his hostility difficult to detect. The true meaning of the game to the player is to appear harmless when his motives are quite the opposite.
- He invariably substitutes idiosyncratic methods of coping with a situation for rational and direct methods whenever faced with a difficult situation.
- He has a payoff, i.e., he has to get some sort of satisfaction from the behavior at the expense of the other person.

Once you understand what constitutes a game, you can spot it when a person plays it. Armed with that knowledge, you, as a manager-leader, can prevent games from disrupting the effectiveness of your work group or team.

Self-managed people don't play games, but because of their self-esteem and respect for others, they might inadvertently find themselves caught up in someone else's game. As a self-managed manager-leader, you can not only learn to detect games and avoid participating in them, but you can also help people get out of the game-playing habit by taking the following steps:

1. Don't play the game once you uncover it. The lack of payoff extinguishes the game quickly.
2. Watch out for "hooks," ideas or values or feelings that catch you up in a game. Game players say or do things that could get you angry, agitated, or unnecessarily concerned about events or other people.
3. Invite differences of opinion and listen to them without reacting emotionally or with hostility.
4. Check out the truth of what you're told by one person about another.
5. Confront game players with the fact that they're playing a game.

The key to eliminating game playing is to make it clear that it won't be tolerated. People will play games as long as they think the group or you will let them get away with it.

Ineffective Management or Leadership

Storms usually arise when the people involved have differences of beliefs, semantic disagreements, differences of attitudes, or they play games. But you, as a manager, can also create the conditions for conflict by not managing your group's task and process dynamics. Managing or leading a work group or semiautonomous team requires that you prevent task-oriented and process-oriented people from clashing over what has to be done and how to do it.

Very task-oriented people just want to get the job done and don't want to bother with the relationships among people. Very process-oriented people want to get the job done also, but they also want to make sure that the relationships between people are smooth and mutually satisfying, even if it means delaying getting the job done. I've seen very task-oriented people attack the group or walk out of meetings whenever process issues are raised. "I've got too much to do to be sidetracked by all this touchie-feelie stuff" is a common task-oriented complaint. On the other hand, I've seen very process-oriented people delay decisions past their deadlines until hurt feelings are mended. "It's not fair that . . ." is their common complaint.

The work has to get done, and group members must feel good about working with each other. As you set the stage for the group, the harmony of the two dynamics must be a specific criterion of group success.

As I pointed out earlier, when I described disagreements of attitudes and values, the very thing that gives a group its power can also create its biggest storms: diversity, the differences that exist among all people. The only thing that can keep a diverse group of people from flying apart anytime the members disagree with each other is the level of *synergy* the group creates.

Managing the Storms Through Synergy

The word *synergy* describes a group's ability to pull together (synthesize) the energies of a group of people, to focus them on a common goal, and thereby to achieve a positive result—a result that no one person working alone could accomplish and that no one could predict on the basis of an audit of team member skills or experience. (Synergy is the sine qua non of an effective team.) Some people use the metaphor "the whole is greater than the sum of its parts" to describe the process as a property that emerges from how the group manages its natural dynamics: task relationships and process relationships.

Groups can get through their storms by calling upon the synergy that comes from managing the task and process dynamics that influence and move them. The way you and the other group members manage the dynamics determines whether or not the group can create synergy and fulfill your mission as a group. Mismanaging or poorly managing these relationships can whip up ordinary disagreements (task or process problems) into frenzied storms.

Useless, unproductive meetings are a clear symptom of process and task dynamic problems, but they're also the best place in which to forecast the weather and to evaluate the causes of conflicts. High-performance teams encourage and manage disagreements to help the group prevent conflicts.

Task Problems

The mission is the group's prime directive, which mismanaging the group's task relationships (e.g., missing deadlines, producing waste, giving misinformation, not asking for information) can undermine. Yet, an overwhelming task orientation (e.g., driving to meet production goals) wreaks havoc with the group's process relations. Whether goals are not met, as in the first case, or they are, as in the second, mismanagement of task dynamics profits no one.

Process Problems

Groups fall apart when their members don't get along, in particular, when differences of beliefs, values, attitudes, and game playing interfere. Not getting along subverts productivity because people don't listen to each other, or because they're playing games and have lost sight of the common goal, or because one or more people dominate the group while others withdraw. Meetings may suffer from a lack of direction and coordination. People may feel left out or believe that others are receiving special treatment. Disagreements get out of hand and become conflicts.

Guidelines for Weathering Storms

Typically a difference of opinion or a general disagreement kicks up a mild storm in which two or more people experience a situation differently, or hold different beliefs or values, or believe different versions of the same so-called facts, or differ in their interpretations or feelings about a situation. They "knock around" their differences for a short time and reduce the storm to a few breezes, if any. Encouraging these storms usually leads to new or different ways of getting the results you want. Mishandling these disagreements usually leads to a severe storm in which disagreement turns into conflict.

You're in for quite a storm whenever at least one party believes, rightly or wrongly, that his right to satisfy his needs or interests has been denied. When storms strike, you can reestablish the synergy by following five basic guidelines.

1. Understand the Scope and Intensity of the Process Problem

Watch how people react to the group's mission, to you, and to one another and listen to what they say. Through careful observation, you'll see and hear the signals you need for knowing how big or severe the storm really is, but you can't rely on your own perceptions alone. To grasp the full force of what is happening requires that you engage in three self-management behaviors:

1. Solicit feedback and actively listen to what people say about how the group's processes affect them.
2. Role-model the problem-solving process by using nonjudgmental paraphrasing of what you hear, mirroring feelings or emotions you sense; that is, paraphrase or mirror without interjecting your own feelings or values into the feedback. Then work on behalf of the group to eliminate any disagreement.
3. Maintain reciprocal channels of communication in which everyone gives feedback, actively listens to one another, paraphrases, brainstorms, and provides means for achieving goals or maintaining relationships. This gives everyone—including you, the manager-leader—a chance to participate, to air opinions or feelings, to contribute, and to produce consensus. However, keeping those channels open and free of managerial

obstructions requires you to refrain from pushing your own passions, beliefs, and values onto the group. The ultimate goal? To prevent hidden agendas from surfacing at inopportune times.

2. Review and Reaffirm Commitments

Storms spring up when differences within the group take precedence over its vision (its purpose and its self-image) or mission (its objectives and tasks). They also pop up if the group's vision or mission no longer applies or if it changes. Then:

1. Review group assumptions, goals, objectives, and composition; make sure they still apply.
2. If they do, get everyone to look at what's happening in the group to determine why targets are not being reached.
3. If you see the group really is off target, you, as the manager-leader, can revitalize it by setting it back on course or by redirecting it to new challenges. The ideal, however, is for the group to reach these conclusions on its own.

Proactively, as a matter of course, you and the group should periodically review the group's assumptions, goals, objectives, and composition. Change them, if need be, while reaffirming to yourself your passion for the group and its purpose; transfer that passion to the group by energizing yourself and the group with positive energy.

3. Encourage Healthy Dialogue

The unwillingness to confront issues, opinions, or values ("group think") flattens the group. Encourage self-management behavior by creating healthy disagreement and dialogue. Play devil's advocate and force dialogue that leads to consensus through open communication and discussion. Shouting and pouting, contrary to group think, can also scuttle the group's process dynamics. In either case, take these steps:

1. Deliberately create opportunities for problem solving by beginning a dialogue that allows the group members to confront

the various sides of an issue. You can summarize the disagreement: "You, Joe, think . . . and you, Mary, think . . ." Then ask
Joe and Mary, "How are your positions alike or different?"

2. License everyone to disagree, adopting an "anything goes"
   attitude to encourage participation and creativity.
3. Respect and accept differences.
4. Participate in the discussions rather than dominate them to
   avoid becoming the clog in the channels of communication.
5. Confront the issue causing the storm until it is settled permanently, no matter how many meetings it may take, in order to
   prevent the storm from gathering an unforeseen intensity.

4. Harmonize Task Orientation and Process Orientation

A group's life, just as an individual's, consists of competing demands
and goals. When task and process dynamics are out of harmony,
storms are generated. Driving a meeting to complete a task by beating
down all debate creates a dominating task orientation. Becoming
overly concerned with how people get along produces a dominating
process orientation. Either way, stormy conflicts can swamp the
group and everyone loses. When orientation problems threaten, encourage high levels of mutual respect (concern for the task needs of
some and the process needs of others). Follow these four steps to
bring the group's task and process dynamics back into harmony:

1. Evaluate how the group uses its energies to determine if it has
   emphasized productivity at the expense of relationships, or
   vice versa.
2. Encourage the group to think about *both* what it is doing and
   how it is doing it.
3. Personally model the equal importance of rational thought,
   emotional appeals, and action by engaging in all three. Action
   without thought is deaf and blind, while thought without action is useless. Expect the unexpected and recognize the need
   for the sometimes irrational.
4. Encourage fun and celebration as well as work by having fun
   and by celebrating with the group. The group's mission is its
   reason for being. People should enjoy making personal contributions that produce results, and good results should be cele-

brated by everyone. Your failure to recognize people's success will create a "what's the use" atmosphere.

5. Confront Process Problems With Diverse Yet Unified Resources

Don't put yourself into the center of every storm and presume that you can be the final arbiter of all disagreements and conflicts. Group members need to learn what to do or how to do it when storms pop up. Taking control denies people the power to take corrective action even when they know better than you what to do or how to do it.

1. Empower group members to battle their storms on their own without deferring to authority.
2. Give people opportunities to make decisions that affect their work and their lives, and let them act on those decisions. Unless they feel they have that power, they lose respect for the process and see the system as co-opting them for hidden organizational ends.
3. Teach them the skills they need, if necessary, then allow them the freedom to take risks with one another, to make mistakes, to take corrective action, and to learn (or else you will find yourself and the group forever battling the storms instead of doing productive work).

Notes

1. Bob Messing, *The Tao of Management: An Age-Old Study for Modern Managers* (New York: Bantam New Age Books, 1989 and 1992), p. 11.
2. Al Hendershot (VP of Allied Signal Aerospace) and George Bailey (Price Waterhouse consultant), "How We Brought Teamwork to Marketing," *Wall Street Journal* (August 26, 1996), p. A12.
3. Terry Eastland, "Federal Set-Asides: Just Another Name for Discrimination," *Wall Street Journal* (July 9, 1997), p. A15.

Other Sources

Berne, Eric. *Games People Play.* New York: Grove Press, 1964.
Harrington-Mackin, Deborah. *Keeping the Team Going: A Tool Kit to Renew and Refuel Your Workplace Teams.* New York: AMACOM, 1996.

James, Muriel, and Dorothy Jongeward. *Born to Win: Transactional Analysis With Gestalt Experiments.* Reading, Mass.: Addison-Wesley, 1971.

Masterson, James F. *Psychotherapy of the Borderline Adult: A Developmental Approach.* New York: Brunner/Mazel, 1976.

Simmons, Annette. *Territorial Games: Understanding and Ending Turf Wars at Work.* New York: AMACOM, 1997.

Weiss, Donald H. *Keeping Teams Together.* Watertown, Mass.: American Management Association, 1993. This training video was developed to help teams to manage their storms.

———. *Managing Conflict.* Watertown, Mass.: American Management Association, 1981 and 1993.

———. *Conflict Resolution.* New York: AMACOM, 1993.

———. *How to Deal With Difficult People.* New York: AMACOM, 1987.

Section 6

High-Performance Teams, How to Make Teams Work, When Not to Form Teams at All, and Self-Managed Teams

18

High-Performance Teams

Teams are the way ordinary people do extraordinary things.
—Author unknown

It takes the whole flock of geese to fly home. Older geese show younger ones the way to their winter digs. The young in turn find their way back. While in flight, when a lead bird tires or falters, another one takes its place. All the geese cheer each other on with loud honking, and together, as a group, they add power and commitment to each other. Since migrating geese travel a great distance, they have a good reason for flying in V-formation: Individually, no one goose could fly as far as the gaggle as a whole.

> People have a good reason for working in teams, a reason tied to business goals and strategies. Not so oddly, the reason is the same as that underlying the goose's V-formation: Individually, no one person can accomplish as much as the group as a whole.

Traits That Distinguish Teams From Other Groups

Your mission, if you choose to accept the role of manager-leader, is to take steps to reduce the chances that your team will start out in trouble or run into hurricane-force storms. To create a team that works, everyone (but especially you) has to deliberately incubate, hatch, and nurture the traits that distinguish a high-performance team from an ordinary group that works well together. You also have to ensure an atmosphere of mutual respect (reciprocity) and pride in the group. Only then will group members identify with each other and with the team as a whole. High-performance teams are characterized by a high degree of collaboration.

Three major traits distinguish a team from other work groups:

1. A team is a relatively small group of people, formed around common interests, values, and history.
2. A team is formed to meet a specific set of relatively short-term goals or objectives that support the work group or organization's goals and objectives.
3. Team members have identifiable roles designed to satisfy the demands of team goals.

Relatively Small Size

It's okay to titter when the CEO of the giant corporation you work for announces that the whole company is the team that got the company to where it is. Giant corporations (even small companies) may implement a *team-based strategy* and may consist of many teams, but they are not, as a whole, *a team.*

A team has to be relatively small to work together as a team. The people on the team must have direct, personal face-to-face (or, these days, direct, personal *intra*net) relations; they must know one another, communicate with one another, trust one another, feel comfortable with contributing to and influencing one another. A major-league baseball team is a giant organization, but *the team* has only 25 players on the roster, and only nine of them ever take the field at any one time. (And, usually, only one or two of them ever seems to be playing at peak performance on any given day.)

Size also makes a difference as to whether or not team members have common interests, values, and history. All the employees of General Motors have an interest in the success of the corporation as a whole, that's true, but that success is so remote from each individual's life that it's impossible for any one person outside of the executive team to form a personal identity around it. What you do in a team makes a dramatic difference as to *who* you are, as well as to *what* you are.

"I'm a machinist for General Motors" has a definite ring to it, but it doesn't carry the same sense of personal pride as "I'm a member of the design team producing the prototype of GM's newest-concept car." You may work for General Motors, but you contribute to and influence the design team, the end product of which another person can recognize and admire immediately. "Gosh, you're building *that*?"

Short-Term Goals and Objectives

The corporation's goals are (or should be) long-term in scope and application. Big vision, big plans, big income, big expenditures. Not so a team. You form a team to meet a specific set of relatively short-term goals or objectives that support the work group's or the organization's goals. The baseball team plays to win a pennant and a world series. A Navy SEAL team clears a harbor of mines. A design team produces a new style automobile. Each team belongs to a larger organization, and some of their organizations belong to a still larger organization (e.g., the Navy SEAL team belongs to a squadron, which belongs to a fleet, which belongs to the Navy, which belongs to the U.S. armed services, which belongs to . . .).

Large organizations go on forever (or try to). Many teams don't last beyond achieving their objectives. Ad hoc teams (such as project teams or product launch teams) come into existence for one purpose and one purpose only and go away once they fulfill that purpose (sometimes to be re-formed at another time). Team identities rarely expand beyond the scope of their mission.

Identifiable Roles

Perhaps the only thing team members have in common with everyone else in the organization is that they have identifiable roles designed to satisfy demands of the organization's goals and objectives. Well, everyone in the organization is *supposed* to have identifiable roles and is *supposed* to perform those roles effectively to achieve their goals. However, investigative reporters have discovered that there are people in some organizations (e.g., the federal government) who have no identifiable roles at all.

Not so a team. Nonproductive people can't happen in a high-performance team. It's too small to enable them to hide. Everyone can see what everyone else is doing, and since collaboration depends

on everyone's contribution and influence, if someone isn't doing anything, everyone will know it. A team performs at peak levels because
it consists of self-managed people. Employee characteristics prized
by IBM's field teams provide a good example of what to include:
"high job competence," "good business judgment," "dependability,"
and *self-disciplined, self-starter.*" IBM wants self-managed people on
its high-performance teams.

General Characteristics of High-Performance Teams

Although team members operate in groups with the above-mentioned
traits that are unique to teams, they, like all other group members,
must perform the activities associated with task and process dynamics, the activities listed in Exhibits 15-1, 15-2, and 15-3. Likewise,
members of successful teams harmonize those dynamics to achieve
team and individual satisfaction.

Mutual Respect and Pride

High-performance teams operate in an atmosphere of mutual respect
(reciprocity) in which members identify with each other and take
pride in the team as a whole. I must point out here that you can
respect people without necessarily liking them. Baseball fans will remember the Oakland Athletics of the 1970s and 1980s in this regard.
Most of the players disliked or even despised each other. They bick-
ered among themselves in the clubhouse and snubbed one another
socially, but on the field they were champions. What made these men
so successful as a team?

First, the team was efficient insofar as each player executed the
basics flawlessly. They were individually among the best ball players
in both major leagues, and they worked hard at staying the best. They
respected each other for it, and they played together with the "arro-
gance" of competent ball players, believing they were the best and,
because of that belief, winning (when no one thought they could).[1]
As in the case of the A's, in a business environment, team members
have to acquire and practice the skills that make them peak performers at whatever they do.

Second, the A's were effective. As ball players, they did the right things, at the right time, and in the right way. They extended themselves beyond the normal expectations for ball players, raising the bar on themselves individually and as a team at every possible turn. Likewise, in a business environment, team members have to understand what they are doing and why they're doing it, and they have to do the right things, at the right time, and in the right way in order to fulfill the mission they assume as team members.

At Baxter International of Deerfield, Illinois, a medical products supplier, "hundreds of working-level employees [working in teams have figured] out ways to streamline the operation," to change the way the company does business, to install cutting-edge warehousing equipment, and to reorganize the way they do their work. The company and its employees underwent traumatic change (some making the "ultimate sacrifice" of redesigning themselves out of jobs), but in the process they rationalized the whole supply chain, saving *many* jobs as they brought the company greater prosperity.[2]

Specific Characteristics of High-Performance Teams

A business team has to go beyond mutual respect and pride and efficiency and effectiveness. Its members have to exhibit six basic traits that are similar to or are corollaries of the traits of self-managed people. The result of internalizing those traits is the empowerment of the team's members.

Self-Generated Commitment

Each member has to have a self-generated commitment to the other members of the team, to the task of the team, and to the team concept itself. When you read Jim Lovell's account of the Apollo 13 mission, in *Lost Moon,* you get a sense of what this means.

As the damaged moon vehicle limped toward the moon, after the shift of the White Team at Mission Control in Houston ended, no one on "the White Team showed . . . signs of leaving the auditorium." The White Team controllers "stood or crouched behind their replacements [on the Black Team], their eyes focused on the screens they had been monitoring for the previous eight hours and their headsets plugged into auxiliary jacks. . . ."[3] Major catastrophes usually bring out the best in teams.

But, you don't need a major catastrophe to show your loyalty to (1) team members and (2) the team. When Tom Mattingly was exposed to measles and scrubbed from the flight of Apollo 13, Lovell argued strenuously to keep him on board, but after the flight surgeon "thumbed Mattingly out of the lineup," Lovell transferred that loyalty to the backup command module pilot, Jack Swigert.[4] Lovell felt no guilt in doing so, and no one blamed him for it: At this point, the team members needed to subordinate their personal interests to those of the team.

Trust as a Basis of Agreement

Usually abjuring majority voting, high-performance-team members reach agreement through one of two ways: (1) trust in each other's judgment or (2) by consensus. Don't be dazzled by the myth that teams make *all* their decisions by arriving at a consensus; on the other hand, don't minimize the effectiveness and importance of consensus decision making. Members of high-performance teams depend on each other to think for the group when their independent judgment adds value to the group's success. When time allows, and other conditions make it possible, they use consensus to achieve their good results. It all depends on the situation, the level of expertise the members have, and the distribution of skills or talents within the group.

In the movie version of the Lovell/Kluger book, *Apollo 13*, Gene Kranz's White Team collectively solved the CO_2 scrubbing problem. In reality, the solution occurred to one person, Ed Smylie, chief of the Crew Systems Division, as he drove to the Command Center. To test his idea, he had to get Cape Canaveral to jet their spare canisters to him, which they did without discussion. Once tested, he took his "strange, unwieldy invention" through the doors of Mission Operations Control Room, where no one questioned that his contraption "would likely save [the astronauts'] lives."[5] They trusted their ace's judgment and went with it.

Consensus as a Basis of Agreement

At the same time, decision making by consensus commends itself when time permits, when the needed expertise is in the group, when long-term decisions are involved, and when many people have a stake in the decision. The experience of Tamara Sager, the quality inventory control supervisor, at the Midwest center of Baxter International, in Indianapolis, makes the point. Charged with telling upper management if they should shut down the center or not, she "pulled together ten distribution, transportation, and sales colleagues from the Chicago area and Indiana." This team made the thorough assessments that could have led to tough decisions, including those that could have cost them their own jobs. Given the appropriate information, they recommended keeping the center open, but changing how business was done there. A decision a skeptical management wisely implemented in April 1995. The savings came to $150,000 that year *with no loss of customers.*[6]

Encouraging Disagreement

Effective team members encourage each other to disagree among themselves. They also turn potential conflicts into creative problem solving. When Don Kozlowski took over the C-17 program at McDonnell Douglas, "he spent his first three days in the assembly area" asking people questions. He didn't want to know what they liked about what they were doing; he didn't want a bunch of people telling him what they thought he wanted to hear. He wanted to know what was wrong with what they were doing, how to simplify or how to improve the system. He wanted disagreement with the status quo, and he got it.[7] The production team then made the necessary improvements in their processes to get building the C-17 back on track.

Communication

High-performance teams function at peak levels because the members communicate, not only face-to-face but through embedded electronic performance support systems as well. At Baxter, for example, to make communication at the Waukegan, Wisconsin, distribution center complete and instant, computers "rule in nearly every process" of the three around-the-clock shifts. They've even put computers on board the trucks headed to Waukegan to "give electronic notification of what supplies are en route and when they will arrive" and on forklifts to tell the drivers "where to stow newly arrived stuff."[8] *Detailed, instant communication.*

Empowerment

Members of high-performance teams take their destinies into their own hands. They are empowered; they have the right and the ability to make decisions as well as the right and the ability to act on the basis of those decisions. The National Center for Employee Ownership, in Oakland, California, concluded in a 1986 study that employee stock ownership by itself did little to increase sales or improve employment levels (which, in those days, signaled "business success"). On the other hand, "when companies gave workers a say in *running* the show as well as *owning* the business . . . a participative management culture . . . [they] realized jumps in sales and employment levels in the range of 8 percent to 11 percent."[9] Significant gains come only with an increase in employee power to make the decisions leading to those gains.

Testing Team Productivity

The Team Productivity Assessment (Exhibit 18-1) asks the team members to evaluate their ability to work together as a team to get things done. That means the team needs team performance standards based on behaviors that make a team successful. Criteria for acceptable contributions or influence also help the team measure the value of each person's task-related participation, as well as to measure the team's process dynamics.

The assessment also makes each person aware of the task dynamics that keep the team on track toward accomplishing its objectives. Once more, you see why self-managed people are central to the success of a team. To determine if the team is in fact productive, each person has to assume personal responsibility for properly testing and measuring how the group, and each person in the group, is functioning. Everyone should ask for the reasons why they are asked to adopt a procedure, should require that production levels be maintained or that quality inspections be conducted; this testing should become so

Exhibit 18-1. Team productivity assessment.

Part A. From my experiences so far, I think the team:					
	Low				High
1. Is productive	1	2	3	4	5
2. Helps me in the work I do	1	2	3	4	5
3. Helps me meet personal needs during meetings (e.g., expressing my opinions, having people listen to my ideas, etc.)	1	2	3	4	5
Part B. From my experience during this meeting, here's how I estimate the following:					
	Low				High
4. The contributions (information, opinions, ideas) of other people to the team's productivity	1	2	3	4	5
5. My contributions to the team's productivity	1	2	3	4	5
6. The trust level of members (willingness to be open, candid)	1	2	3	4	5
7. My trust level	1	2	3	4	5
8. My influence on the group	1	2	3	4	5
9. Other members' influence on me	1	2	3	4	5

commonplace that no one feels put off by the demands of the team. Positive confrontation is a norm of high-performance teams.

Periodic process checks, like the Team Productivity Assessment, measure candor, openness, and perceptions of team productivity, and they help head off team-rending problems. The possibility of doing this evaluation should be discussed when the team is formed and carefully explained to each new member coming into the team. Everyone should be familiar with it as a prerequisite to having planned assessment sessions that help the team keep itself on track.

You can find the complete assessment instrument (including interpretations) in Appendix F. The questionnaire portion, reproduced here, asks individual members to circle the rating after each item that best represents what they think or feel. Each person copies his individual scores and gives the form to someone designated to produce a statistical summary of the results of the assessment. That person presents the results at a subsequent meeting or immediately, depending on how the team wants or needs to use the instrument. A smoothly functioning team may not want or need immediate results; a team experiencing storming may prefer to discuss the results "right now." Regardless of how and when the tool is used, the group can discuss the results and decide on what actions can sustain the good scores and improve on the poor ones.

A discussion of the assessment's results helps the team identify how group process dynamics and behaviors may be suppressing personal feelings and agendas. Suppressed feelings and agendas can emerge at inopportune moments and generate conflicts and other nonproductive activities that destroy the group's ability to function. After discussing suppressed feelings or any other negative reactions, you, as the team leader, can prevent those nonproductive activities from endangering the team. Using the instrument and discussing its results can help you and the team:

🕇 Monitor who participates and who does not.
🕇 Deliberately probe in order to surface feelings or opinions.
🕇 Encourage open, candid exchanges of opinions and feelings among the members.

Careful management of this probing/testing behavior obviously supports the team's process dynamic, as well as the team's task dynamic during the productivity aspect of team life. In essence, combining team tests with customer tests constitutes 360-degree feedback of the team and of its members.

Testing Ad Hoc Teams

A long-lived or permanent team has to assess its performance on a regular basis in order to continue producing up to standards. An ad hoc, or temporary, team, which puts an end to its existence by producing whatever product or outcome it was set up to produce, on the other hand, needs to evaluate how well (or poorly) it has done its completed job. An ad hoc team can be considered, in a sense, "suicidal," because neither the norms that make its work possible nor its maintenance requirements are perpetuated beyond the short life of the team.

Temporary teams need feedback as follow-up to their activities.

Evaluating the end product and talking over the process by which the team achieved its ends serve to identify how standards (e.g., deadlines) were met or why they weren't met. They identify what went wrong and what went right. The results of this debriefing provide you with a baseline for creating and managing other teams—and for improving on the team process.

Notes

1. Paraphrasing a conversation between sportscasters Steve Stone and Harry Caray about championship teams, during a Cubs baseball game in Chicago, September 20, 1996.
2. Mary Connors, "Baxter's Big Makeover in Logistics," *Fortune* (July 8, 1996), pp. 106C–106N.
3. Jim Lovell and Jeffrey Kluger, *Lost Moon: The Perilous Voyage of Apollo 13* (Boston and New York: Houghton Mifflin, 1994), pp. 140–141.
4. Lovell and Kluger, p. 82.
5. Lovell and Kluger, pp. 250–253.
6. Connors, p. 106L.
7. Christopher Carey, "A Triumph of Teamwork: After Initial Nose Dive, C-17 Helps Transport McDonnell Douglas to Stratospheric Heights," *St. Louis Post-Dispatch*, December 31, 1995, pp. 1A, 6A, and 7A.
8. Connors.
9. Cited in David Stamps, "A Piece of the Action," *Training* (March 1996), p. 66.

Other Sources

Holpp, Larry. "The Betrayal of the American Work Team." *Training* (May 1966), pp. 38–42.
Weiss, Donald H. *How to Build High Performance Teams.* Watertown, Mass.: American Management Association, 1991, Chapter 2.

19

When to Fly in Formation

The surest way for an executive to kill himself is to refuse to learn how, and when, and to whom to delegate work.

—James C. Penney (1875–1971)

Wild geese don't always fly in a V-formation. When they hang out together at a pond, one might fly off by himself, a couple of others might pair up for a short hop around the neighborhood. Most of the time, however, individual geese waddle around with both feet planted on the ground. They hunt for food, play goose games, and mate. Yet, when the time comes to move on to other climes, up they go into formation and head for "home." In short, in their secret way of doing things, wild geese know when to form a team and when not.

Before committing to creating formal teams, especially before forming self-managed teams, decide whether or not your organization or your situation calls for creating or supporting them; then consider whether the results you want lend themselves to a team approach.

> General rule: Create a high-performance team only when the team is likely to outperform an individual or a number of individuals working separately.

When Not to Form Teams

Not every organization or situation calls for creating a team. How long do you think a gander would last if he relied on the whole gaggle for food? You're more likely to see a mother goose waddling around the pond, a troop of goslings trailing behind, foraging for food—unless some human treats the gaggle to a loaf of bread.

Then, many of the geese will fight over the food, and, in fact, some ganders would rather fight than play. You can watch them at the pond beating on one another with their beaks and wings, scrapping over scraps or over a potential mate. And, speaking of mating, goose procreation would screech to a stop if it became a team effort. Individual geese do much better at taking care of their own basic needs than they would if they relied on the whole gaggle or subgroup of the gaggle to do it for them. If the work doesn't call for it and if the employees or managers are not ready for it, teams may not be the way to go.[1]

When the Knowledge or Skills of Only One Person Are Required

In the workplace, individuals can make the right decisions and work quite effectively without team membership. In Chapter 18, you saw that Ed Smylie, chief of Systems Operations for the Apollo 13 mission, cooked up the CO_2 absorption unit all by himself while driving to Mission Control. Sometimes the work itself doesn't call for a team. Who doesn't know the old joke, "How many (whatever) does it take to screw in a light bulb?" You don't need a team if the task calls for the knowledge, talents, or skills of only one person.

And even when a task does call for a team, it doesn't automatically follow that every individual will be suitable as a team member. There are people who don't work well in teams and/or are more effective working alone. Why try to force a lone eagle into the confines of the flock? Lone eagles often disrupt a team. They're not "bad" employees because they don't work well in teams. Some exhibit self-management traits and characteristics. (A good many don't, especially eccentric geniuses and a good member of CEOs.)[2]

Although the issue is open to debate, recent research suggests that about only 15 percent of the populations studied are genetically predisposed to seek out novelty and are prone to risk taking.[3] Frequently these risk takers rise to the top of the entrepreneurial heap, but sometimes we find them imbedded in R&D departments or in other recesses of the corporation. On the whole, though, businesses don't encourage and reward risk taking; too often they force creative loners into collective behavior ("go by the book," "play the game"), even if they should be allowed their freedom to create or innovate.

Professor/consultant David Newton suggests identifying these free spirits and "physically hiving off [i.e., separating] a unit [comprising them] to another site away from corporate headquarters and its bureaucracy."[4] But, hold on. If you do that, you lose the rich diversity of thought they provide. Since Newton himself believes you can develop risk taking in non–risk takers, what's the point of isolating the risk takers? Why not, instead, give them their freedom, recognize them for the work they do, and let them role-model the independent thinking you want from everyone? You develop self-managed risk takers only by encouraging people to act accordingly and then by rewarding them for it.

When There Is Insufficient Time

A conventional team isn't needed and is actually counterproductive if time doesn't permit discussion, debate, or dialogue to solve problems. If you're hauled into an emergency room, dying from a heart attack, you don't want a team of doctors and nurses who are debating alternatives and arriving at a solution by consensus. They'd better know what to do, and they'd better do it STAT.

On the other hand, putting people under artificial time pressures ("hurry up and wait," as they say in the Army) can be counterproductive. Time pressure, *without a legitimate reason,* can lessen the quality of key decisions and hamper organizational output.

When There Are Bureaucratic Constraints

Some bureaucratic policies create stumbling blocks. Union contracts, and rules promulgated by the National Labor Relations Board can prevent creating teams at will.[5] In particular, if you establish a team to deal with collective bargaining issues, such as compensation, benefits, work rules, or work hours, you could run afoul of the Labor Relations Act, which proscribes the freedom of organizations to form what even resembles a company union.

When Employee or Management Readiness Is Lacking

It takes a group of self-managed people to make up a high-performance team. You need people who are ready to accept the philosophy and who are ready to do what it takes to make a team succeed. That someone has reached the age of maturity or earned an M.B.A. doesn't automatically qualify him or her to perform as an effective team member. People need to learn how to work together well in teams, especially where teamwork is countercultural.

The lack of readiness at the Caribbean facility of an international metals mining and manufacturing company (which remains anonymous because of confidentiality agreements), nearly scuttled the entire operation. The mother company decided in 1990 to convert from individual responsibilities in different departments to team-based responsibilities, but no one was ready to meet that challenge. Consultants helped them see that (1) management came mainly from the U.S., was predominantly white, and was, as a group, untrained in the local culture and ignorant of team management; (2) the nonmanagement personnel were predominantly islanders, largely undereducated, and, as a group, untrained in team functioning, group problem solving, and group decision making. Forming a team when people aren't ready or trained leads to missed opportunities, poor results, grievances, or legal problems.

When to Form Teams: Organizational Conditions

Forming teams, especially self-managed teams, can be risky business. The people should be capable of using self-management skills or should be willing to learn; either way, don't ask them to take on responsibilities before they're ready. Indeed, you have to prepare even self-managed people for new roles. Most of all, before forming temporary, or ad hoc, teams or permanent semiautonomous or self-managed teams, consider the organizational conditions that may or may not call for their creation.

Condition 1. Specific business goals or strategies should call for creating teams at all levels of the organization and for specific reasons. Simply tacking on teams to a strategy that doesn't include them as an integral part of the strategy invites failure. Instead, adopt the Corning, Inc. model. Turning Corning plants over to self-managed teams fulfilled specific business goals or strategies that mandate creating a team or teams. Corning management planned for long-term results it

wants teams to produce: e.g., more employee ownership of the processes of production, reduced costs, greater customer satisfaction. The
lesson is thus clear: Carefully define team goals and spell out why a
team would better achieve them than would an individual or a gorup
of individuals working separately.

   *Condition 2. Strategic requirements should permit sufficient time
for teams to do their work.* When the strategy requires and the organization provides sufficient time for discussing and debating decisions,
teams work well. Teams grappling with long-term problems, in particular, need the time to collect the data, interpret it, identify and prioritize the issues, and give alternative solutions or plans sufficient time
to percolate and to take operational shape. Taking a long view regarding how to do business may have a sense of urgency about it but it
usually doesn't demand immediate action. That doesn't preclude giving ad hoc, problem-solving teams sufficient time as well.

   Strategic teams and ad hoc teams differ in kind and in objective.
A strategic team has long-term objectives affecting large portions or
the whole organization and is best served by multidisciplined people
representing different parts of the organization. Ad hoc teams usually
meet an emergency and are usually best served by people who have
the expertise or skill for solving a specific problem. Gene Kranz, Mission Control director for the Apollo 13 mission, formed his Tiger
Team to help save the lives of the Apollo 13 crew by pulling experts
from one shift out of their usual rotation and setting them aside for
solving specific problems as they arose.

   Still, successful ad hoc teams don't just happen. The Apollo 13
team's success derived, in part, from protocols NASA has built into
strategic plans for creating Tiger Teams. Life-and-death events drove
the team's time pressures, but they rose to their challenges because
the organization had given them time to practice being a Tiger Team.
That the fifteen men in Kranz's Tiger Team knew one another and
had worked together in the past as a high-performance team made
them as effective as they were. Additionally, they had been trained
and prepared for "SWAT Team" tactics: worst-case planning, problem
identification, and creative problem solving. You can't have that kind
of readiness without strategically expecting the unexpected.[6]

   *Condition 3. Strategies must recognize the value of two heads
working together and reward them for doing so.* When fulfilling a

strategy requires knowledge or skills one person alone can't provide, especially in today's high-tech world, two heads probably are better than one. No one, not even the CEO, should presume she can answer all the company's major problems. Why should one person assume that sort of responsibility? It can only jeopardize the success of the organization.

Jack Stack, CEO of Springfield Remanufacturing Corporation, takes advantage of the synergies created by working together, not only in business but in everything he does, including coaching his son's Little League baseball team. Teaching each child the fundamentals and the rules of the game worked well, up to a point, but he and his co-coach realized that they also had to teach the boys the fundamentals of winning as a team. This paid off handsomely when the team was confronted by an unusual pitcher, a bigger, heavier kid, with "an unbelievable fast ball."

By the third inning, neither coach had figured out how to get their kids to hit that fast ball, and defeat seemed inevitable. Rather than let the young players flounder to defeat, however, they asked them for ideas, and one boy had the answer: "He's too fast for his own catcher. He can't catch the third strike if you swing at it." The rules permit the batter to steal first base on a dropped third strike, and the team made use of them, "stealing like crazy, scoring runs [and] in the end [winning] the game, 5 to 3—without getting a hit."[7] Using all the heads you've got, when it's appropriate, makes awfully good business sense.

Condition 4. Strategies should create flexible, permeable relationships among separate groups that allow teams to recruit what they need when what they need is not immediately available. Not having the knowledge or skills a team needs in your own work group shouldn't present a barrier to forming one. Recruit the talent from another part of the organization and create a cross-functional team. If the talent needed is not available anywhere in the organization, time permitting, use headhunters. *Warning:* Make sure the talent you recruit has team skills as well as technical abilities.

Condition 5. Strategy needs to make provisions for training people to do the work of teams. Take people out of different individual roles (management and nonmanagement alike) and form them into teams only if they can do the work of the teams. Not only do people have to know how to do their individual jobs, they have to have team-related task and process skills. Here's where training people to be self-managed helps teams succeed. Self-managed people are competent at what they do, and they are also capable of relating well to the needs of other people and to the group as a whole. Hark back to Kranz's Tiger Team, if you will. His White Team members were properly prepared to take on the emergencies they faced.

One way to raise people's readiness to accept teams is to provide them with "as needed real-time" training. Instead of creating artificial classroom situations or simulations, training should focus on solving real problems or on making actual changes from a current condition to a desirable future state. The consultants working in the situation on the Caribbean island described earlier began the change process by bringing together groups of expatriate managers and island supervisors to work on production or equipment maintenance problems—not to sit through classes on team building. They learned the basic principles of team effectiveness *by working together as a team* to solve a specific and real-life problem. At the end of their sessions, they not only had solved some production and maintenance problems, they could also transfer the process to other group activities. They had learned how to become a team by being a team.

When to Form Teams: Desired Results

Form teams when the results you want lend themselves to the way in which teams work. You can use teams most effectively when you want to raise the quality of decisions or actions, prevent emergencies, lower the risk of failure, increase the acceptance of decisions, improve vertical or horizontal relationships, and increase collaboration and improve implementation.

Raising the Quality of Decisions or Actions

Getting more brain power to work on a problem usually raises the quality of the decisions made or actions taken. Most managers assume that in times of emergency more than one head is working on the problem, but assumptions can lead to disaster. A *deliberate effort* to add the competencies of one person to those of another removes the risk associated with assuming that different opinions or talents have been brought to bear on the problem.[8] Unless a team's objective is to consciously improve on what an individual or a group of individuals working alone can achieve, why bother?

Preventing Emergencies

Another danger: Remember that old saying about closing the barn door after the cows got out? Waiting for and reacting to emergencies closes the barn door too late. Staying alert to signals (experiencing a healthy anxiety about the future) prevents the barn door from flying open. Low employee morale or apathy, high turnover, late deliveries, defects: Sound the alarm when you see these wisps of smoke.

That's what Eric Gershman, president and founder of Published Image, did with his small but multimillion-dollar newsletter publishing house. Although the company didn't suffer any serious troubles, he sensed something was wrong (low morale, high turnover); in spite of steps already taken, the company wasn't doing as well as it could. To prevent further erosion, he created self-managed teams that took responsibility for making the operation work better. Almost immediately morale increased, turnover dropped, and company revenue doubled, while profit margin increased from 3 percent to 20 percent. Once each employee felt that he had a stake in his part of the business, he saw to it that his part succeeded.[9] Don't just react to emergencies, prevent them.

Lowering the Risk of Failure

Preventing emergencies means planning for them and for what to do should conditions indicate they're imminent. Teamwork lowers the risk of failure. People from diverse backgrounds and different skills or values can work together to test new designs, processes, activities, or new ways of serving your customers' interests before they're rolled out. Asking several people with different viewpoints and skills to evaluate something new, rather than make the decision on your own, gives it a better chance of succeeding. Almost all new product marketing campaigns, in almost all organizations, are the products of multidisciplined teams rather than of one "marketing genius." Multidisciplined teams (users, designers, managers, trainers) always produce the electronic performance support systems designed by RWD Technologies, a consulting firm in Columbia, Maryland; this approach reduces the possibility that the system won't do what it's supposed to do for the user and for the company.[10] Following good models like these will reduce the number of emergencies you face and lower the risk of failure when trying something new; not following those models can produce a disaster.

Increasing Acceptance of Decisions

One common reason new ideas fail is that the people most affected by them or who have to implement them don't accept them. Consider the disaster MCI Communications Corp. experienced when, in 1991, "the chief technology officer . . . decided to relocate MCI's . . . 4,000 employee Systems Engineering division . . . from MCI's Washington, D.C., headquarters to Colorado Springs." Why? In spite of warnings from other executives, the CTO, an avid skier, "believed the mountains, low crime rate, healthy climate and rock-bottom real-estate prices would be 'a magnet for the best and brightest' computer-software engineers." Many of the rank-and-file employees accepted generous relocation packages, but "numerous key executives and engineers, and hundreds of the division's 51 percent minority population said no, or fled . . . soon after relocating." The cost to MCI for the chief's single-minded decision has been in the hundreds of millions of dollars, as well as in the loss of many of its finest minds.[11]

Consider the sound approach Robin Landew Silverman took when she and her husband felt compelled to move their large, well-established downtown haberdashery business in Grand Forks, North Dakota, to a suburban mall. In her words, the couple "decided to let the staff lead us."[12] They explained the situation in detail to everyone, and, taking them on a field trip to the unfinished new location, she told them that the success of the move wouldn't "be possible without the full, unconditional efforts of all of you."

The staff then formed a team to oversee the moving sale, another to handle the details of the move itself, and a third to organize the grand opening of the new store. Only three people out of their very large management and retail staffs failed to make the transition with them, and the Silvermans had to let two of those three go because they couldn't meet the demands of their new jobs. The company was much smaller than MCI but not much smaller than the MCI division that moved to Denver, but the lesson is clear nonetheless. The greater the employee involvement the more readily they will accept decisions and the lower the risk of failure during any dramatic change.

Here's another common, wrongheaded practice: recognizing a problem exists and calling in an outside expert (an industrial psychologist, an engineering consultant, etc.) to fix it. In a typical case, an expert drawing from her previous experience and education made suggestions that looked good on paper. Her fix-it recommendations failed, however, in spite of her good intentions, because she did not ask for input from the people who live with the problem and or get their buy-in to the final plan. Use experts, by all means, but, to promote acceptance of a decision or to maintain employee morale, ask the people who will be affected by the decision or will have to implement the new ideas to make the choices.

The moral: Listen to what people on the front line have to say, and act on what you hear if it makes good business sense. Consider also how important the decision is to those people; the greater its importance, the more morale will be affected if you make the decision without involving them.

Improving Vertical or Horizontal Relationships

The same reasoning applies when what the team produces could affect either vertical or horizontal relationships within the larger organization. Different people at different times in different positions have to work together. Cross-functional work teams or problem-solving teams "grease the skids," and take the rough spots out of transitions (including transitioning from an individual-centered to a team-focused organization). When representatives of different parts of the business work together to invent a new way of doing business or to solve a problem, it becomes easier to promote their decision or action throughout the organization. These are the principles applied in many of the companies I've described in this book, including General Electric.[13]

Increasing Collaboration and Improving Implementation

Transitioning during times of dramatic change, implementing new ideas, and reorganizing processes are in many ways a lot like operating a restaurant. It sometimes takes more than one cook to make the soup, at least one other person to serve it, and several people to clean up the mess if the customer throws the soup onto the floor in disgust. Otherwise, you're sure to hear: "Not my job," "Not my fault," "I didn't do it." Not only won't customers come back, but they will take two or three (or more) potential customers out the door with them. When implementation depends on the collaboration of a variety of people, giving them the opportunity to plan the implementation almost always guarantees the success of the final product.

Notes

1. Dick Richardson, "Teams not always the best way to get work done," *HR News* (August 1996), p. 1. See also Brian Dumaine, "The Trouble with Teams," *Fortune* (September 5, 1994), pp. 86–92.
2. Interview with Richard Hagberg (consultant), in Linda Grant, "Rambos in Pinstripes: Why So Many CEOs Are Lousy Leaders," *Fortune* (June 24, 1996), p. 147.
3. Reported in *Nature Genetics* (January 1996) and summarized in *St. Louis Post Dispatch* (January 2, 1996), p. 4A. For the business school debate, see Marc Hequet, "Risk," *Training* (June 1996), p. 86.
4. David Newton, cited in "Risk," p. 86.
5. Genaro C. Armas, "Plant's Work Teams Ignite Debate," *St. Louis Post-Dispatch* (February 10, 1996), p. B1. See also Glenn Burkins, "Senate Debates Right to Set Up Worker Teams," *Wall Street Journal* (July 10, 1996), pp. B1, B7; "Unions Win One and Lose One in Senate," *St. Louis Post-Dispatch* (July 11, 1996), pp. 1A, 10A; "Senate Vote Gives Employers Leeway on Labor Teams," *Wall Street Journal* (July 11, 1996), p. A18; Leon Rubis, "TEAM Act sent to Clinton," *HR News* (August 1996), pp. 1, 9.
6. Lovell and Kluger, p. 159.
7. Jack Stack, "That Championship Season," *Inc.* (July 1996), p. 27.
8. Jim Lovell and Jeffrey Kluger, *Lost Moon: The Perilous Voyage of Apollo 13* (New York, Boston: Hougton Mifflin, 1994), p. 159.
9. Michael Selz, "Testing Self-Managed Teams, Entrepreneur Hopes to Lose Job," *Wall Street Journal* (January 11, 1994), pp. B1–B2.
10. Robert Riner and Catherine Witt, "Methods and Skills for Designing Electronic Performance Support Systems," unpublished paper presented at the National Conference of the American Society for Training and Development, Orlando, Fla., June 1996.

11. Alex Markels, "Innovative MCI Unit Finds Culture Shock in Colorado Springs," *Wall Street Journal* (June 25, 1996), pp. A1 and A8.
12. Robin Landew Silverman, "A Moving Experience," *Inc.* (August 1996), pp. 23–24.
13. Mary Buchel, "Accelerating Change: Three Approaches for Making Organizational Transitions Easier, Quicker, and More Effective" *Training and Development* (April 1996), p. 48. See also Noel M. Tichy and Stratford Sherman, *Control Your Destiny or Someone Else Will* (New York: Harper Books, 1994), pp. 83, 240–244.

Other Sources

Harrington-Mackin, Deborah. *The Team Building Tool Kit: Tips, Tactics, and Rules for Effective Workplace Teams* (New York: AMACOM, 1994).

20

How to Harness the Power of Wild Geese †

Liberty will not descend to a people; a people must raise themselves to liberty; it is a blessing that must be earned before it can be enjoyed.

—Charles C. Colton, British author (1780–1832)

Just as the whole flock supports all the birds in the formation, the whole organization must support the people in all work group configurations. Harnessing the power of a gaggle of geese depends not only on the efficiency of individual group members but also on how well manager-leaders, from the senior executives to the team leaders, follow the three rules of organizational behavior I listed in Chapter 15. Manager-leaders can help people raise themselves to liberty.

> To make a team as good as a gaggle of geese requires the support of the entire organization and requires manager-leaders to provide the systems and opportunities for the team to flourish.

In the storm window factory where I worked (described in Chapter 15), our interaction with units downstream essentially formed an ad hoc, self-managed team. We often discussed shapes and sizes of cuts (glass or frames) that would make assembly easier or safer for both the framers and the glass. We talked about rough edges and how to eliminate them. Sometimes we came in early to talk about those things. Sometimes we talked them over during lunch. No foremen were involved. No one told us to do this. Without knowing what we were doing, we had formed quality circles of our own. (An added bonus: A racially mixed group, we did our own sensitivity training by discussing our lives.)

Today the kind of "team" we had created has become mandated in many organizations and takes two basic forms: self-managed teams and semiautonomous teams. Here I'll talk about how to support semiautonomous groups, and in the next chapter, I'll describe how to evolve them into self-managed teams.

Semiautonomous Teams

In most organizations, teams are semiautonomous and are composed of management and nonmanagement employees working together. Here management holds on to the right to finalize decisions, with advice and consultation (not consent) from the team. The most effective semiautonomous teams have manager-leaders who can facilitate team activities and not be "the boss." This is the real meaning of the quote from magazine publisher Carol A. Tabor in Chapter 14: "Hire the people and then delegate."

In the current political atmosphere surrounding work teams, with Congress hoping to change restrictions the National Labor Relations Act places on how work teams are formed, management has to watch how much control it exercises over teams. Controlling what they do, how they vote, and on what they vote undermines the whole purpose of creating teams. Management control of employee-management committees creates a barrier to worker input. In a public show of hands, how many nonmanagement employees will raise a hand in opposition to a management wish? Hand counting happens at some of the most "progressive" companies.[1]

I've witnessed this phenomenon in many organizations, going back to my faculty meeting days in the University of Texas system (over twenty-five years ago). Likewise, administrative-law judge Marvin Roth chides Polaroid for giving "lip service" to the independence of its Employee Owner Influence Council, citing its practice of asking "for a show of hands when members were polled on such policies as the company's employee stock option plan."

To shield teams from even the perception of cooptation do the following:

- ✈ Define their roles carefully to ensure they don't infringe on employee rights to collective bargaining, and involve nonmanagement personnel in the process of defining those roles.
- ✈ Don't ask team members to speak for all employees when discussing work rules, work hours, compensation or benefits plans, and other broad workforce issues, which would place the team in the role of company union (a bargaining group selected by and run by management).
- ✈ Train nonmanagement employees in team leadership and management, which would place team members in a position to perform those roles in the team successfully.
- ✈ Call on trained people to lead teams and to select team members. Managers should either not be involved in these leadership and selection roles, or, if they are, they should work in collaboration with the nonmanagers.
- ✈ Impose as few managers as possible on the teams to ensure that nonmanagement employees make essential decisions.
- ✈ Truly empower teams by giving them as much freedom as possible to make decisions and to act on those decisions.

These are tough prescriptions, but they legitimate and support the team concept.

Harnessing Gaggle Power: Organizational Responsibilities

That African proverb "It takes a whole village to raise a child" can be modified to apply to leading teams: "It takes a whole organization to lead a high-performance team." To understand how to lead a high-performance team, you first have to understand what it takes to harness its power.

Knowing What, Why, and How

Work groups of any kind, high-performance teams in particular, fail when senior executives don't understand the company's core business or don't understand the core business of the work groups they create. They react like Ralph, the VP of Human Resources in the comic strip "Sally Forth." After upper management mandates the HR department to form a cross-functional team, he tells Sally to let the team do "anything that'll sound good to the management weenies who came up with this garbage . . . until it goes in the dumper. . . ."[2]

You may laugh, but it does happen. To prevent that kind of reaction, tie ordinary work group or team goals and tactics directly to business goals as key elements in company strategies. For instance, if an organizational goal includes reducing operating costs by 10 percent, strategy should refer to forming teams to accomplish that goal; the teams formed then have mandates to take steps for reducing operating costs by whatever margins are appropriate to those teams. Otherwise, you can't obey the three rules of organizational behavior or form the right kinds of teams.

Systems for Supporting Teams

Teams differ from ordinary work groups in that a team's activities require high levels of communication and collaboration among members in order to achieve its goals. If team activities are to succeed, management must go beyond the basics of hiring the best people and delegating. It must also provide training and systems support for managing team activities. At the very least, the organization should create mechanisms whereby teams can have regular communication meetings. If it has computers, the organization should provide a local area network (a LAN, the intranet) with e-mail as one way to communicate. Such tools are a minimum requirement for building teams today, especially if the organization is trying to reengineer or redesign the way work is done.

Reengineering or redesigning work should be used for increasing productivity, meeting customer needs, improving the organization's competitive edge, and increasing profits, not merely as an excuse for reducing headcount. A study by the American Management Association asserts that between 1989 and 1994, cost cutting by big companies has increased operating profits by only 50.6 percent and worker productivity by only 34.4 percent, while decreasing employee morale by 86.0 percent. Sales staffs turn in lousy numbers. Chronic complaining about too few doing too much work with longer hours and fewer resources chokes the atmosphere (the so-called survivor syndrome). Productivity falls as morale plummets. Providing the proper training and support systems for working with a leaner workforce avoids what some wags are calling "corporate anorexia"[3] (i.e., reengineering that starves the organization to death).

Redesigning Work for Long-Term Gains

Previously too many senior managers had become too happy with the short-term gains created by laying off people. But very few companies that have downsized before will opt to ever do it again.[4] Downsizing should be a precipitate of reengineering, not its goal. Even when downsizing results from reengineering or redesigning work, the organization should provide for taking care of the people who do the work, the "survivors" (now called "retained employees"). Productivity will improve only if you recognize people's needs and provide a productive work environment for them. That type of reengineering requires proactive management.

Walking the Talk When Creating Teams

If the organization thinks well enough of teams to create them, then the organization has to act as if teams really mean something. Reward outstanding teams and let the teams reward outstanding individuals. Encourage risk taking and accept failing when the effort is made in good faith. Only then will people take risks. Think the way Tom Watson, the former CEO of IBM, did (according to the probably apocryphal) story. An account executive blew a $5 million deal, the oft-told tale recounts, and he figured the boss would fire him: "Fire you?" Watson exclaimed. "Hell! We just invested $5 million in your education." Investing in long-term gains takes the sting out of immediate expense.

Team-Building Roadblocks

The organization also has to take a proactive stance with regard to the problems inherent in team building.

➤ *Many people find the responsibilities of leadership overwhelming.* They have a deadly fear of leading for one or more of four common reasons: (1) fear of failure, (2) fear of being blamed if things go wrong, (3) fear of making bad decisions that affect people's lives, and (4) fear of losing friends. As a manager-leader, you can help such people overcome their fears by providing them with short-lived, easy-to-manage leadership opportunities, such as assigning that person to head a group collecting data for identifying a specific problem.

✦ *In a team-based environment, accountability is ambiguous and easily shirked.* Unless you and the group define the team's mission and individual roles carefully, writing down everything if necessary, it's easier in a team for people to say "Not my job" and let details fall through the cracks. You should help the team write its "constitution" and "contracts" to prevent shirking.

✦ *Not all tasks lend themselves to being done by teams, and not all individuals should or can be team players.*[5] When you create a team where none is needed, you run the risk of interfering with individual productivity. People will be spending too much time talking about work rather than working.

Likewise, as I implied earlier, when you select a person to work on a team whose work life has consisted solely of individual performance and individual achievement, you run the risk that that person will disrupt the process dynamics of the group; she's too task-oriented to fit into a group in which process is important. Find a peripheral role for the loner that contributes to the group's success without making too many process demands on that person, or, if that's not possible, provide the person with extensive group dynamics training.

✦ *Use of teams can create a paradox: Cross-training conflicts with specialization, while "multiskilling" can dilute quality.* Yet, without cross-training, teamwork in teams is impossible. People need to know what other people on the team are doing. For example, in a baseball team, although most players perform best in an individual position, they also may be called upon to play another position—that is, the catcher may be assigned to play first base if the team requires it. Everyone on the team knows the fundamentals of each position and can perform them in a pinch. Only if you permanently place a specialist in one field into the role of a different specialist will you probably hurt group performance.

✦ *Management may expect teams, especially self-managed teams, to be perfect groups composed of perfect people who can pro-*

duce immediate results. The antidote to excessive demands is well known and discussed often by HR professionals: Give people time to climb a steep learning curve; let them learn how to do the basics of their tasks and how to manage group processes before asking them to take on additional or more-complex tasks or processes.

Harnessing Gaggle Power: Organizational Managers' Responsibilities

The single most important thing senior managers can do to help teams is to set the direction and get out of the way. (Okay. So technically that's two things.) Letting high-performance teams perform amounts to managing the vision, not the daily routine.

Managing the Vision

To prevent teams from failing, senior executives have to pull their arms out of the muck of daily activities. Strategy, not process, should concern them. They should stretch their imaginations because the rest of the organization needs them to look ahead and to exercise a healthy anxiety about the future.[6] They need to manage the vision, not the operations. But, what does that mean?

- Develop a customer-focused competitive strategy that drives the system yet remains open to change and expansion.
- Become the eyes, ears, and mouth of the organization. Study the environment and chart the course.
- Build strategic alliances.
- Build relationships with all constituencies, especially with customers, suppliers, vendors, the general public, and (where necessary) the government.
- Communicate, communicate, communicate.

Actually, getting out of the way makes it possible for senior managers to find many other ways for unlocking the competence, coordination, and commitment of high-performance teams.

Cutting-Edge Management Models

You can't rely on outmoded business and management models when installing methods as cutting edge as empowering employees. Too often, managers, no matter what else they do, are still *talking to* employees when they should be *listening to* them. Orit Gadiesh, chairman of Bain & Company, pointedly states that "trouble starts when people are afraid to talk to the boss and ideas don't reach the top."[7]

Many old-style managers can learn new tricks, but they don't always like to do it. Ralph, in "Sally Forth," responds in an all-too-familiar way. Two days after their first conversation, Sally has put Ralph on the team. He then complains: "I asked you to form a team, not to put me on it." When Sally replies that the mission statement defines the department manager's new role as that of *coach*, he dismisses the title with, "I prefer to be called, 'O Exalted One.'" In another strip, Sally reminds Ralph of their new managerial motto: "Influence without authority," to which he replies that he likes his old motto better: "Authority without question."

So, laugh again, but many senior executives today reflect Henry Ford's turn-of-the-century values with regard to employees. "Why is it," he lamented, "I always get the whole person when what I really want is a pair of hands?"

To manage teams successfully, you can't be a Ralph or a modern-day Henry Ford. No one likes to be treated as a pair of hands—as less than a whole person. It's a truism that the whole person comes to work. Treat employees only as a pair of hands, demand obedience to authority, and you'll create a hostile workforce willing to destroy their own jobs in order to sink the company's ship. Many sources can provide you with the latest fads that claim to manage human factors business, but how do you find cutting-edge management models that work?

Copying Success

Redesign your own thinking about how work gets done in your organization by becoming more process-oriented. Replace thinking of individual contributions in terms of jobs and think of them as aspects of a flow of events. (The idea of *the job* may already be a dinosaur.)[8]

Benchmark practices from companies closely related to your

own, especially if they are complementary rather than competitive. Some highly regarded companies include:

Saturn:	where anyone can stop the line
AES:	which includes making work "fun" in its corporate mission
SRC:	which practices Open Book Management
American Standard:	where working capital works

When looking for new management models, find new and flexible forms of work organization in your industry or type of business; seek out HR systems and work practices linked to processes that enhance commitment and learning. When copying these new models, link any new or different system to your company's organizational goals and strategies and create a culture that is consistent and compatible with those goals and strategies. That means aligning individual, work group, or team goals and objectives with company strategies, values, and day-to-day work practices. It means setting "decision boundaries" among different levels of the organization, thereby making responsibilities, accountabilities, and limits clear to everyone. It also means using all of the organization's resources—human, material, and technological—hooking them together in a coordinated system of interlocking processes or activities designed to create products or deliver a service.

When bringing resources to bear, support teams with team-oriented technology and management systems. Then design team-based performance management and appraisal systems through which you can manage team accountabilities. Senior managers should manage the team's *organization process.* They should then let the team leaders and team members manage *individual accountabilities.* The reward system may have to be changed to manage rewards for outstanding teams while letting the teams reward outstanding individual members. Open all communication networks, including informal channels, to everyone.

Supporting Teams

Support for teams includes modeling team behavior, providing "as-needed real-time training," tracking performance, creating "guerilla teams" (ad hoc groups) where appropriate, and, most of all, listening. These five means of support are described as follows:

1. *Modeling team behavior.* Encourage collaboration, if not teams, by creating an atmosphere of trust, openness, and mutual support. Model teamwork by creating and working with teams in the executive suite (as they do at Xerox and Microsoft Corp, where both permanent and ad hoc teams "reap productivity benefits through responsiveness and adaptability").[9] Not only does the company reap the benefits, so, too, do the employees, but no one benefits unless they know what to do and how to do it.

2. *"As-needed real-time" training.* Training is the most neglected aspect of team building. Experience with companies shows that most of them that do create teams throw them into the deep end of the pool without providing the floaties of training. Tie team training to strategies responsive to the demands of business goals and of teamwork: "as-needed real-time" training. Here's a *partial* list of topics to integrate into team development:

- Process improvement methods and tools
- Creative problem-solving skills
- Meeting management skills
- Team/group dynamics
- Leadership skills
- Conflict management skills
- Stress and self-management skills

3. *Tracking team performance.* After helping teams design and implement their tactical plans, design appropriate tracking systems. Many companies, especially closely held companies, have no methods, or at best sketchy methods, for tracking individual performance, let alone team performance. Performance tracking tools measure improvement applications, such as focus, accountability, cycle time, and responsiveness. Without baseline data and tracking systems, you have no way of knowing whether or not team building has had any added value for the company.

4. *Supporting guerilla teams.* Support guerilla teams, like the "skunkworks" team at Data General Corp. that "developed a new

minicomputer way ahead of competitors."[10] Guerilla teams don't have to be renegade squads of corporate Rambos if given a chance to provide creativity and innovation. Let ad hoc teams, especially R&D teams, do their own thing as long as they contribute to the organization's overall vision. Make resources available or at least don't punish people for "midnight requisitioning." Maintain a hands-off policy and restrain that impulse to look over people's shoulders. Satisfy requests for shifting duties, if necessary, for time to contribute to the guerilla team's efforts. These teams can give your company a competitive edge regardless of the size or type of industry you're in.

5. *Listening, the springboard to action.* Telling is only half of communicating. Listening is the other, more important, half. Open the system to all participants. Open the books to all employees. Use both formal and informal channels to spread your messages and, then, to hear the messages coming at you from all directions. Listen and you might be amazed at what you hear.

After listening, act on what you hear—especially if it makes sense—even if it means reshaping the organization's vision. When no one heeds what people say, opportunities are lost. For many years after World War II, railroad workers said out loud that passenger and freight transportation would grow but that customers would seek new ways of transporting themselves or goods from one place to another. If anyone was listening, they didn't do anything. So they let trucking and airline companies take their customers away. Management assumed they were in the railroad business rather than in the transportation business. They were narrowly product-oriented rather than customer-focused and were deaf and blind to their own future.

In sum, to create an environment that nurtures teams, senior executives should lead as well as manage. Set the direction, launch the ship, and let the crew sail it to its ports of call. And, why not? That's why you hire crews in the first place.

Making the ship available, provisioning it, charting a course around the reefs and shoals, sending out the right messages to everyone at the right time—those are senior executives' most effective roles. Even the U.S. military recognizes these principles. When's the last time you saw a general leading a reconnaissance platoon (which is a semiautonomous team in the mold I've described)?

Harnessing Gaggle Power:
Team Leaders' Personal Responsibilities

Now, what's your role in leading high-performance teams if you are given the title *team* leader? To be a coach, as Sally Forth told her boss, Ralph? Or is there more to it than that?

It used to be that team leaders thought they were responsible for improving the group's work, setting priorities, or solving problems. Well, that doesn't work any more. Team members have to take responsibility for improving their own work. They have to set their own priorities within the limitations of the team's priorities (or justify stepping outside the boundaries). They have to solve their own problems. Set goals and/or priorities, or lead the team through the process, and get out of the way, as well as coach the team when you can or when it's appropriate. Along with internal and external communication, getting commitment, and training people to work together as a team, there are other steps you can take.

Share Leadership

Understand and take advantage of the fact that even a self-managed team is not leaderless, and if you are appointed to be team leader, you have to share that leadership. Leadership in a high-performance team is fluid, following expertise, skill, interest, or influence. Encourage team growth and team learning by sharing leadership when appropriate (e.g., rotate meeting chairpersons). By constituting teams with self-managed people, you can empower team members to take responsibility for themselves and for the team's results.

Allocate and Track Work Assignments

Work with the team to analyze or allocate the way work is performed. Establish baseline performance data. Without this baseline, you have no way of knowing if the team is getting any better results than before there was a team. Define areas of work to be studied and the way things could be or should be. Describe the current situation. Identify conditions or processes in need of change. Design action plans. Implement and monitor progress. You can't reward the team for process improvement unless you can prove they improved the process.

Facilitate Team Process Dynamics

You also have to work with the team to analyze the way the group is working (its norms, its decision-making processes, its communication). Since this is critical, it might be better done by someone outside of the team itself. An outside facilitator has no ax to grind and can remain above the storm when one breaks out.

But, if you must act as team facilitator, here's a list of essential steps you can and should take to help the team facilitate its task and process activities:

1. *Manage meetings.* Managing meetings involves four basic rules. First, publish an agenda and distribute it before the day of the meeting. Second, stick to the agenda during the meeting. Third, review the meeting's results. Fourth, set flexible plans and a date for the next meeting.
2. Help the team agree on clear meeting goals, member roles, and operating procedures.
3. Create an open, trusting, and candid environment in which all members contribute.
4. Discourage disruptive behavior. Use the Group Process Feedback when appropriate.
5. Encourage problem-solving discussions of differences and disagreements; discourage conflict.
6. Guide team decision-making processes using consultative techniques; don't tell people what to do or solve their problems for them.
7. Communicate clearly with all team members, actively listening as well as telling.
8. Observe and accurately interpret team task and process dynamics. Use the Team Productivity Assessment when appropriate.

Facilitating its own process-oriented behaviors and taking corrective action when necessary are essential for raising the team to high performance.

Not only do you have to analyze how the team is functioning as a team, you need also to analyze the relationships among team members. Here's another way you act as a linking agent, not only with the world external to the team but with the individual members themselves.

Although you'll want to encourage the team to facilitate its own process-oriented behavior and to take corrective action when necessary, you don't want to abdicate this responsibility. Everyone has their own way of making contributions to the team (i.e., their contribution behavior preferences). So, identify your own contribution behavior preferences and those of your team members, and don't overlook the able-bodied sailors—the administrators—who prefer to carry out orders rather than to create or to enhance ideas.

Without these people, the ship can't sail. High-performance work teams, composed of very creative people, generate great ideas, debate them, argue them, hash out marvelous plans. Then they turn the plans over to the administrative people to flesh out the details and execute them. Thank goodness for that; otherwise nothing would ever get done.

Rewarding

Just as the organization has to reward teams as a whole for outstanding work, so too do you have to reward your team as a whole. Then allow the team to devise ways to reward individual members for outstanding work. That way you can't be accused of playing favorites, and the team takes responsibility for holding its members accountable for what they have to do.

Managers from "the old school" have difficulty with conducting a performance appraisal for someone they may not observe doing the work of the team. Some of their employees may never do any work apart from cross-functional teams. Others may work on network-based virtual teams and rarely come into their managers' presence.

Traditional performance appraisals won't work in these situations, and to that extent, W. Edwards Deming was correct in excoriating performance appraisals.[11] However, you're appraising other people's work whenever you accept it, pat them on the back for it, or take corrective action to improve it. Without a formal system, you can run into a pack of avoidable legal hassles. Only by redesigning how individual performance is appraised and rewarded can you make the system work. You can use 360-degree feedback for helping people identify areas in need of improvement (but not as a performance appraisal) and then use peer reviews for performance management. You can also base rewards on some sort of gain sharing or other bonus system in which everyone gets a fair share of productivity gains.

Self-Management

If you're appointed or elected to be the team leader, don't panic. Susan Caminiti, writing in *Fortune,* makes this important point: "The job of team leader is an unscientific blend of instinct, on-the-job learning, and patience."[12] The skill sets of self-management (wholeness, self-confidence, self-awareness, self-respect/self-esteem, drive, and respect for others) also characterize effective manager-leaders of semiautonomous teams. People are not born leaders. They have to learn how to do it, just as they have to learn any other skill.

Some teams may not have managers, but all teams have leaders. Most are appointed or elected, but status means little in a high-performance team. Each member of the team can and should think of himself as playing the dual role of leader-follower. Expertise, skill, knowledge, influence dictate the role each person should play at one time or another.

As a leader, you model what you expect other people to do. Your commitment to the team concept as well as to the team's mission does more to guide the team than anything else you can do. To revert to the ship metaphor: As a team leader you are a helmsman.

To see if you and your organization are ready for this role, complete the questionnaires in Appendix G before moving on to the next chapter.

Notes

1. Glenn Burkins, "Senate Debates Right to Set Up Worker Teams," *Wall Street Journal* (July 10, 1996), p. B7.
2. All references to Greg Howard and Craig MacIntosh's "Sally Forth" come from the *St. Louis Post-Dispatch,* week of June 19, 1995.
3. Bernard Wysocki, Jr., "Lean and Frail: Some Companies Cut Costs Too Far, Suffer Corporate Anorexia," *Wall Street Journal* (July 5, 1995), pp. A1, A5. See also Robert J. Grossman, "Damaged, Downsized Souls: How to Revitalize the Workplace," *HRMagazine* (May 1996), pp. 54–62.

4. Wysocki. See the American Management Association study cited earlier, and Alex Markels and Matt Murray, "Call It Dumbsizing: Why Some Companies Regret Cost-Cutting" *Wall Street Journal* (May 15, 1996), pp. A1, A6; and see Jack Stack's opinion of managers who define redesigning work as downsizing: "Our job is to prevent layoffs," in "Mad About Layoffs," *Inc.* (May 1996), p. 21. See also "Downsizing Firms See a Down Side," *St. Louis Post-Dispatch* (October 3, 1997), p. BP3.

5. See, Jack Gordon, "The Team Troubles That Won't Go Away," *Training* (August 1994), pp. 25–33; Thomas Petzinger, Jr., "The Front Lines: At Deere They Know a Mad Scientist May Be a Firm's Biggest Asset," *Wall Street Journal* (July 14, 1995), p. B1.

6. See Kenneth Labich, "Why Companies Fail," *Fortune* (November 14, 1995), who refers to this anxiety as a "wide-ranging, creative paranoia."

7. Cited in Labich.

8. William Bridges, "The End of the Job," *Fortune* (September 19, 1994), pp. 62–74.

9. Amanda Bennett, "Firms Run by Executive Teams Can Reap Rewards, Incur Risks," *Wall Street Journal* (February 5, 1992), pp. B1–B2.

10. Jon Katzenbach, "The Right Kind of Teamwork," *Wall Street Journal* (November 9, 1992), p. A10; Beverly Geber, "Guerilla Teams: Friend or Foe?" *Training* (June 1994), pp. 36–39.

11. W. Edwards Deming. *Out of the Crisis.* Cambridge, Mass.: MIT Press, 1986.

12. Susan Caminiti, "What Team Leaders Need to Know," *Fortune* (February 20, 1995), pp. 93–100.

Other Sources

A useful instrument from Carlson Learning Systems (C.A.R.E.) separates team member preferences into four categories: creating, advancing, refining, executing.

Beckhard, Richard. "Optimizing Team-building Efforts." *The Journal of Contemporary Business* (I:3, 1972).

Dumaine, Brian. "The Trouble With Teams." *Fortune* (September 5, 1994).

Holpp, Lawrence. "Applied Empowerment." *Training* (February 1994).

Labich, Kenneth. "Why Companies Fail." *Fortune* (November 14, 1994).

McCann, Dick, and Charles Margerison. "Managing High Performance Teams." *Training and Development* (November, 1989). McCann and Margerison divide team member preferences into exploring, advising, organizing, and controlling. It doesn't matter what instrument you use as long as it encourages people to contribute according to their own behavior preferences.

Self-Management Communications, Inc. "Get Organized! The Workgroup and Personal Performance Manager (for Windows), Version 2.0."

Sherriton, Jacalyn, and James L. Stern. *Corporate Culture: Removing the Hidden Barriers to Team Success.* New York: AMACOM, 1996.

Smith, Lee. "New Ideas From the Army (Really)." *Fortune* (September 19, 1994).

"The Journeys of Father Goose." ABC News' *20/20,* August 26, 1994. The story has since been fictionalized in the movie *Flying Home.*

Tosti, Donald, and Stephanie Jackson. "Alignment: How It Works and Why It Matters." *Training* (April 1994).

"Training Today: Tips for Teams." *Training* (February 1994).

21

Self-Managed Teams, or How to Soar With the Wild Geese

To be what we are, and to become what we are capable of becoming, is the only end of life.

—Robert Louis Stevenson (1850–1894)

Lo! the magnificent eagle darting across the sky to catch its prey. However, when it comes to teamwork, an eagle can't hold a goose's feathers. A gaggle of wild geese, whose coordination and commitment you see when they fly in formation, provides a much more usable model for self-managed teams than does any group of eagles.

Semiautonomous teams, no less than ordinary work groups, defer decision-making authority to management. Self-managed teams (SMTs), on the other hand, have decision-making authority delegated to them. SMTs therefore require more nurturing than other teams to make them successful. Their ability to take advantage of the best traits and behaviors of self-managed people separates SMTs from run-of-the mill teams. However, the whole organization has to be ready to create and support them, take responsibility for overcoming barriers, and see to it that each team has the resources necessary to succeed (not just survive).

> A self-managed team has to be free to function with little more than guidance and direction from the organization's management.

Self-Managed Teams

Theoretically any team is capable of becoming self-managed. To be one, any kind of team—an executive team, a work team, a project team, or an ad hoc team—has to be free to function with little more than guidance and direction from the organization's management. It's a team in which every member is a leader according to his or her abilities and responsibilities. In self-managed teams, all the members are leaders.

SMTs are composed of self-activated "leader-followers" committed to the team and to the team's mission (although no one is appointed leader or manager).[1] The name refers to *how* the team functions rather than to *who* sits on it or to *what* its task objective is.

In one sense, a self-managed team is leaderless. Yet, it has many leaders committed to the team and to the team's mission. That's the model set for others by the Saturn plant, Spring Hill, Tennessee, which has proven itself to be very popular with the workers as well as with management.[2]

In spite of the labor-management conflicts at McDonnell-Douglas, according to a recent report, by the end of 1998, 90 percent of the company's machinists will be organized into Saturn-like teams that will:

↑ Select their own leaders.
↑ Determine work schedules.
↑ Decide on what training they need.
↑ Take responsibility for quality.
↑ Decide how the team and its members will work.
↑ Take responsibility for cross-training their members.

These are just a few of the tasks assigned to SMTs.

The decision to create self-managed teams can't be made because it's the fad *du jour.* Creating SMTs requires dedication to action, not just to words. Experience shows, however, that only a small percentage of managers will do more than talk the talk about SMTs.[3] Leadership expert James O'Toole notes that, based on his experience, "Ninety-five percent of American managers today say the right thing. Five percent actually do it." Therefore, before you decide to make the move, look at what SMTs are and whether you should create them.

Empowerment of SMTs

You create a semiautonomous team when conditions (e.g., management policy) dictate that you retain decision-making authority. You create an SMT when management agrees that employees should be empowered to act on their own.

Empowerment in an SMT means allowing team members to act on the basis of team decisions without fear of being reprimanded or of being overruled by an executive decision rather than by a team decision.[4] This level of empowerment exists at Johnsonville Foods and is what makes SMTs at the company the model for SMTs everywhere.

Empowerment also means encouraging people to influence each other and then recognizing them as influencers. Empowerment like this happens only when an organization and all its people put these values into *practice* in the following ways:

- ➤ Leadership is shared. Team members contribute to and influence the team in ways appropriate to their individual abilities, skills, and preferences.
- ➤ The team's vision and mission are shared. Everyone is forward-looking, seeking challenges, initiating change.
- ➤ Responsibility for the team's results is shared.
- ➤ Responsiveness is shared. The entire team is willing to seek out opportunities for growth as well as to act on team decisions.
- ➤ Rewards for success are shared.

In practice is the operant phrase. The values have to be real rather than only espoused and must provide a tangible or intangible payoff of some kind for team members. As Thomas A. Stewart, contributing editor of *Fortune*, says, "You can blather on endlessly about teamwork and trust, but if your people don't see what's in it for them, don't expect them to listen."[5]

Remember, however, that self-managed teams are more appropriate in some environments than in others. Before deciding to create them, look carefully at what they are, how they function, and what barriers you may have to overcome to make them work effectively.

Self-Managed People and Self-Managed Teams

What kind of people do you need on an SMT? The short answer to that question is self-managed people. What that means to an SMT is expressed by a production worker at Corning, Inc.: "Everybody that works here is competitive . . . willing to work long hours . . . to be multiskilled and [to] learn how we can make the product better so we can be the best in quality and service to the customer."[6]

Those words put the values of an SMT in perspective. Its members want to be the best and to do the best they possibly can. Such people are truly empowered, self-managed people.

From an individual perspective, self-management consists of a set of skills that forms the foundation of leadership. It flows from within but can be learned and perfected through practice. As self-management transforms you as a person, it also becomes the tool through which you lead others and transform them from followers to leader-followers.

From a team perspective, self-management means that you harmonize the two dynamics of team life and work (task and process), recognizing which dynamic is important or immediate at any given time (prioritizing) and emphasizing it. Simultaneously, the team gives appropriate measure to the other dynamic as well. It's the same for a team as it is for an individual: Harmonize the various aspects of the team's life and work. That takes having a vision for your team and an action plan for getting out of it what you and the organization want or expect of it.

Just as a self-managed person integrates thoughts, feelings, emotions, values, and actions, so does a self-managed team. We can categorize the behaviors and values of SMTs under all six headings that describe a self-managed person: wholeness, self-confidence, self-awareness, drive, self-respect/self-esteem, and respect for others.

1. *Wholeness of a team.* Wholeness of a team, as in the case of the wholeness of a person, provides the background and support for managing the team, principally by recognizing and harmonizing to

the extent possible the experiences, thoughts, feelings, emotions, values, and actions of each team member. The wholeness of the team is also provided by harmonizing both the task and the process dynamics of the group. You might liken the task dynamics to linear thinking, the step-wise and analytic methods we use for organizing life and work that takes place only within the bigger context of the mission for your team. Executing that mission includes emotional values, creativity, flashes of insight, subjective decisions, and interpersonal or social relations. Team wholeness then comes from integrating both the linear, analytic side of its life and the nonlinear, subjective side.

2. *Self-confidence of a team.* Self-management comes in part from having a vision for the team, and believing in the rightness of that vision and in what you and the team, working together, can accomplish in regard to that vision.

3. *Self-awareness within a team.* Ongoing, honest self-assessment prevents a self-managed team from being smug and cocksure.

4. *Drive.* SMTs have task-related goals they have to achieve. To succeed, the team and its members need the energy to do what they have to do. They have to be self-starting and strong-willed with regard to meeting the team's and the members' goals and objectives. They also have to be willing to take risks and to make the most of the team's independence. And, they need the capacity for revitalizing the team regularly, renewing its sources of energy through proper doses of group recreation and celebration over successes, as well as by taking on new and exciting challenges.

5. *Self-respect/self-esteem.* Everyone has to take pride in the team, in the abilities and accomplishments of any of the teammates. Athletic teams make such excellent models of teamwork because of the pride they take in their team's success and in the statistics individual players roll up. Walter Payton's offensive line on the Chicago Bears took responsibility to see to it that he became the greatest running back to ever carry a football. To them that meant more than just being good individual linemen. They rejoiced (even more than he did) with every record Payton set.

6. *Respect for others.* This magic bullet of self-managed people makes possible the work of a self-managed team. As I said early on and repeat here for emphasis: Without respect for others, throwing a

group of self-confident people filled with self-esteem into a room and
telling them to solve a problem could lead to open warfare. For other
people to give you respect, to care about you, they must feel you
respect them and care about them as well.

Take all of these self-management behaviors and values into account when creating self-managed teams, and apply the one integrating principle that pulls all five categories together: having a vision for
your teams. Unless that vision is built into the organization's strategies, and unless that strategy includes a demand for self-managed
teams, the teams and their members won't live up to any of these
prescriptions for self-management.

Operating Rules of an SMT

A whole team of totally self-managed people? Can you imagine what
that would be like? And, are you and your organization ready to
create an SMT? The key is that members of an SMT must recognize
that they are far from being leaderless. The SMT performs the functions of a traditional supervisor.

That means all the members have to assume the responsibilities,
accountabilities, authorities, and standards usually associated with *excellent* manager-leaders. Each member of an SMT exhibits, to some
degree, the characteristics of self-managed people: leaders who can
also follow. As self-managed people, they experience their own importance and the importance of what they do in the team. They participate as equals, as leader-followers, playing either role in response
to the group's needs. By virtue of their participating and sharing responsibility and accountability, they don't experience the we-they di-
chotomies that ravage so many teams. And that translates into three
usually unspoken rules:

1. Each member contributes to the team's success.
2. Each member is empowered and is influential; therefore no
    one has to struggle to gain power.
3. Each member performs his or her function and plays a variety
    of functional roles at different times (such as seeking informa-
    tion or giving information).

Anyone violating the rules must face whatever team self-regulating processes have been set in place, e.g., a "hearing" and expulsion from the team if a serious breach of trust has occurred.

Organizational Readiness

Deciding to create SMTs follows from considering if the organization *needs* them and is *ready* for them. If upper management wants to maintain traditional management controls over the teams, semiautonomous teams will suffice; they report directly to a manager and look to the manager for approval of or veto over many of the team's decisions. If the organization is willing to turn over many if not all managerial functions to the team, then it's ready to create an SMT.

To determine if a team is likely to outperform an individual or a group of individuals working separately, you need to see if the willingness to share leadership and responsibility is present in the group. If not, only radical changes can make it happen.

Before you can form an SMT, you, the senior managers, and nonmanagement personnel need to rethink your roles and revise your perceptions of your various objectives to focus on one and only one outcome: to achieve positive results for all stakeholders. How managers and nonmanagers achieve that outcome may vary, but their goal is the same. Therefore, managers have to learn not only how to assign certain of their responsibilities to the team but also how to delegate their authority and their accountability. The organization can form successful SMTs only after these changes in perceptions, values, and roles are made.

To change people's perceptions, values, and roles requires a reexamination of cultural demands and customs. These changes may require changing the limits of authority and making resources available to teams of nonmanagement employees that in the past were reserved to managers only: the account books, customer service reports, and the like. And most of all, the organization must create systems of communication that convey:

➤ What management wants
➤ Why management wants it

➤ The benefits of SMTs to nonmanagement employees as well as to
   managers and to the organization as a whole
➤ The obstacles the SMTs may face

Why are these communications most important of all? Sudden
changes in organizational behavior, without proper communication,
are threatening and overwhelming. Even with communication, nonmanagement employees have long ago learned to distrust any shift of
responsibility from management to nonmanagement. How you communicate is therefore important as well. Openness, honesty, fairness,
and listening with an open mind are not common management behaviors, but only they can help overcome the inertia most organizations
experience when they try to shift gears to SMTs.

By now you probably have realized why I told you to complete
the readiness assessments in Appendix F. If you don't think you or
your organization is ready for SMTs, it could be that you really
aren't. Typically, when people don't hold those systems in high regard, they aren't ready. On the other hand, you could be underestimating yourself and the organization. Until you put both to the test,
you can't know for sure.

Barriers to SMTs

Readiness is the result of everyone's willingness to make radical
changes in how work gets done and how business is done. However,
traditionally, management attitudes and perceptions, and many union
contracts, block what you want: productivity, competitiveness, and
growth.

Management Barriers

Often, people think the buck does have to stop where some one person must take responsibility for decisions for which she will be held
accountable. Sometimes, for example, regulatory agencies (e.g., the
Environmental Protection Agency) demand holding a specific person
(or persons) accountable because agencies have a public charge they
must protect or rules to uphold. Therefore, in some industries, such
as defense, utilities, medicine, a perception of social responsibilities

(whether right or wrong) will outweigh the desire for employee-based, self-managed teams.

Still, if the organization isn't ready, don't place all the blame on top management. Creating the appropriate climate, setting up the proper technological and management systems, and initiating and supporting cultural change are executive responsibilities. However, managers in the middle often create their own barriers by failing to delegate authority when they assign responsibility or by failing to hold teams accountable for what they're supposed to do. Often the best technicians (which is no guarantee that they are good managers) are reluctant to delegate work they think they should do and can do better than anyone else. Additionally, as they give up their technical or traditional management chores, they feel very threatened.

Managers promoted out of line positions often feel that they are not making what they think is an appropriate contribution. Being "doers" by training and experience, they feel that management duties are themselves trivial or mere paper shuffling. With thousands of managers complaining that managing is "nothing more than going to one useless meeting after another," none of which seems to be real work to them, you can imagine how they feel about self-managed teams.

The prospect of SMTs raises the possibility that not only can people do their technical work at least as well as they can, but they can also do that "trivial" stuff, too. Suddenly, management responsibilities become real work that only they can do. And top management often reinforces middle management fears of being redundant. Flattening the organization has meant, in practice, flattening the number of middle managers needed. However, that may be a big mistake, since given their expertise, the organization needs these people to advise rather than to closely supervise. Ralph, the VP of Human Resources in "Sally Forth," is resisting the most important role middle managers can play: coach to self-managed teams.

Employee Barriers

Nonmanagement employees can also create barriers to effectiveness. They are usually not trained for it and are not ready to take on the responsibilities of self-management. Typically, they suffer from conditions based on previous experience and so prevalent we've given them names: imposition, ignorance, stagnation, fear, eagerness, and power playing.

🠞 *Imposition.* People often complain that SMTs are just another way for managers to shirk their own responsibilities and pass them on to the workers' backs. They need a clear picture of both management's roles and their own, or they won't accept being self-managed.

Many people in low-paying jobs will do only what is minimally required of them, working for their paycheck and that's all. They find it pretty hard to motivate themselves in a job they probably had to fight to get and that is probably a dead end as well. "Tell me what to do, and I'll do it," they usually respond to work in general. Enriching their work, as hard as that may be, is the only way to move them painstakingly from carrying out orders to managing their own work.

🠞 *Ignorance.* Often, employees don't realize what they have to do to get more from their work. Not understanding that new skills are needed to get ahead is a barrier people throw up in their own paths. The slow disappearance of automatic cost-of-living adjustments (COLAs) distresses these people because they don't see themselves ever doing anything other than what they do. They may want more for themselves than they have, but they don't know how to get it. Managers have a responsibility to coach and counsel employees as to the possibilities that lay ahead for them as well as for the organization.

🠞 *Stagnation.* Some employees may understand what's required to grow and develop, but they're willing to stagnate; they just don't want to change. Happily nestled in their own niche, they exclude themselves from the possibilities for their own lives. They don't want to be cross-trained, and some union contracts encourage them by prohibiting cross-training. This doesn't necessarily make them bad employees.

Indeed, some people with highly technical skills shouldn't be removed from their ordinary work. They're the best in their field, and they're satisfied with their jobs. They just want to be left alone to be the good soldiers they are, out of the limelight, away from public notice, doing jobs that can be done quickly and safely. If you have a work group made up of people like them, creating an SMT is probably impossible.

➤ *Fear.* Fear can be the source of satisfaction with the status quo too. Many people fear the demands change makes on them. They fear the unknown, and they fear failure. "Better to be locked into a dead-end job I know well then to stretch out into the unknown."

Sometimes people are afraid of imagined or actual peer pressure about cooperating, especially of being seen as a management stooge if they do. A person's fear of being isolated from his peers may lead to his conforming, even if his peers aren't in fact demanding it. A more common fear is that the teams will become so effective they will encourage more downsizing. Distrust of management exacerbates that fear, especially at companies with a history of labor/management strife, as in the cases of Caterpillar and McDonnell-Douglas.

Only by involving everyone in the successive planning and implementing phases of a change can you overcome these fears. People gain self-confidence by gaining control over the processes in their work and lives. The more fairly the company treats its employees and the more it supports employee teams, the more relaxed the employees will become. They need to see their effort not only cuts costs but also generates new business, which they recognize grows jobs on the line.

➤ *Eagerness.* At the other end of the spectrum from all the above are the eager beavers willing to plunge into changes without thinking about what they mean. Eager to please, with a need for social and management recognition, they jump out ahead of themselves before they're properly trained and ready. The setbacks they encounter then become demoralizing.

Their enthusiasm is necessary and shouldn't be stifled, but you need to carefully nurture these people and slow them down. Bring the team up the learning curve slowly and carefully, and assign tasks in proportion to people's abilities to complete them successfully. Then build on those successes.

➤ *Power playing.* Enthusiasm can mask power playing. Power players interfere with team effectiveness by taking on additional tasks only under conditions that favor them at the expense of other people. They will take advantage of the situation and literally blackmail other people as they attempt to usurp control of the team. Either the manager or the team itself has to bring anyone attempting to do this into alignment with the team goals and team guidelines. Negative consequences for power playing should be made clear from the outset.

Responsibilities for Creating SMTs

Everyone needs to take responsibility for the success of SMTs or they won't survive, let alone succeed.

Responsibilities of Management

Freedom, like self-management, consists of learned behaviors. Think about your own slow evolution from childhood to adulthood, graduating from one level of control over your own life to another level. At each level, you had to learn how to be independent in thought and in action, and some people never pass from one stage to another. Assuming that leaders can be made through training, then SMTs can be made through training as well.

Managers who wish to create SMTs must first get themselves the training they need to learn how to properly delegate work. They must learn how to delegate authority and accountability as well as assign responsibility, and they must gradually delegate those opportunities at a level appropriate to the employees' abilities to assume them. That requires training other people as well as the managers not only in technical and problem-solving or decision-making skills, which we do to create quality improvement teams, but also in many skills previously reserved to management development: basic accounting for managers, projecting, communicating, meeting management, and of course self-management.

Management shouldn't try by itself to orchestrate all the changes for self-management. Everyone at every point in the organization will need to help, and no two people are at exactly the same level of independence and readiness. Identifying the different levels of readiness, designing, and delivering the necessary training may require outside help. Outsiders can take a larger, more accurate picture than can insiders. They can help the managers develop the skills they need for creating SMTs and letting them do their work. It isn't easy, and it takes time; however, the money spent in proper preparation comes back quickly and several fold.

Responsibilities of Nonmanagement Employees

Since everyone has to take responsibility for the changes that support SMTs, nonmanagement employees have to accept responsibility and accountability for planning, coordinating, ordering supplies, monitoring quality, satisfying customer needs, and continuously improving the way work is done. They need training that includes, at the very least, reading about SMTs at the Saturn plant, at Atlantic Bell, at SRC, at Hewlett Packard, at 3M, and other up and running groups. (Site visits are even more mind-expanding.)

Most of all, nonmanagement employees have to create and support SMTs. They must feel ownership of these teams. To do that, they have to have a sense of ownership of the organization and its goals. Actual ownership, as in profit sharing or stock ownership, is one sure way to guarantee a workforce driven by self-interest. It's hard for employees to resent management or owners when the enemy they resent is themselves.

Team Responsibilities to Itself

Assuming that everyone on the team will act responsibly on behalf of the team could lead to storms up the road. Even self-managed people need to secure the team's future by planning ahead (proactive team management). As part of the team's stage setting, it helps to move beyond a purely psychological contract to a written document that sets out what team members can and should expect from one another. Rules help prevent individuals or small subgroups from dominating or otherwise subverting the team. Rules, in short, help prevent self-managed, permanent teams from devolving into a madhouse run by the inmates. But who should write this document and what should it include?

First, the team should write the prescriptions. Taking into account the organization's mandate for the team, the group should take responsibility for producing the norms it will honor. This process can evolve from the Probing/Testing experiences that usually go on early in the team's existence.

Second, when writing the prescriptions, the members have to anticipate problems any team, and their team in particular, could run into. Members of an SMT would like to think that they are above these possibilities, but everyone's human. The written rules and the group responses to their violation therefore have to protect team members and the team from the following possibilities:

➤ Chronically late or absent members
➤ Passive or uninvolved members
➤ Dominating, carping, or complaining members
➤ Distracting or overly long discussions, especially about trivia
➤ Missing information or failure to involve people who could supply that information
➤ Inadequate preparation or failure to properly follow up on the part of a member
➤ Domineering task-orientation by the team that overwhelms individual members
➤ Domineering process-orientation by the team that prevents the group from meeting its work-related goals

Getting people to function within the rules will help modify the behavior of people experiencing self-management for the first time. The rules, coupled with training, will help them assume responsibility for themselves and for the demands the team makes on them.

If you decide to adopt this formal process, how you frame the document depends on how legalistically your team views the situation. Either a constitution-style document with specific "articles" or a "code of conduct" will work as long as what you produce contains a preamble identifying a general set of expectations concerning contribution and empowerment listed (see "Empowerment of SMTs," earlier in this chapter) and a list of specific unacceptable behaviors (e.g., "Chronic tardiness: being late for meetings more than twice in a month"). Consequences for repeated unacceptable behavior must also be spelled out ("Anyone late to two or more meetings will not share in the short-term bonuses the team earns until that tardiness stops"). Experience with SMTs shows that if consequences are taken seriously, team members follow the rules.

For every unacceptable behavior, you need to contrast it with an acceptable alternative ("Members are expected to be early for or on time for all meetings unless reasonable and unavoidable circumstances delay them"). Rewards for acceptable behavior can be anything the team decides.

A caution: As with any attempt to formalize a process, you need to avoid rigidity and micromanagement. Since no cookbook provides recipes for freedom, creativity, or innovation, there's a fine line between protecting a group from self-destructive behavior and the tyranny of the group over individuals.

Notes

1. See James MacGregor Burns, *Leadership* (New York: Wiley, 1978), pp. 9–25.
2. Robert Manor, "McDonnell's New Teams Mean Changes for Machinists: Old Work Rules Will Disappear," *St. Louis Post-Dispatch* (September 15, 1996), pp. 1E, 5E.
3. Quoted in John Huey, "The New Post-Heroic Leadership," *Fortune* (February 21, 1994), pp. 42–50.
4. Joann S. Lublin, "My Colleague, My Boss," *Wall Street Journal* (April 12, 1995), pp. R4, R12.
5. Thomas A. Stewart, "Why Value Statements Don't Work," *Fortune* (June 10, 1996), pp. 137–138; Stewart, "Company Values That Add Value," *Fortune* (July 8, 1996), pp. 145–147.
6. John Hoerr, "Sharpening Minds for a Competitive Edge," *Business Week* (December 17, 1990), pp. 72–78.

Other Sources

Gardner, John. *Self-Renewal: The Individual and the Innovative Society*, rev. ed. New York: Norton, 1981.
Waterman, Robert H. *The Renewal Factor: How the Best Get and Keep the Competitive Edge*. New York: Bantam Books, 1987.

Appendix A

Three Exercises for Increasing Personal Power

The first three exercises will help you apply the process approach to increasing personal power (Chapter 2). Who and what you are, what you accomplish, consist of processes that culminate in identifiable events. To make events happen the way you want them to, you have to design a plan based on the realities of your life. The exercises that follow will give you the opportunity to make decisions about the kind of future you want to create for yourself.

The first exercise, "My Personal SWOT Analysis," asks you to look at yourself in terms of your own *strengths,* your own *weaknesses,* the *opportunities* you see for yourself, and the *threats* or perils you have to face. The second exercise, "The Center of Your World, You," asks you to use your SWOT Analysis and look at yourself in relation to other people, to the organization in which you work, and to the environment that surrounds the organization. The third exercise, "Ben Franklin, John Venn, and You" (a two-parter), gives you a chance to refine the opportunities for yourself. The last exercise, "Venn Diagram of My Future," lets you use the information you generated from the other three charts to diagram a chart that points toward where you should be heading in your life.

If you are in a position to influence strategies in the organization

Inasmuch as the instruments and exercises in these appendices have appeared in several of my other writings and have been used in a large number of my seminars, I have no idea how many people have completed them; however, from the feedback I do know, the responses have been overwhelmingly positive. They have helped quite a few people increase their personal power, improve the quality of their lives both off and on the job, and increase group effectiveness.

for which you work, you can apply all of these exercises to the organization. Just replace the personal pronouns with words or phrases
that refer to it.

Exercise 1. SWOT Analysis

Step 1. Strengths

List all the talents, skills, capabilities, and interests you think you
have. Use the same format as the example in the accompanying chart.
Since you probably won't think of all of them, ask other people close
to you to contribute to this list.

Step 2. Weaknesses

List all the areas of knowledge, skill, capabilities, and interests you
need to improve on to make you more effective. Include specific in-
abilities or disabilities that could prohibit you from doing something.
Use the same format as the examples in the chart. Since you may not
think of all of the areas in need of improvement, ask other people
close to you to contribute to this list.

Step 3. Opportunities

List all the advantages you have for exercising your strengths or improving on your areas in need of improvement. If you believe it possible to develop an ability listed as an inability or to overcome a
disability, don't hesitate to include it in this list. Use the same format
as the examples, and ask for other people's suggestions.

Step 4. Threats

List all the possibilities you can think of that could get in the way
of your exercising your strengths or managing your weaknesses.
Use the same format as the example, and ask other people to help
you do this.

My Personal SWOT Analysis

Strengths Accomplished singer.	*Weaknesses* I lack stamina. I have an impaired leg.
Opportunities I can join a fitness center to improve stamina.	*Threats* Competition extremely high. No medical correction for my limp, limiting my singing career to nondancing roles.

Exercise 2. The Center of Your World, You

How to Read the Diagram

Use the diagram in Exhibit A-1 (called a Euler Diagram) to complete an "environmental scan," that is, to describe the world in which you live and how you and it relate to each other. The inner circles constitute aspects of the outer circles. One way of reading the diagram is to say, "What and who I am consist of aspects of what is uniquely me *and* aspects of everyone and everything else in my world."

"Other people" refers to significant others, e.g., my spouse, my children, my parents. "The organization" refers to the company or agency for which you work (if you are employed full- or part-time), the school you attend (if you are a full-time student). The phrase *my*

Exhibit A-1. Environmental scan.

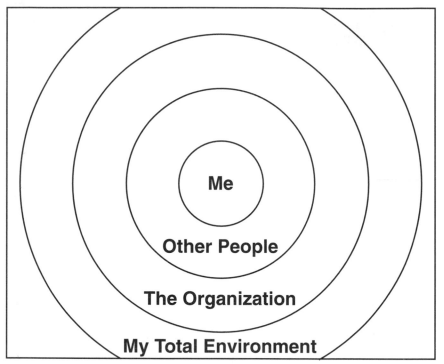

total environment refers to everything else: your social and physical worlds. The largest circle deliberately runs out of the border because no one can possibly experience "everything else," even if it does affect their lives. Now answer these questions:

1. Who or what surrounds you and affects your life (for example, your manager, your family, your community leaders)?
2. How does the environment around you support your strengths?
3. How could the environment help you improve on your weaknesses or overcome your disabilities (if you have any)?
4. What opportunities do specific aspects of your environment provide for advancing your aims?
5. What threats do specific aspects of your environment present?

Exercises 3a and 3b. Ben Franklin, John Venn, and You

Salespeople are familiar with the decision-making device known as the Ben Franklin Close. Our T-chart, below, is a variation of this tool in which you list the answers to these two questions:

1. What can I do or have the capacity for doing after study and practice?
   Your answers identify your strengths, and they also *limit* your efforts to those things with the greatest potential for paying off. Others may disagree with this, but it's okay to recognize what you *can't* do. That's a mark of a genuine self-assessment.
2. What from among my strengths do I want to do?
   Your answers identify your values, attitudes, and interests, and you will get your greatest payoffs from doing those things you value, that you feel good about doing, and in which you have a genuine interest. That way you don't waste your energies on dead-end opportunities.

You can now refine your lists of strengths by reviewing your lists in this chart and assigning a weight to each item (5 = the highest or most important, 1 = the lowest or least important). Now compare the items of "What to Do" with those you rated "Can Do." Where the Want to Do items and the Can Do items match up, you can pretty well decide whether or not you should do them.

Ben Franklin Analysis

Can Do	Want to Do
Sing professionally (5)	Sing (5)
Dance professionally (1)	Dance (1)

Exercise 3c. Venn Diagram of My Future

Many businesspeople* have seen the power of borrowing a tool from logical analysis to create their organization's vision and mission: the Venn Diagram, the method the logician/mathematician John Venn designed for analyzing logical arguments. You can use the diagram for personal planning by refining your previous analyses to a simple chart, such as the one in Exhibit A-2, that consists of answers to the three questions below. You can apply the Venn Diagram to group planning as well simply by changing "I" to "we."

1. What can I do? (See your own Ben Franklin Analysis.)
2. What does my potential market (people who might ask for and pay for what I do) want? Include only those things for which you have good reason to believe a genuine market exists.
3. What do I want to do? (See your own Ben Franklin Analysis.)

To make decisions about where you might head, look at the point at which the "Can do" and "Want to do" circles overlap one another. Then, if you're doing career or work planning, the overlapping third

Exhibit A-2. Venn Diagram of the future.

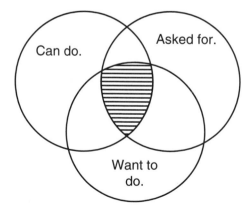

*For example, Candace Ulrich, a former associate of mine at the Citicorp Executive Development Center (now also in private practice), calls this diagram "The Three W's."

circle ("Asked for") represents a profitable application of the other two. The diagram also represents several other possibilities, none of which would be appropriate for you:

➤ What you can't do, whether you want to do it or a market exists
➤ What people want but that you can't do and don't want to do
➤ What you can do but don't want to, and no one else wants it either
➤ What you want to do but can't do, and no one wants it
➤ What you can't do and don't want to do, and no one would pay for it anyway

Appendix B
Eulogy Exercise

Yogi Berra, the former New York Yankees catcher and baseball coach, reportedly said, "It ain't over till it's over." The tale of your life will not be told until you die. What do you want that tale to say about you?

This is one way of creating a vision for your life. Write the eulogy you would want someone to read at your funeral. By the time all is said and done, how do you want your résumé or vitae to read? Writing in the past tense, develop a broad picture of how you fulfilled the life you now think you want to live. Think in terms of the seven dimensions in Chapter 3: Career, Community Relationships, Family, Finances, Material Goods, Personal Values, and Social Relationships. Use your master list and chart in "What Drives You?" to guide you toward the payoffs you want from all your efforts. Dream a little, but don't fly in the face of reality. When you finish, you'll have produced a broad vision statement that will guide you when you set goals for your life and work.

Then, if you wish, have someone read this eulogy to you. Listen to how it sounds. Pin it up on a wall in front of you to refer to it whenever you can. After all, it's your eulogy.

Over time, don't be afraid to make changes in it. Remember, "It ain't over till it's over."

Appendix C

What Drives Me? Work-Related and Personal Goals Self-Assessment

Introduction

Every action produces some kind of result, whether you know the reason you're doing it or not and whether you plan for it or not. Unless you plan for the result you want, the one you get may not satisfy the (deliberate or unconscious) reason for which you took the action. To align your organizational goals and your work or personal goals, it's important for you to know what results you want from the effort you put out.

Organizational goals are all very compelling, while some personal goals (motives) are more compelling than others. The reasons that motivate you most forcefully are your drivers—your most important reasons for doing what you're doing. Satisfying those drivers becomes your most important activity because reaching those goals means getting the payoffs you want for yourself. So, what goals drive you?

The list below consists of twenty-five possible reasons for doing anything. Each word or phrase can be used to answer the question "What do I want to get out of the effort I'm putting into my life?"

See adaptations in two other products from Donald H. Weiss and American Management Association, *Managing Stress* (New York: AMACOM, 1987); *Successful Delegation* (Watertown, Mass.: American Management Association, 1978 and 1987).

Instruction 1

This is important. Read the **entire** list of possible payoffs **before** continuing. **Stop here** and read the list.

_____ 1. KNOWLEDGE: To pursue and learn about new things and ideas; to search for truth, or information; to be known by others as an intelligent person and to feel intelligent.

_____ 2. WISDOM: To understand and frame for myself a meaning of life, perceiving experience from a broad frame of reference.

_____ 3. POWER: To lead and direct others; to influence or control others—that is, to get them to do what I want them to do.

_____ 4. AESTHETIC PLEASURE: To enjoy and respect the things from which I derive pleasure—art, nature, work, people.

_____ 5. ETHICAL STANDARDS: To believe in and maintain a code of ethics, a sense of right and wrong; to be moral; to conform to the standards of society, my family or spouse, my profession, and my personal or religious ideals.

_____ 6. INDEPENDENCE: To achieve my own goals in the manner best suited to me; to have freedom to come and go as I wish; to be myself at all times; to control my own actions.

_____ 7. ACCOMPLISHMENT: To achieve my personal objectives with a sense that I've done something as well as, if not better than, someone else would have; to experience self-satisfaction when I rise to a challenge, accomplish a task or a job, or solve a problem.

_____ 8. RECOGNITION: To receive attention, notice, approval, or respect from others because of something I've done; to generate a feeling in others for who I am and what I achieve.

_____ 9. FRIENDSHIP: To have many friends; to work with others, enjoying their camaraderie; to join groups for companionship; to look forward to and enjoy social relations.

_____ 10. RESPONSIBILITY: To be held accountable to others or to organizations to which I belong for a job or task; to possess something and care for it.

_____ 11. CREATIVITY: To be free to and have the ability and desire

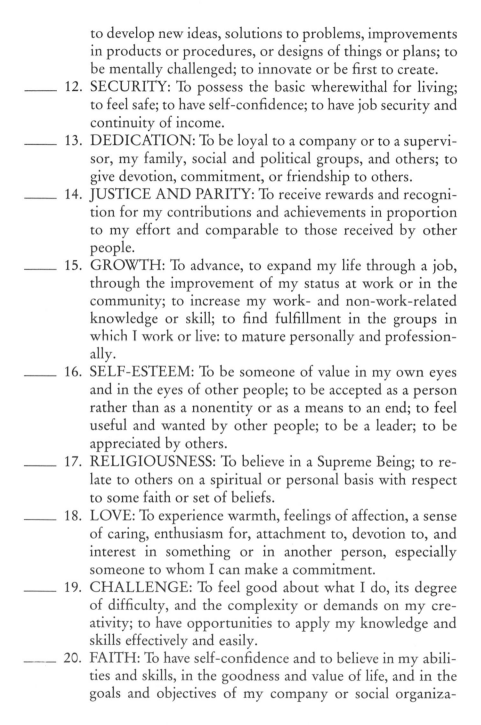

to develop new ideas, solutions to problems, improvements in products or procedures, or designs of things or plans; to be mentally challenged; to innovate or be first to create.

_____ 12. SECURITY: To possess the basic wherewithal for living; to feel safe; to have self-confidence; to have job security and continuity of income.

_____ 13. DEDICATION: To be loyal to a company or to a supervisor, my family, social and political groups, and others; to give devotion, commitment, or friendship to others.

_____ 14. JUSTICE AND PARITY: To receive rewards and recognition for my contributions and achievements in proportion to my effort and comparable to those received by other people.

_____ 15. GROWTH: To advance, to expand my life through a job, through the improvement of my status at work or in the community; to increase my work- and non-work-related knowledge or skill; to find fulfillment in the groups in which I work or live: to mature personally and professionally.

_____ 16. SELF-ESTEEM: To be someone of value in my own eyes and in the eyes of other people; to be accepted as a person rather than as a nonentity or as a means to an end; to feel useful and wanted by other people; to be a leader; to be appreciated by others.

_____ 17. RELIGIOUSNESS: To believe in a Supreme Being; to relate to others on a spiritual or personal basis with respect to some faith or set of beliefs.

_____ 18. LOVE: To experience warmth, feelings of affection, a sense of caring, enthusiasm for, attachment to, devotion to, and interest in something or in another person, especially someone to whom I can make a commitment.

_____ 19. CHALLENGE: To feel good about what I do, its degree of difficulty, and the complexity or demands on my creativity; to have opportunities to apply my knowledge and skills effectively and easily.

_____ 20. FAITH: To have self-confidence and to believe in my abilities and skills, in the goodness and value of life, and in the goals and objectives of my company or social organizations; to feel secure in the availability of help from others and to recognize help received.

_____ 21. HELPFULNESS: To provide assistance, support, empathy, or protection to others; to be open, responsive, and generous.

_____ 22. HEALTH (PHYSICAL/MENTAL): To feel energetic and free of physical pain from injury, disease, or infection; to feel free of worry and anxiety and of emotional blocks to success in all aspects of my life; to have peace of mind.

_____ 23. MONEY: To have sufficient income or other assets to use as I wish; to be materially comfortable or well off.

_____ 24. GOOD TIMES/PLEASURE: To have fun; to enjoy myself; to do things I like to do rather than only things I have to do.

_____ 25. BEING LOVED: To experience warmth, feelings of affection, and a sense of caring from other people, especially from someone from whom I can expect a commitment.

Instruction 2

Return to the beginning of the list. Slowly review each item, *ranking* each payoff as to its *importance to you*. In the spaces provided, write 1 for the most important and up to 25 for the least. For example, if you feel that KNOWLEDGE is important but not the most important reason for doing things, you might write an 8 on the line next to item 1. It may make things easier if you hunt out the item that represents the most important reason before you rate the rest.

Instruction 3

From your master list, transfer the top five goals you want from your *work* to the chart below. For example, you could list RECOGNITION as the most important work-related goal even if it ranks lower than that on your master list.

From your master list, transfer the top five *personal* goals you want to satisfy outside the workplace. These help you balance and maintain your well-being and your relationships with other people, e.g., your family.

Use the following model as a guide. When you complete the list of goals in *each* group, compare them with one another. Note which side of the chart contains the highest ratings in the master list—work-related or non-work-related.

In some cases, goals may be both work- and non-work-related. For example, many people seek FRIENDSHIP at work as well as outside of work. The model shows you that you can list a driver on both sides of the chart.

When you finish, you'll have a personal profile, a picture of your own most important reasons for doing things. Check your list of goals to see which of them you think you should pursue most vigorously. Then, the decisions you make should fit with those goals. Unless you integrate your goals, you may feel a great deal of frustration and stress.

Model

RANK	WORK-RELATED DRIVERS	RANK	NON-WORK-RE-LATED DRIVERS
2	Recognition	1	Love
4	Friendship	3	Being loved
5	Accomplishment	4	Friendship
15	Money	20	Religiousness
9	Responsibility	8	Aesthetic Pleasure

Your Goals

RANK	WORK-RELATED DRIVERS	RANK	NON-WORK-RE-LATED DRIVERS

Appendix D
Ways to Evaluate Motivation

No one has designed a foolproof method for evaluating what encourages people to do their best. You could ask each of them to complete a copy of "What Drives You?" and discuss the results with them. That would profit everyone. Or, you can use the following guide to make *fair estimates* of what you think you need to do to provide the proper incentives for each person.

Of course, you can't always supply exactly the reward or incentive another person wants. Be creative to hit on one you can provide that would come as close to the employee's payoffs as you can get. You and the other person working on this assessment together could make your job a lot easier and reduce much of the speculation involved.

Instructions

In Part 1, Self-Concept, consider how the employee sees him- or herself. Then, think of what you can offer as an incentive to help that person stay motivated. Whatever you offer, it has to match with how the individual sees him- or herself or it won't work.

In Part 2, Preferred Working Conditions, consider under what conditions the employee produces the most and the best work. Not every one of the items in the list will fit for any one employee. Some are mutually exclusive. Decide on what you can allow or provide

Adapted from Donald H. Weiss, *Successful Delegation* (Watertown, Mass.: American Management Association: 1978 and 1987) and Weiss, *How to Get the Best Out of People* (New York: AMACOM, 1988).

and what you can't in order to help the person work under the best conditions possible for him or her. Take into consideration accommodations you might have to make with respect to a person's disabilities.

Use a separate copy of the form for each person. The first two response lines are models, and add anything you think is relevant to the person whose behavior you're evaluating.

Name: _____

Behavior	Ways to Encourage the Behavior
Part 1. Self-Concept: How does _____ see him-/herself? As a self-starter As a hard worker _____ _____	Let him/her set his/her deadlines. Praise his/her punctuality. _____ _____
Part 2. Preferred Working Conditions: ⊤ Detailed instructions to carry out faithfully ⊤ Work things out him-/herself ⊤ Work slowly and give a lot of attention to detail and logical thinking ⊤ Work at a fast pace, making quick but intelligent decisions ⊤ Take responsibility for other people (lead) ⊤ Work autonomously but get along well with others ⊤ Work in a team with close	_____ _____ _____ _____ _____ _____ _____

work and social relations
- ➤ Little recognition or attention from others   _____
- ➤ A lot of recognition or attention from others   _____
- ➤ To express his/her feelings easily and constructively   _____
- ➤ Receive feedback whether positive or negative (as opposed to receiving none at all)

_____

_____

_____

_____

_____

Appendix E

Am I Already a Leader?

Instructions

On the spaces provided, answer the items in this unscientific but useful survey either *yes* or *no*. Then, read the interpretations to determine whether or not you are already doing the things that people do to distinguish themselves as vision leaders.

_____ 1. It's important to me that individuals in the group get what they need or want for themselves.

_____ 2. When I look at a situation, I look for more than what affects me immediately and directly.

_____ 3. When I talk with people about what we are doing or how we are doing it, I relate what I'm saying to the group's needs, aspirations, and feelings.

_____ 4. When dealing with a problem, I look for the wider implications of what I know or believe.

_____ 5. I attack everything I do with vigor and a willingness to give it my all.

_____ 6. I get excited by new challenges presented to the group.

_____ 7. I represent my group to people outside it in such a way that they can understand what the group wants or needs to be successful.

_____ 8. I spend as much time as I can afford helping build people's morale, especially when they feel down or not receiving what they think they deserve.

_____ 9. When talking with other people about situations that affect

Adapted from Donald H. Weiss, *Becoming an Effective Leader* (New York: AMACOM, 1993).

us, I try to explain how I see the relationships between us and other people or with the organization as a whole.

_____ 10. Usually, I express the group's needs, aspirations, and feelings clearer than and more thoroughly than most people in the group.

_____ 11. I keep myself physically and emotionally fit and feel vigorous most of the time.

_____ 12. People are more than mere instruments or tools for meeting my objectives or the goals of the organization.

_____ 13. As often as I can, I encourage people to act on the basis of long-term goals rather than on the basis of immediate returns.

_____ 14. I care about how people in the group feel or what they want for themselves.

_____ 15. I feel good about what we're doing and how we're doing it.

_____ 16. I believe that anything can be improved, and I welcome change.

_____ 17. I help people see where we're going and how we're trying to get there.

_____ 18. It's important to me that the group fulfill its goals and meet its needs.

_____ 19. I know we can do better than we are doing, and I will do whatever it takes to make it better.

_____ 20. The people with whom I associate are important to me and have my respect.

_____ 21. Whenever I get the chance, I talk with other people about how the group is doing, what it wants, or what it needs to be successful.

_____ 22. Whenever the situation seems confused or dismal, I encourage people to look toward the future and to concentrate on achieving our goals or objectives.

Interpretations

Each pair of statements represents one generally agreed-upon trait of vision leadership. Add up your yeses and noes. If you answered yes to every item, you're already a super leader (or you're kidding yourself). If you answered yes to most of the items, you're on your way to being a superior leader. If you answered yes and no equally, you're somewhat confused as to how to be a leader and this book will help you improve the quality of your leadership. If you answered most of them no, you're either underestimating yourself grossly or you have a long way to go.

➤ The ability to see the whole picture
  2. When I look at a situation, I look for more than what affects me immediately and directly.
  4. When dealing with a problem, I look for the wider implications of what I know or believe.
➤ The ability to communicate the whole picture to other people
  9. When talking with other people about situations that affect us, I try to explain how I see the relationships between us and other people or with the organization as a whole.
  13. As often as I can, I encourage people to act on the basis of long-term goals rather than on the basis of immediate returns.
➤ The ability to interpret and articulate the group's needs, aspirations, and feelings
  3. When I talk with people about what we are doing or how we are doing it, I relate what I'm saying to the group's needs, aspirations, and feelings.
  10. Usually, I express the group's needs, aspirations, and feelings clearer than and more thoroughly than most people in the group.
➤ Concern for the needs, aspirations, and feelings within the group
  14. I care about how people in the group feel or what they want for themselves.
  18. It's important to me that the group fulfill its goals and meet its needs.
➤ Respect for the needs, aspirations, feelings, and abilities within the group
  20. The people with whom I associate are important to me and have my respect.
  12. People are more than mere instruments or tools for meeting my objectives or the goals of the organization.
➤ The ability to communicate the group's needs, aspirations, and feelings for, to, and outside the group

21. Whenever I get the chance, I talk with other people about how the group is doing, what it wants, or what it needs to be successful.

7. I represent my group to people outside it in such a way that they can understand what the group wants or needs to be successful.

➤ A grasp of what people need or want for themselves that will encourage them to do what they otherwise might not do for themselves or for others

1. It's important to me that individuals in the group get what they need or want for themselves.

8. I spend as much time as I can afford helping build people's morale, especially when they feel down or not receiving what they think they deserve.

➤ The ability to provide people with direction and to focus their energies on specific goals while maintaining a high group morale

22. Whenever the situation seems confused or dismal, I encourage people to look toward the future and to concentrate on achieving our goals or objectives.

17. I help people see where we're going and how we're trying to get there.

➤ Enthusiasm for the group's mission, objectives, and standards

15. I feel good about what we're doing and how we're doing it.

6. I get excited by new challenges presented to the group.

➤ An avid desire for change, growth or improvement

19. I know we can do better than we are doing, and I will do whatever it takes to make it better.

16. I believe that anything can be improved, and I welcome change.

➤ The energy necessary for conducting the business of the group

11. I keep myself physically and emotionally fit and feel vigorous most of the time.

5. I attack everything I do with vigor and a willingness to give it my all.

Appendix F

Team Productivity Assessment

Instructions

In both parts of the assessment, circle the number that best reflects your opinions or feelings about the team's effectiveness. Make a copy and turn in the original for scoring.

Part A. From my experiences so far, I think the team:	Low				High
1. Is productive	1	2	3	4	5
2. Helps me in the work I do	1	2	3	4	5
3. Helps me meet personal needs during meetings (expressing my opinions, having people listen to my ideas, etc.)	1	2	3	4	5

Part B. From my experience during this meeting, here's how I estimate the following:	Low				High
4. The contributions (information, opinions, ideas) of other people to the team's productivity	1	2	3	4	5
5. My contributions to the team's productivity	1	2	3	4	5
6. The trust level of members (willingness to be open, candid)	1	2	3	4	5
7. My trust level	1	2	3	4	5
8. My influence on the group	1	2	3	4	5
9. Other members' influence on me	1	2	3	4	5

Scorecard

Instructions

Add the individual scores for each item and divide the sum (total) by the number of scores to find the average.

Part A. From my experiences so far, I think the group:	Individual Scores								Total	Average
1. Is productive										
2. Helps me in the work I do										
3. Helps me meet personal needs during meetings (expressing my opinions, having people listen to my ideas, etc.)										
Part B. I think this about what happened during this meeting:										
4. The contributions of other people to the group										
5. My contributions to the group's productivity										
6. The trust level of members										
7. My trust level										
8. My influence in the group										
9. Other members' influence over me										

Interpretations

The averages reflect the opinions and feelings of the group. We told you to keep the original assessment form in order for you to record your individual opinions or feelings, especially if you rated down the group. Only if you own up to your score can you deal with the issues that bother you. Discussions should focus not on the numbers but rather on what the numbers mean.

A group score of between 4 and 5 is either very good or no one wants to downgrade the group's performance. Discussions should focus on how your group can sustain this level of effectiveness. What are we doing right? What can we do even better than we're doing?

A score between 3 and 4 suggests that someone in the group is having some problems, and this has to be discussed. Each person who rated the group down should 'fess up to the issues, and questions to answer should include: What are we doing poorly? What can we do to improve on what we're doing?

A score between 2 and 3 suggests significant problems in the group's activities. Most people in the group think something's wrong; therefore, surface the problems now or else suffer severe consequences later. You may want to call in a trained facilitator to help the group open up and deal with the issues.

A score between 1 and 2 shouts out the seriousness of the problems. An outside facilitator is undoubtedly a wise choice.

Caution: Don't let problems ever reach the seriousness of a mean score between 1 and 2.

Appendix G

Are You Ready? Is Your Organization Ready?

Instructions: Are You Ready?

Respond yes or no (not often, sometimes, maybe) to the following twenty-five items. If you cannot respond yes to an item with multiple parts, the answer must be no. Be honest with yourself. Unless you show it to someone, no one else will see this self-assessment.

Yes	No	Readiness for Self-Management
____	____	I recognize both my strengths and my limitations.
____	____	I communicate and interrelate well with other people.
____	____	I know what I want for myself both in the short term (daily, weekly, etc.) and in the long term (for my life).
____	____	I am a good listener, hearing what other people feel as well as what they believe.
____	____	I am flexible and competent in coping with change.
____	____	I feel in control of myself in all situations.
____	____	I feel strongly (even passionately) about what I believe and want for myself.
____	____	I feel comfortable when under pressure, prioritizing tasks and completing them.
____	____	I am proactive rather than reactive (initiating activities rather than waiting to be told or waiting for things to happen to me).
____	____	I am able to get myself going at the beginning of my day and to revitalize myself periodically during the day.

Yes	No	Readiness for Self-Management
___	___	I keep people issues and task issues in proportion to their importance under the circumstances.
___	___	I usually solve my own work-related and personal problems effectively.
___	___	I motivate myself and do not rely on others to motivate me.
___	___	I help other people stay motivated.
___	___	I am aware of how I come across to other people.
___	___	I have a high regard for other people (i.e., I care about how they think and feel).
___	___	I recognize that I am as dependent on other people for information, support, and direction as other people are on me.
___	___	I encourage people to disagree with me in a constructive dialogue designed to solve problems.
___	___	I understand the overall goals and functions of the organization and feel a sense of ownership (commitment) to them.
___	___	I feel a sense of obligation to the organization and to the people with whom I associate.
___	___	I communicate openly and candidly with people.
___	___	I strive to be dependable and knowledgeable.
___	___	I am willing to work toward a consensus when resolving disagreements or solving problems.
___	___	I can follow the leadership of other people and of the group without feeling that I'm giving up my individuality.
___	___	I feel a responsibility to the organization to be an agent for change or renewal.

Interpretations: Are You Ready?

If you responded yes to:

➤ All 25 items, you're super self-managed; you're ready to be a member of a self-managed team. (Either that, or you weren't honest with yourself.)

☛ 20 to 24 items, you're ready, but you need to work on those to which you responded no.

☛ 15 to 19 items, you have some work to do before you're completely ready.

☛ 10 to 14 items, I suggest you seek out training and coaching if you are asked to participate in a self-managed team.

☛ Fewer than 10 items, all is not lost or hopeless, but I recommend you don't join or let yourself be placed on a self-managed team. You need a lot of help to become self-managed.

Instructions: Is Your Organization Ready?

Respond yes or no (not often, sometimes, maybe) to the following twenty items. If you can't respond yes to an item with multiple parts, the answer must be no. Be candid. Unless you show it to someone, no one else will see this assessment.

Caveat: Your responses to this assessment do not signify that the organization is in fact ready or not ready to adopt the principles and practices of self-management. They reflect only your perceptions of the organization's readiness.

Yes	No	Readiness for Self-Management (in Your Organization)
____	____	Management encourages all employees to solve their own problems, even if it means accepting some mistakes.
____	____	Management has created an environment in which employees can figure out what needs to be done and then do it.
____	____	Managers believe that they do not have to solve all problems by themselves.
____	____	The managers and nonmanagement employees of the organization all have a clear picture of the organization's vision and functions and feel a sense of ownership of it.
____	____	Leadership is shared by all employees and is not just a management role.

Yes	No	Readiness for Self-Management (in Your Organization)
___	___	Managers share information with nonmanagement employees; there are no "company secrets."
___	___	Everyone understands his/her responsibilities and accountabilities.
___	___	Everyone has authority to carry out the responsibilities appropriate to his/her work.
___	___	Resources are always available or made available for people to do their work.
___	___	Managers take a long-view approach to the development of the organization.
___	___	Managers make time available to stop and examine the work and its results.
___	___	Everyone believes in the importance of learning and personal development and takes advantage of available opportunities.
___	___	The technology is available for people to work together in teams.
___	___	Communication and performance management (including appraisal) systems are flexible and enable teams to work effectively.
___	___	Organizational goals and priorities have been clearly established and communicated.
___	___	Communication with upper management is open and candid.
___	___	Everyone feels a commitment to the organization.
___	___	Everyone feels a commitment to the team concept.
___	___	Everyone has a sense of competency and willingness to take risks.
___	___	Management is not threatened by changes in management/nonmanagement relationships.

Interpretations: Is Your Organization Ready?

Again, your responses reflect only your interpretations of organizational readiness. If, however, everyone in the organization completes this assessment and a significant majority of people respond no to a significant number of the items, it might be advisable to find out why they think as they do before installing a system of self-managed teams.

If you responded yes to:

➤ All 20 items, you believe your organization is super ready. (Or else, you haven't been honest with yourself.)
➤ 15 to 19 items, you believe your organization is ready but needs some help.
➤ Fewer than 15 of these items, you believe your organization is not ready and needs a great deal of help before being able to support self-managed teams.

Index